Pragmatic Spatial Planning

Instead of seeking theory to justify practical professional judgments, this book describes how professionals can and should use theory to guide these judgments.

Professional spatial planning in the US, and globally, continues to suffer from a weak conceptual grasp of its own practice. Practitioners routinely recognize the value and wisdom of practical judgment finely attuned to context, nuance and complexity; but later offer banal testimony and glib stories of 'just so' best-practice discrediting the ambiguity of their own experience. The chapters in this book provide a vocabulary tailored to the conventions of practical judgment, challenging students and practitioners to treat professional expertise as work in progress rather than 'best' practice. Instead of seeking theory to justify practical professional judgments, Hoch describes how professionals can and should use theory to guide these judgments. The pragmatist plan helps cope with complexity rather than control it, making it invaluable in the anyone's pursuit of a planning career.

This book will appeal to a wide cross section of students and scholars, especially those working in urban planning, public policy and government.

Charles Hoch studies planning activity across scale and discipline. He has spent four decades studying and proposing that we treat planning as an inherently pragmatic enterprise. Hoch received his doctorate in Urban Planning from UCLA in 1981. After a short stint at Iowa State he settled in Chicago, teaching urban planning in the College of Urban Planning and Public Affairs at the University of Illinois, USA.

Pragmatic Spatial Planning
Practical Theory for Professionals

Charles Hoch

NEW YORK AND LONDON

First published 2019
by Routledge
52 Vanderbilt Avenue, New York, NY 10017

and by Routledge
2 Park Square, Milton Park, Abingdon, Oxon OX14 4RN

Routledge is an imprint of the Taylor & Francis Group, an informa business

© 2019 Taylor & Francis

The right of Charles Hoch to be identified as author of this work has been asserted by him in accordance with sections 77 and 78 of the Copyright, Designs and Patents Act 1988.

All rights reserved. No part of this book may be reprinted or reproduced or utilized in any form or by any electronic, mechanical, or other means, now known or hereafter invented, including photocopying and recording, or in any information storage or retrieval system, without permission in writing from the publishers.

Trademark notice: Product or corporate names may be trademarks or registered trademarks, and are used only for identification and explanation without intent to infringe.

Library of Congress Cataloging-in-Publication Data
Names: Hoch, Charles, 1948- author.
Title: Pragmatic spatial planning : practical theory for professionals / Charles Hoch.
Description: New York : Routledge, 2019. | Includes bibliographical references and index.
Identifiers: LCCN 2019009027 (print) | LCCN 2019011122 (ebook) | ISBN 9780429021275 (eBook) | ISBN 9780367075385 (hardback) | ISBN 9780367075392 (pbk.)
Subjects: LCSH: Land use. | Planning. | Space--Social aspects.
Classification: LCC HD113 (ebook) | LCC HD113 .H63 2019 (print) | DDC 711.01--dc23
LC record available at https://lccn.loc.gov/2019009027

ISBN: 978-0-367-07538-5 (hbk)
ISBN: 978-0-367-07539-2 (pbk)
ISBN: 978-0-429-02127-5 (ebk)

Typeset in Sabon
by Taylor & Francis Books

Contents

List of illustrations	vi
Acknowledgments	vii
Book chapters drawing from prior published work	viii
Introduction	1
PART I	**7**
1 Practical Judgment and Planning	9
2 Emotional Intelligence in Planning Judgment	17
PART II	**37**
3 Integrating the Planning Field, Movement and Discipline: Planning Theory for Practice	39
4 Anticipating Complex Spatial Change	48
5 Planning Imagination: Utopia, Scenario and Plan	65
PART III	**83**
6 Crafting Plans	85
7 Evaluating Plans	110
8 How Planning Theory Informs Planning Practice	132
PART IV	**157**
9 Planning Spatial Community in a Complex Society	159
10 Ethical Planning Judgment	175
Index	189

Illustrations

Figures

3.1	Planning theory domains.	40
6.1	Diagram for local government plan making in California.	98
6.2	Burnham used misleading residential precedent based on styles popular in European cities like Paris and Vienna (Burnham & Bennett 1909, p.100).	100
6.3	The confluence of grids at Octavia Hill in San Francisco.	101
6.4	The San Jose urban renewal plan offers a stakeholder guide.	102
6.5	Planning scenario selection from the Valley Futures Project.	104
8.1	Orland Park planning districts.	136
8.2	Layered Orland Park land use map detailing many plans in play.	138
8.3	Zoomed in portion of Figure 8.2 land use map showing plans in play.	140
8.4	Frankfort projected population growth from migration.	141
8.5	Sketching other plans in play for Will County in 2010.	143
8.6	2010 Village of Frankfort land use map.	143

Tables

6.1	Urban complexity conditions and adaptability.	88
6.2	Practical plan making.	97
8.1	Comparison of planning theory analyst approach.	145

Acknowledgments

I am indebted to my many teachers. Jim Clapp and Marco Walshok at San Diego State University helped direct my early critical leanings. John Friedmann's work inspired my pursuit of doctoral study at UCLA and Peter Marris provided crucial intellectual mentorship. Alan Heskin sparked my interest in the role pragmatist thought played justifying early 20th century progressive reform and how these lessons might still prove useful for conceiving and conducting contemporary planning. John Forester from Cornell and Howell Baum from the University of Maryland generously offered critical conversation and friendship as we worked together to do theory through the study of professional practice each in our own way. My colleague Sanjeev Vidyarthi provided invaluable advice on my journey. I am especially grateful to my wife Susan for respecting and supporting my intellectual work.

Book chapters drawing from prior published work

Chapter 1, Practical Judgment & Planning, was adapted from: "Making plans: Representation & intention," *Planning Theory*, 6(1), 15–35, published 2007.

Chapter 2, Emotional Intelligence in Planning Judgment, was adapted from: "Emotions and planning," *Planning Theory and Practice*, 7(4), 367–382, published in 2006.

Chapter 3, Integrating the Planning Field, Movement and Discipline, was adapted from: "Viewpoint: The planning research agenda: planning theory for practice," *Town Planning Review*, 82(2), published in 2011.

Chapter 5, Planning Imagination: Utopia, Scenario & Plan, was adapted from: "Utopia, scenario, plan: A pragmatic integration," *Planning Theory*, 15(1), 6–22, published in 2016.

Chapter 6, Crafting Plans, was adapted from: "Planning craft: How do planners compose plans?," *Planning Theory*, 8(3), 219–241, published in 2009.

Chapter 7, Evaluating Plans, was adapted from: "Evaluating plans pragmatically," *Planning Theory*, 1(1), 53–75, published in 2002.

Chapter 9, Planning Spatial Community in a Complex Society, was adapted from: "Planning to keep the doors open for moral communities," *Planning Theory*, 5(2), 127–145, published in 2006.

Chapter 10, Ethical Planning Judgment, was adapted from: "Learning from groundwater: Public, private and common goods," *Environment and Planning C: Government and Policy*, 36(4), 629–648, published in 2017 and coauthored with Sanjeev Vidyarthi.

Introduction

Why do we plan for our lives and for the settlements that we build and inhabit? We hope to anticipate and prepare for the risks and uncertainties that challenge or promote our expectations for the future. We use plans to craft mental pathways of pursuit whose impacts we imaginatively compare. This vicarious testing helps us select a promising path informing our intentions. We may follow these intentions or not. This seemingly uncontroversial idea deserves special attention because professional planners and many planning analysts do not recognize and understand this idea. Many believe plans rely upon other kinds of knowledge and skill; namely rationality and expertise. Others believe planning serves progressive social efforts to remedy and replace global capitalist enterprise. Plans possess a kind of authority all their own. I disagree with this view.

The arguments in the chapters that follow describe plan making as a practical minded activity that attends to purpose, context and use more than principles of rationality and method. The judgments people make about the future come to us through tacit intuition that combines thought and feeling. We plan as part of our cognition and conception. The varieties of plan making conceived as blueprints, strategies, scenarios and visions emerge less the products of rational methodical analysis and more the result of practical use and experimentation. I dub this small 'p' planning in contrast to the large 'P' spatial planning professionals do.

Do spatial planning professionals need theory to justify the advice they offer about the future for a place? Not if people already know how to anticipate and prepare for the future. Instead of seeking a kind of philosophical foundation justifying professional planning judgment, I describe how professionals can, do and should use social and moral theories to improve the practical effectiveness of spatial plans. Instead of adopting rational planning I urge professionals to adopt pragmatic planning.

Professional planning continues to suffer from a weak conceptual grasp of its own practice. Practitioners routinely recognize the value and wisdom of practical judgment finely attuned to context, nuance and complexity; but later offer banal testimony and glib stories of 'just so' best-practice discrediting the ambiguity of their own experience. I am offering a pragmatist approach that provides a vocabulary tailored to the conventions of practical judgment resistant to simple lessons and handbooks.

This may prove disheartening for those professionals in search of best practices or doctrinal assurance. Treating planning as a functional activity means that I am wary of efforts to treat planning as the source of normative and ethical guidance. Professionals make plans to help form and guide the intentions that sponsors, clients and other stakeholders take toward the future. How professionals make plans follows norms and sets expectations for the conduct of the craft within institutional settings. But the moral and political meaning of the plans comes from the social and cultural beliefs of the people shaping the problems the plan addresses, the beliefs of those making plans and those beliefs projected for those people the plan envisions inhabiting the future. The complex interaction does not submit to a simple moral or ideological pathway.

This pragmatist approach presumes that people inhabiting and using places should be the ones with whom and for whom spatial plans get made. Spatial plans cannot and should not reconcile the multiple beliefs and expectations that come into play animating the places we inhabit. Plans do not tell people what to do but compare and assess the imagined consequences of what these people might do. Improving how we make spatial plans for places can improve the quality of the judgments about future collective consequences. Plans inform intentions. Plans do not make these intentions.

The pragmatist approach does not avoid moral and political conflicts, differences in social standing or asymmetries of political power. It treats these as inescapable conditions like the physical features of the environment, demographic trends, transportation technology and the multitude of influences shaping what the future holds. The pragmatist outlook looks to the future imagining horizons for social improvement that rely upon intelligent democratic collaboration. In this view, communities of people sustain and animate individual virtue, critical inquiry, economic exploitation, technical innovation, institutional design, religious belief and all that together compose the layers of relationships building and sustaining the places we inhabit.

The professional spatial planner should not try to shoulder the burden of knowing what to do and how to do it before events unfold. Prediction, control and certainty generate the very spatial problems that people face in urban places. The pragmatist recognizes that everyone plans, but seldom do people understand how to make plans for the places they inhabit that anticipate and use the plans of others. People do make plans all the time that coordinate the flow of daily activities with others. But how do they learn to put that skill to use anticipating and preparing for the kind of spatial problems looming on the horizon? I believe that question should animate the professional work of spatial planners in the 21st century.

Overview

The book draws upon arguments honed over the past two decades. The argument details how a pragmatist approach contributes to understanding the complexity of places and how to make spatial plans. The chapters generously tap the expertise of diverse planning scholars. I involve the reader in the development of insights for planning, keeping the bridges I travel across disciplines, beliefs and methods intact. I purposely choose authors whose theoretical ideas come from different disciplines outside urban planning or different specialty areas within the planning field to show how a pragmatic outlook can find common value for practical judgment among disparate and sometimes competing views.

I divide the book into four parts that highlight the major contributions of a pragmatist approach. First, the finding that everyone plans. This basic insight links the practical efficacy and democratic promise of the pragmatic approach to human development everywhere. Second, the complex uncertainties of modern places arise mainly from human system interactions generated by the rational pursuit of plans. Resolving these requires a robust pragmatist approach. Third, the pragmatist approach integrates diverse disciplinary expertise composing plans that inform practical judgment: conceiving future possibilities, composing relevant problems, assessing tradeoffs, anticipating conflicts and finding compromise. Professionals have plenty to learn about improving how people collaborate in diverse places to improve practical judgments that anticipate and prepare for the future of these places. Finally, the conclusion emphasizes how pragmatist adaptability contributes to the public good. Good advice helps us cope with wicked complexity reconciling moral aspirations through critical compromise.

Part I uses two chapters to make the case that everyone plans and that they do this in ways well captured by a pragmatist approach to inquiry. The often restrictive and exclusive limits of rationality need not be imposed on the practical inquiry that people use as they make plans. People offer reasons to justify judgments and choices made after the fact. Rational arguments support the claims we imagined and deployed for a specific situation demanding attention and decision. The composition of plans in the messy context of practical inquiry does not rely on foundational argument but responds to disruptions in the flow of experience searching for causes and solutions by framing problems, creating solutions, imagining future consequences and assessing different impacts. This pragmatist rationality has a provisional quality fueled by emotional and social relationships with the surrounding world. Learning remains the most valuable resource people possess to prepare for the future. A pragmatic orientation helps us in practice to learn, to integrate learning into plan formation, and it helps us to improve the practical judgments that professional and other planners must take as they make plans.

4 *Introduction*

Part II includes three chapters that focus on the emergent complexity of urban places in our still modernizing world. The physical and organizational engineering set in motion by the scientific and industrial revolutions has spawned infrastructure that increases economic growth, social interdependence and expectations for human progress. The uncertainties generated by the very success of human ingenuity and dominance now challenge those imposed by Mother Nature. Cities and their surrounding hinterland became the crucibles cradling the interactions generated among the firms, households, governments and individuals pursuing their own plans. The rational system building that inadvertently created the uncertainty posed by carbon emission pollution and global warming, global pandemics and diminished health (aka obesity, diabetes), coastal flooding and ground water depletion and so much more cannot resolve complex problems. Instead of pursuing clever strategies to avoid or control complexity, a pragmatist approach anticipates and embraces complexity with open inquiry. Instead of subduing Mother Nature with ever more powerful rational tools, the pragmatist searches for ways to emulate and integrate human activities with the forces of nature.

Part III describes how to make pragmatic spatial plans that address the challenges of urban complexity. Professional planners, engineers, architects, managers and administrators who face these problems daily will find support for the insights common sense often provides facing the limits of rational expertise. Students will find arguments, examples and stories that help put technical skill in the service of practical judgments attuned to the demands of complexity. This need not mean abandoning utopian dreams, even as it requires attention to context and conflict. Making plans for places is more craft than science. Plans compose diverse options imagining future effects susceptible to anticipation and preparation. Objectivity flows not from abstract detachment, but the comprehensive consideration of relevant strategic interest subject to varieties of democratic deliberation. Showing how values shape causal attribution and interpretive assessment enhances the validity of practical judgments, including adjustments to both ends and means. Spatial plans cannot be made to demand consensus or consent for a place beset with complex challenges; but can offer useful provisional advice about practical options relevant actors may take to resolve current problems that include impacts on imagined future effects. In the final chapter of this Part, I show how very different planning theories may be pragmatically adapted to compare how professional planners made different comprehensive plans for similar suburban places.

Part IV affirms how a pragmatist planning can release professional advisors and public officials from contemporary conventions that exalt rationality and expertise as theoretical foundations for practical insight and improvement. Three lessons stand out. One, instead of knowing first what to do and how to do it, the pragmatic approach emphasizes contextual inquiry closely tied to social learning, practical experimentation and democratic deliberations among those touched by the plan. Lesson two, everyone can learn to make better plans by paying more attention to the craft of plan making in different cultural, institutional and geographic settings. Disciplined professionals can do even more as they learn to build a scaffolding of comprehensive spatial breadth and temporal reach across disciplinary expertise. Lesson three, the complexity of human interaction and interdependence require flexible and provisional practical judgments about the arrangement of future settlement. We cannot know the future, but we can and must work together to create it with intention. These lessons speak to a conception of public good that embraces democratic social learning as the building block for resilient place communities.

Part I

1 Practical Judgment and Planning

Introduction

Professional spatial plans take for granted the expectation that a plan provides a guide for the future. The architect provides a blueprint, the social scientist a policy, the public bureaucrat a regulatory protocol and the politician some provisional combination of them all. The meaning a plan inhabits varies with provider, sponsor and clientele. But regardless of this diversity composing public advice about the future requires backup – a rationale that can pass professional muster even as it speaks to all the diverse voices and interests that set the plan in motion. Professionals routinely claim rationality as a foundation for these sorts of claims.

Professional planners may disagree about the kind of rationality a plan includes, but few would support a plan that lacks reason. Reasons justify the content of the plan, providing arguments for the quality of the advice. This protocol deserves our attention and respect because it offers coherent reflective advice about what to do in the future to coordinate multiple purposes in a complex spatial context. Disputes between substantive and procedural rationality or between modernist and postmodern rationality matter because the kind of rationality we adopt shapes the kind of planning advice we give – the kinds of plans we make.[1]

This rationality places planning outside the reach of religious prophecy or sentiment, emotional attachment or intuition, and other sources of judgment considered irrational or non-rational. Much planning theory takes this distinction for granted as analysts offer competing conceptions of rationality (e.g., instrumental versus substantive). The emphasis on rationality generates a separation between rationality and other kinds of thought. Rational theory tells us how to think about planning, but not how to do it. Rational theory discerns the truth, but not what to do with it. Theory and practice travel different paths. Furthermore, the association with rationality holds planning hostage to the debates about rationality as form and guide.

Instead of arguing that rationality shapes planning, I will argue planning shapes rationality. In a nutshell the argument goes something like this: As humans we learned to make plans to anticipate future events and coordinate actions as a matter of inescapable habit. We communicate plans to others and in so doing coordinate conduct about and towards our respective goals. We deliberate together about future options and outcomes. In so doing we use plans to help turn desires into intentions; intentions we may also use to construct a rationale for what we do.[2] Instead of modeling plans on rational belief, we use plans to organize rational intentions. This pragmatic approach uses plans to bind ideas and feelings about what to do as intentions for practical judgment.[3]

The argument does not discredit debates over planning theory but implies that the outcome of such debates may not be important for how professionals do planning – but mainly about our beliefs about important social purposes and methodological technique. This shift provides a strong rationale for the value of historical and other types of case study research in addition to more conventional tools of analysis. We learn to improve how well we anticipate and cope with complex problems – whether making plans or planning – comparing how others cope in very specific contexts with similar problems. The context might include the analysis of probabilities for sample data, but it may also include relevant interpretations of a problem using prior experience and case comparison. How did you solve that rush hour traffic congestion problem or reduce the incidence of homelessness among the urban poor? The research allows for the inclusion of the full range of human emotional responses and values. As we get contextual and relevant, the details of narrative, dialog, and the full complement of human interaction provide useful insights about the meaning and motivation of our plans and the planners who make them.

Planning and Practical Reason

People possess the capacity to act purposively; and to form and execute plans (Bratman 1987, p.2). Other animal species act purposefully, but none plan (Mithen 1999).[4] Planning grows out of the cognitive powers of our species that enable us to attend to time and others as we make our way in the world. We anticipate future action making our own plans and so coordinate our action in relation to the plans of others.

We rarely make deterministic or complete plans (aka blueprints), but provisional ones that we adjust in response to unexpected obstacles in our path or changes in other plans that conflict with our own (Sunstein 2000).[5] We also form habits that turn what were once planned decisions into a predictable routine. As we commit to following a plan the situation that prompted the effort disappears from attention, at least until unexpected changes generate new forms of uncertainty.[6]

Planning analysts adopting popular conceptions of rational decision making often presume that plans follow preferences linking desires with belief. A pragmatic approach views plans actively shaping intentions by anticipating and comparing future consequences and relationships.

Theories of rationality conceive of rational action as the employment of appropriate means for achieving a desired end. Rational action is thus thought of as a product of two vectors. One is the vector of belief, or knowledge, or probability. The other is the vector of desires, or wants, or utility. I act rationally when I act to promote what I want on the basis of what I know (Ullmann-Margalit 1999, p.73).

Instead of conceiving cognition as mental modeling that represents the world, the pragmatist approach conceives cognition as actively using the world to inform and assess judgments about what to do. Cognition uses memory of behavior in similar situations to construct and assess imaginary options testing and comparing consequences. Research on judgment uncovers a more complex set of influences shaping how people respond to uncertainty about the future. The inferences we draw about possible actions and consequences flow from emotional responses following the contours of social convention and experience.

As we seek to coordinate our conduct with others we do not deliberate about what to do from moment to moment but use plans to guide our choices.[7] Pragmatist conceptions of cognition presumes: the cognitive agent joins or inhabits a task domain, system states acquire meaning in the context of action, and the functioning of cognitive systems inseparable from embodiment (Engel et al. 2013); extends to social interaction (Clark 2008; Gallagher 2013). Plans provide scaffolding for joint coordination. We each form our provisional plan and then follow it jointly until we encounter problems that require adjustment.[8] Plans shape conduct, resist reconsideration and provide inputs for further practical reasoning.

Plans are also provisional. We do not fill in all the possible details – but leave room for revision. Plans typically exhibit a hierarchical structure. Some aspects are more important than others. Provisional and hierarchical plans enable us to assess the consequences of different goals using the same means; review how different means might achieve the same goal and more. The deliberate comparison of the differences in anticipated effects informs my intention.

Using provisional, hierarchically organized plans has a pragmatic rationale. The complexity, uncertainty and ambiguity of our social world make unilateral versus joint planning too rigid. The incomplete and hierarchical format of small p planning enables us to cope with a changing world and social partners with diverse goals. We use planning to guide our daily conduct, but also to set and fill in the larger and more general plans for our future and that of others with whom we associate. The research by cognitive and social psychologists provides evidence supporting the role for plans shaping intentions, but also the follow through associated with execution. Evidence from social psychological research on counterfactual thinking demonstrates that people do anticipate and prepare for future action. How people value plans depends on their conception of the future; a conception shaped by the plans they make (Kahneman & Lovallo 1993; Roese & Olson 1995).

Stability, Confidence and Commitment in planning

We do not deliberate from a blank slate, but in the context of predispositions tied to earlier plans, the taken for granted plans we follow all the time. How do we describe the reasonableness of such plans? We envision taken-for-granted plan following as the execution of deliberate decisions that meet the consistency and coherence tests without encountering disruptive problems. We recognize that people follow reasonable plans that might be revised using different goals offering more advantageous outcomes. Changing plans has costs that may not balance reconsideration and redirection. The less stable my current plans, the more susceptible they become to distraction based on new opportunities or difficulties. But if the stability becomes too great, so great that the coherence of the plan no longer holds, then I cannot describe my action as reasonable. "That was just a fantasy."

The stability of a plan may not dispose each individual in the same way or to the same extent. We may hold different beliefs even as we cooperate. We possess different levels of sensitivity and competence that lead us to act differently even though we hold the same beliefs and plans. The plan does not predict action, but shapes the intentions that motivate action. I may not possess the competence to sustain the plan we share and so turn away or drop out.[9]

Evaluating Plans

How do we know when our plans work well or fail us? Plans need to meet two types of demands: consistency constraints and means–ends coherence. We do not make a plan to take parallel routes on our journey to work. We must choose one or the other. Insisting that we take both is inconsistent with regard to constraints.[10] As for means, choosing air travel for a ten mile commute is inconsistent and incoherent. It makes no sense. A plan need not spell out all means ahead of time, but it should include enough means to support the underlying intention, otherwise the plan becomes means–ends incoherent. [Plans that say little about how to turn policy into projects may be said to lack means–ends coherence.] Dewey argued that we can also reconsider ends if the means entail unacceptable consequences. He envisioned the relationship as a means–ends continuum. For instance, supporters of home ownership for all Americans learn about implementation costs using current housing industry and market practices and revise the goal downwards to 65 percent (Blanco 1994, pp.68–69).

These two demands reflect a pragmatic orientation. You cannot coordinate and control future conduct if your plans are not consistent with constraints (realistic) or means–ends coherent. Our fantasies or utopias (which are unconstrained by reality and do not worry about how ends follow from means) do not qualify as plans informing our intentions. When we intend to do something, we place this intention within our planning framework and the intention is subject to the demands of consistency with constraints and means–ends coherence (Bratman 1987, p.32).

Prior plans channel future deliberations in effect narrowing the scope of what options we need to consider in coordinating our conduct. The consistency and coherence filter the options we consider based on prior plans.[11] Preferences and interests may generate expectations that motivate action; but the expectations do not become intentional without a plan (Hendricks-Jensen 1996). Planners often imagine that the meaning of the planning effort flows downward from goal to policy. But reasoning practically uses planning to move in the either direction. We learn to articulate and clarify our purpose as we form a plan. How we do science and present our scientific findings differ, and so does planning conduct and plan presentation. We put the fully articulated goals at the beginning of a finished plan, but these goals did not appear so vivid and complete at the outset of the planning process.[12]

Planning Makes Practical Reasoning Work

We make plans not to reduce complexity into predictable routine, but to anticipate, prepare for and cope with complexity in ways that better meet our needs, fulfill our purposes and respect our limitations. Plans combine instrumental inquiry with deliberation to form intentions that guide joint action and improve coordination. Deliberation invites participants to persuade one another to adopt a modified version of the descriptions, analysis, programs and policies that compose a plan, and to inspire a willingness to treat these versions as a guide for the practical judgments used to put the plan elements into action (Forester, 1999, Hoch 2002).

Once we recognize planning as a crucial ingredient for practical judgment then we no longer need to find a theoretical justification for planning. We need not search out some foundation for planning, some deeper or wider rationale beyond the practical anticipation we use every day. When analysts argue that planning need apply the rules and conventions of rationality used in the sciences they are not providing a foundation or justification for planning but trying to squeeze a practical and robust planning activity into a too specialized theoretical framework.[13]

How do we make plans that improve the rational coordination of the purposes of many people who do not know one another? How do we make plans that improve the rational assessment and inclusion of a variety of desires, purposes and beliefs held by many different groups of people? Rationality is not something we need to make sure we possess before we plan, but a practical accomplishment that may help or hinder the plans we make. Susan Haack offers a wonderful analogy to capture how we compose epistemic judgments – a socially constructed crossword puzzle. The gradual testing of words tied to the ongoing interdependent meaning across the assembly of prior commitments combines experiential evidence with the demands of a coherent fit (Haack 1993, p.120). How do we take the wisdom of the practical deliberations we use to make plans and use it to provide rational plans for more complex relationships?

In the next chapter, Chapter 2, I explore how emotions shape human judgment. The findings and insights provide a much more robust account of the ways that intuition and feelings shape not only expectations, but the very organization of how humans think and judge. Feelings shape how people compose and use plans. Professionals should understand and include their experience and knowledge of emotions as they compose plans for places. Professional objectivity flows not from detached expertise, but a compassionate grasp of the meaning future consequences may pose for people inhabiting a troubled place.

Notes

1 I am avoiding a strong distinction between plan making and planning. I believe the meaning varies with the context of use, but that making and doing plans retains enough common meaning to make the argument that follows coherent. See Verma (1998) on the importance of similarity in theoretical approach.
2 Rationality refers to how we use reason to guide choice and conduct. Rationale refers to the reasons we offer when responding to questions about the choices we make and our conduct. Deliberation refers to the inherently dialogical and social quality of both. How we choose and how we act on the choices are distinct but closely related.
3 Gerald Nadler distinguished between research inquiry and problem solving or planning. We can conduct research through solitary reflection but solving problems or making plans requires joint inquiry.
4 Studies of chimpanzees have uncovered highly developed social intelligence including theft, deception and cooperation; and evidence of the use of tools to collect termites and crack nuts. But there is no evidence that chimps can use tools to improve social activity or social learning to improve the use of tools
5 Cass Sunstein describes this sort of adjustment as an incompletely theorized agreement. When people in groups (e.g., planning commission or committee) disagree about the meaning of an abstract value (e.g., equality versus liberty) they improve their understanding by conceptual descent. They move down levels of abstraction to a level where conceptual agreement becomes possible. People may believe in the protection of an endangered species but hold different reasons such as ecological contribution or contribution to human life. We may agree that traffic is bad without agreeing on a rationale.
6 Most of social life consists of habits for individuals, customs for communities and rules or laws for societies. The dynamics of planning change as we increase the scale of the social relationships and as we increase the temporal reach.
7 Plans accompany intentions in this sense across the full range of contexts. We can describe cases where people make intentions without plans, but then we describe them as impulsive and irrational.
8 Heuristic models for decision making adopt this insight, for instance, when studying 'consumers' with little time and money coordinate with others in learning about and choosing a product. Consumers mimic others not only to reduce transaction costs, but because we learn that if others like the product we will as well. Advertisers understand how we make plans and use this feature of human cognitive and social adaptation to shape our purchase intentions and choices. That we make judgments in such ways does not mean that we should do so. We can adopt clever forms of resistance.

9 The idea of stability of commitment represents a virtue of sorts for individuals and an institutional or social property that proves especially rare. When the very survival of the institution requires the stability, then the plan will hold, but for more peripheral issues of taste the change will be more frequent and plans will become obsolete. A complementary quality is flexibility and the more targeted notion of adaptability. Flexibility refers to a capacity for change that does not alter the integrity of the commitment, while adaptability refers to a capacity that denotes a flexibility that will alter the commitment to fit changing circumstances to produce improved consequences.
10 From this viewpoint we cannot say that we plan to provide affordable housing or adequate flood control without intending to carry it out. We would find it impossible to coordinate plans with others if they were not consistent in this way.
11 Local municipal planning in the US often occurs without paying attention to prior plans. The apparently imaginative and innovative posturing does not build upon how we use planning, but falsely imagines plans as an image of the future independent of current policies and activities. The idea of the comprehensive plan stumbles badly when it adopts a concept of rationality that relies on assumptions about the future not closely tied to local context, institutional practices and favored purposes. Bratman does not consider the various sources of cognitive and emotional bias that can clog the filter of admissibility.
12 Local plans that use the same goal statements as neighboring communities skipping the time-consuming process of starting with the more detailed and prescriptive plans or policies that link purpose to context not only lack relevance for those who might use it, but the goals may perversely distract or misguide people inspiring disbelief or cynical acceptance with little practical regard. If elected officials can adopt a plan and then ignore it, the document failed to do planning.
13 Here is where I deploy the insights of the post-structural critics of rational planning. We can learn how desire subverts misleading rational assumptions and claims. Since the critics identify rationality with planning they do not consider how desire fuels the plans we make and so provide practical insights about what to do with our feelings. At times they seem to treat feelings as strangers to the cognitive infrastructure for judgment – something that happens to us rather than something that accompanies what we experience, and that we might modify as we make plans for the future.

References

Blanco, H. (1994). *How to Think About Social Problems: American Pragmatism and the Ideal of Planning*. Westport, CT: Greenwood Press.

Bratman, M. (1987). *Intentions, Plans and Practical Reason*. Cambridge, MA: Harvard University Press.

Clark, A. (2008). *Supersizing the mind: Reflections on embodiment, action, and cognitive extension*. Oxford: Oxford University Press.

Engel, A. K., Maye, A., Kurthen, M. and Konig, P. (2013). Where's the action? The pragmatic turn in cognitive science. *Trends in Cognitive Sciences*, 77(5), 202–209.

Forester, J. (1999). *The Deliberative Practitioner*. Cambridge, MA: MIT Press.

Gallagher, S. (2013). The socially extended mind. *Cognitive Systems Research*, 25–26, 4–12.

Haack, S. (1993). Double-aspect foundherenstism: A new theory of empirical justification. *Philosophy & Phenomenological Research*, LII(1), 113–128.

Hendriks-Jensen, H. (1996). *Catching Ourselves in the Act*. Cambridge, MA: MIT Press.

Hoch, C. (2002). Evaluating plans pragmatically. *Planning Theory*, 1(1), 53–76.

Kahneman, D. and Lovallo, D. (1993). Timid choices and bold forecasts: A cognitive perspective on risk taking. *Management Science*, 39, 17–31.

Mithen, S. (1999). *The Prehistory of Mind: The Cognitive Origins of Art and Science*. London: Thames & Hudson.

Roese, N. J. and Olson, J. M. (1995). *What Might Have Been: The Social Psychology of Counterfactual Thinking*. Mahwah, NJ: Lawrence Erlbaum Associates.

Sunstein, C. (2000). Practical reason and incompletely theorized agreements. In E. Ullmna-Margalit (Ed.), *Reasoning Practically* (pp. 98–122). New York: Oxford University Press.

Ullmann-Margalit, E. (1999). On not wanting to know. In E. Ullmann-Margalit (Ed.), *Reasoning Practically* (pp. 72–84). New York: Oxford University Press.

Verma, N. (1998). *Similarities, Connections and Systems*. New York: Lexington Press.

2 Emotional Intelligence in Planning Judgment

Objectivity Versus Sensitivity

As professional planners make plans, they judge the value of current acts in relation to future consequences. They construct pathways for intentions tied to future expectations that anticipate and evaluate these consequences. Planning analysts and practitioners pay close attention to these pathways studying how the beliefs people hold carry them along this path from concept to intention; and intention to action. Analysts study whether and how environmental, political, social, economic and cultural influences shape beliefs as descriptions or guides. Practitioners seek to understand how people comprehend beliefs about the future and how the plans practitioners make may modify these beliefs. Both emphasize the role of ideas, thinking and argument in plans that link knowledge with purposeful action. Urban plans should rely on rational judgment.

But attention, perception and reflection used in planning judgment also rely upon emotional dispositions and sensitivity. The practical activity people take learning and adopting a belief involves more than cognitive judgment about the value of the belief (its truthfulness or goodness). Belief also draws upon emotions and feelings (its meaning and significance). Most people recognize that emotions and feelings shape beliefs. The desires and preferences we hold direct our attention, motivate our interests, compel our assent and alert us to risks. Yet, despite the ubiquity of emotions and feelings, planning practitioners and analysts rarely focus on them as a resource for comprehending future oriented, purposeful action. Practitioners and analysts learn to treat emotions a source bias and distortion. They need control their emotions lest feelings bias rational judgment.

Two arguments justify the strategy of detachment. First, the influential method of experimental scientific inquiry relegates emotions and feelings to an inferior role in human judgment. Emotions and feelings in this view undermine the quality of intellectual judgment (Forgas 1990; Goldie 2005). The metaphor of hard science denotes this kind of inquiry. Hard implies indifference to the force of passion. Professional planners reflect this outlook embracing expert judgment that relies upon a cool and precise reason that keeps affect at bay. Planning analysts similarly discourage rhetorical expressions of emotional significance in the organization and reporting of research. This is the objectivity approach. Second, paralleling and complementing the objectivity tradition is another that directly studies how emotions and feelings influence cognition. These analysts (psychologists, neurophysiologists and social scientists) conceive the impacts of instincts, drives and feelings as pressures originating from physiological and psychological conditions and social experience (Forgas & Smith 2003; Rolls 2000; Elster 1996). Analysts who study the effects of emotions and feelings on cognitive judgment retain the hard methods of experimental science. These analysts argue that although we cannot easily avoid or control emotional impacts on our judgment, we can learn how to adapt, modify and channel them to improve the quality of the cognitive judgment we make to guide successful action. This is the sensitivity approach. In the first approach emotions must be identified and controlled to plan objectively; in the second emotions must be identified and tamed to reduce emotional bias on plans.

Objectivity encourages planners to frame beliefs about the future using concepts that exclude emotions and feelings entirely. Sensitivity prepares planners to anticipate and channel emotional responses to plans for the future. These views show up as distinct styles in the planning enterprise. We adopt objectivity as we conduct a planning study of existing conditions, demographic trends and the like; abstracting from sources of emotional bias to focus exclusively on the quality of cognitive judgments. Professionals offer scientific findings and expect the audience to believe these findings following logical argument and evidence. Sensitivity comes to the fore as planners anticipate emotional responses to the analysis of problems and the evaluation of alternatives; adopting compensatory adjustments that minimize the impacts of feelings and passion. Here planners use images, construct narratives and adopt graphic symbols that attract and channel the emotional attachments of the relevant audience. Planners use the analysis of emotional effects to anticipate and avoid undesirable emotional responses on the part of the audience.

Research Study of Cognition and Emotions

Spatial planners study complex social and institutional plans and planning drawing on a wide variety of professional (e.g., engineering, architecture) and social science (e.g., economics, geography, sociology) disciplines. The systematic study of human emotions and their impact takes place in disciplines less familiar to planning analysts; psychology, social psychology, neurophysiology, philosophy and literature. In this portion of the chapter I briefly summarize some experimental research conducted by psychologists and social psychologists to frame the objectivity – sensitivity contrast and then use work by the neurophysiologist Antonio Damasio and philosopher Martha Nussbaum to frame a pragmatic combination of the two.

Framing the contrast between feeling and thinking informs strategic accounts of emotional manipulation and control. Cognitive psychologists study the relationships between the psychological and physiological dimensions of planning. Using experimental methods, the cognitive psychologists study the relationship between select cognitive problem-solving tasks and select physiological (e.g., brain damage), psychological (e.g., prior learning) or social (e.g., status) conditions. Social psychologists adopt similar methods but focus on social and emotional dimensions of cognitive planning tasks. Both disciplines adopt a strong analytic distinction between aspects of emotion and cognition. Both use this distinction to analyze how individual people plan on their own and in relation to others.

In a book surveying the cognitive psychology of planning Robin Morris and Goef Ward describe plans as cognitive activity used to achieve a goal (Ward & Morris 2005). For decades cognitive psychologists optimistically and abstractly insisted that a useful plan be complete, efficient and foolproof. The analysts devise puzzles to experimentally identify and measure the cognitive components of how individuals plan independent of context and the influence of motivation and emotions. Imagine a psychological version of the synoptic rational planning model (Faludi 1973) applied to a very narrow range of puzzle solving activity. Analysts study variations in puzzle solving plans under different controlled conditions (Morris & Ward 2005; Ward & Allport 1997). They focus mainly on the relationship between cognitive function and behavior analyzing how individuals plan using search heuristics in problem space (Newell & Simon 1972), information processing strategies (Hayes-Roth & Hayes-Roth 1979), and schemes linking knowledge, evaluation and action (Miller, Galanter & Pribram 1960). Recent research has studied planning in ill-defined domains paying close attention to the impacts of expertise and prior learning (Ormerod 2005). Cognitive planning research provides experimental evidence that the complex urban planning that professionals study and use may rely upon underlying cognitive planning behavior only dimly understood.

Other cognitive analysts, instead of studying puzzle solving problems, study the cognitive steps people take when they make plans for simulated activities (e.g., a shopping trip). Studying how people plan errands or other task sequences in simulated experiments add insights that the strategic puzzle solvers miss. The simulation analysts record participant commentary and behavior, documenting how subjects use emotional and historical aspects of their own experience to compare, evaluate and select route choices. For instance, Burgess et al. (2005) use experimental errand plan behavior to challenge puzzle-based plan making emphasizing relevance rather than precision. For instance, the errand analysts criticize puzzle testers for focusing on how well people can 'look ahead' and follow a series of puzzle solving steps using mental representations or images. The errand analysts insist that people do not plan narrowly in their everyday lives. People compose simulated plans that include 'stored preferences' they bring to their planning – preferences based on prior learning and feelings they use to choose routes.

Research on the psychology of cognition uncovers planning at the very core of human judgment (Morris & Ward 2005; Schwarz 2000). The puzzle analysts cast cognitive plan making as a strategic activity testing for correspondence between cognitive behavior models and performance. The simulation analysts conceive cognitive plans as more complex interactions of foresight and reflective adjustment that include emotional responses and communication. But these research analysts retain the conventional bias that subordinates the emotional to the rational – even as recognition of emotional dimensions increases.

Social Psychologists and Counterfactuals

Social psychologists study the relationships between individual planning activity, feelings and social context. Many of these analysts conduct experiments that test for different kinds of emotional impact on cognitive judgments formed in response to social outcomes. Instead of abstracting cognition from emotion, they study their interaction (Forgas & Smith 2003). In this section I briefly describe some of the research findings by those social psychologists studying how people create 'counterfactuals' to make sense of uncertain events from the past and the future.

Social psychologists study how we routinely describe the past in ways that do not fit the facts but run counter to the facts. The social psychologists study why and how people create accounts about prior events that describe for themselves and others how different consequences might have ensued under different conditions. *If I had arrived earlier to the meeting I would have received a copy of the agenda. If the gun had not been loaded I would not have accidentally shot my neighbor.* Social Psychologists want to understand the cognitive functions such counterfactuals play and the emotional dimensions that stimulate and accompany such thinking. They are especially interested in the psychological benefits this activity offers people making and interpreting judgments about prior decisions that produced troubling consequences in relations with others (Roese & Olson 1995).

People also use counterfactuals to imagine a future that contrasts with current factual conditions. As we form a plan we use counterfactuals to conceive alternative activities that will help us reach the anticipated goal. *What would my future hold if I changed my current eating habits or attachment to public transportation?* Turning a desire and belief into an intended goal we conceive a counterfactual plan for accomplishing the goal. The plan will likely be both incomplete and adaptive, but still closely tied to the conditions shaping current practice. Since human life is complicated no complete plan is possible. We expect plans to change, and so plans need adapt to the change.[1] We can use research findings on counterfactuals to understand the psychological aspects of how people make plans (Boninger, Gleicher & Strathaman 1994).

We can use counterfactuals to construct a plan that include only modest changes to current conditions. The plan does not require that we build an entire alternate world, but only a few changes as sequential conditionals guiding choices along the pathway to the goal. The spare decision tree or PERT Chart illustrates the formal choice points along a series of sequential options that once taken lead down distinct pathways that differ from the heading set by current trends. Relying on a comprehensive formal tree that outlines all the possible future choices is a distraction at this point. People use plans to organize their choice (Pollock 2004; Simon 1982).[2]

The counterfactual conditionals may work backwards from the goal or forward from current practice. We do not use the counterfactuals to select an option to help guide our choice of option, counterfactuals help us conceive options as part of a plan. The act of conception uses counterfactual conditions to connect current practice and future goal with an action plan that turns desire into intention. The counterfactual narrates, models, maps, calculates or simulates a plausible future that enables us to act on our desire.

Social Psychologists use the concept of counterfactuals to account for narrative rationales we offer ourselves when reflecting on how past actions might be reconsidered. We do it after the fact and so our thinking is counter factual. Counterfactuals rely upon our linguistic use of conditionals (if, then) in a subjunctive mood (would that it could be so). We learn to ponder the legacy of human choices and actions as we reconsider how events might have turned out differently. The social psychologists do not emphasize the logical and factual reconstruction of past circumstances surrounding the choices made or actions taken. They are not historians or forensic investigators. Rather, they study the functional and emotional impacts that counterfactuals play in shaping the psychological meaning of current activity.

Most of the social psychologists use experimental analysis to test hypotheses about different dimensions of the complex way we reconsider what might happen. The attention to analytic slivers tends to overlook the more encompassing ways that we create stories and arguments, but still provide useful insights for understanding how people make and respond to plans. I will briefly describe some findings about psychological features of human judgment that shape how we plan.

Bias

When planners craft advice they selectively direct attention using emotional cues. Social Psychologists conduct research on how these sorts of cues frame and focus judgments.

1. *Subject over Predicate*: Respondents prefer the subject to the referent when asked to rank the relative merits of competing goods. Analysts tested choices between two equal goods changing only the order. For instance, in the case of two equally good colleges they compared the pairing 'Harvard vs. Stanford' against 'Stanford vs. Harvard' in different test trials. They

found that respondents select the first mentioned subject over the second mentioned referent in each case (Houston & Fazio 1989). This implies that people possess a psychological bias about the order of choice. If we ask people to choose between Plan A and Plan B, all other things equal, they will tend to prefer Plan A based on the psychological response for the subject over the predicate.

2. *Better versus Worse*: People offer different response to the same options depending on how we frame its description (Shafir 1993). If we say an option is better than a competing alternative people will tend to agree more than if we say the same alternative is worse than the same option. So starting out showing our audience how planning options will improve Main Street plays to this approval bias more favorably than beginning with a description of the problems along Main Street and then describing improvements.

3. *Great contrast versus Slight contrast*: How we select and compare alternatives can have psychological effects. Increasing the contrast between options tends to increase the psychological acceptability of the choice above and beyond the inherit merits of the alternatives (McMullen 1997). For instance, if we frame the choice of energy generation options between Nuclear and Solar power we are likely to obtain more acceptance for the Solar option than if we offered the option between Nuclear and Coal. If we offer an alternative that differs greatly from the choice the respondents will select differently than if we offer an alternative that differs only modestly from the choice. We offer a density option that contrasts the choice of town homes against the high rise in Manhattan. Then we compare the same town home choice against a planned unit development that includes a mix of single-family dwellings and apartment buildings.

These examples, and many others I did not include (Forgas & Smith 2003), illustrate how experimental analysts select aspects of a more encompassing judgment arguing that psychological dimensions do shape planning judgments. The underlying analytic framework for most of this research still separates cognition into discreet functions tied to different kinds of planning behaviors. Even after reading a brief litany of these findings the practical minded planner will find the results intriguing and even familiar yet difficult to assimilate to practice. How do we attend to these psychological dimensions without sacrificing the contextual complexity and relevance of practical planning judgment?

Studying Thought and Feeling Together

I want to argue that we leave aside the methodological separation between cognitive objectivity and emotional sensitivity (recognizing the methodological value of the separation for select experimental analysis) and consider both as important resources for human intelligence and judgment. However, combining objectivity and sensitivity proves difficult because most of us inherit the belief that makes their separation appear normal. I want to make the case for such a merger by first arguing, with the help of neurophysiologist Antonio Damasio (2003), that evidence of brain development and use supports a functional integration of emotion and thought. Second, I use the ideas of philosopher Martha Nussbaum to show how we might recognize the intelligence of emotions as we make and evaluate plans. Damasio helps us understand the inescapable features of emotions on the landscape of human judgment. Useful human judgment combines logic and feeling. Nussbaum shows how the careful discernment of feeling can improve the quality of the judgments we make and actions we take. Emotions provide a source of intelligent judgment about complex choices.

The Hierarchy of Emotions and Judgment: Damasio

Psychologists and Social Psychologists studying cognition and emotions do not always agree about the relevant range of human emotions. The following eight appear most common: anger, sadness, joy, fear, shame, pride, disgust, and guilt (Izard 1991). Antonio Damasio offers a richer palette of emotional distinctions distinguishing primary (anger, fear, sadness, happiness, surprise and disgust) and social (sympathy, embarrassment, shame, guilt, pride, jealousy, envy, gratitude, admiration, indignation and contempt) emotions (Damasio 2003, p.44). Damasio interprets emotional function within an evolutionary outlook, assessing the functional merits of each emotion in relation to its adaptive contribution. This outlook does not mean that emotions always prove useful for individuals, but that the study of human behavior will prove more valid and insightful if we consider the emotions as a resource for adaptive learning rather than an impediment to clear thinking and good judgment. For instance, research has uncovered the evolutionary value of emotions like disgust, a response that triggers avoidance of toxic foods or fear that inspires flight from predators. Fridja (1986) labels these emotions "relevance detectors". Emotions inform intelligent adaptive responses to an uncertain environment.

Damasio (2003) describes emotions using the terminology of human anatomy and brain physiology, but from the point of view of practical judgment. He adopts a functional orientation that treats emotions as chemical and neural responses to environmental stimuli that organisms use to activate a state of adaptive behavior. The automatic behavioral responses to danger (e.g. fear), praise (e.g., happiness), loss (e.g., sadness), pain (e.g., anger) and other emotions represents an evolutionary accomplishment of adaptive survival. These emotional responses help organisms respond effectively to a changing environment. Humans, because we possess considerably more brain power, can form sensory maps of the changes that occur in the body as emotions experiencing what we call feelings. Additionally, humans can even anticipate and evoke these feelings without external stimulus accounting for feelings of desire and anxiety generated by memories or fantasies (p.51).

Damasio emphasizes that feelings inhere within a bodily state of response. Feelings occur not only as automatic responses, but as responses linked with the form of mental states associated with consciousness. Feelings provide resources for cognitive reflection and assessment. Additionally, feelings direct our attention to the salience of the objects we encounter within any specific situation that allows time for reflective assessment. Feelings do not operate like a hydraulic system, but more like finely tuned sensors that interact tacitly and subtly to variations in the flow of diverse stimuli (p.177). Damasio argues that the evolutionary architecture of the brain has a hierarchical structure with emotional development preceding and framing the development of feelings.[3] This conception breaks down the functional segregation of cognition and emotion used by most cognitive and social psychologists and insists that we frame our study of human judgment in ways that combine both.

Emotions, Evaluation and Judgment: Martha Nussbaum

Philosopher Martha Nussbaum would agree with Damasio but focuses less on the physiology of emotion and more on the relationship between emotions and moral judgments. She argues that we should think about the emotions that accompany an activity like plan making as both cognitive and evaluative. Emotions mark the salience of the objects we conceive. More specifically, emotions such as grief, fear, love, joy, hope, anger, gratitude, hatred, envy, jealousy, pity and guilt modulate the significance and meaning of our judgment about someone or something. I grieve the loss of my mother, not all mothers. I am angry with your critical remark, not criticism. The local resident stares indifferently at the land use plan and then recoils in anger when viewing the condominium development plan proposed for a nearby parcel. Nussbaum's conception contrasts with the common view that emotions occur outside thought – pushing rather than pulling us toward a judgment. The hydraulic conception removes intentionality from emotion hoping to avoid distortions that may accompany animistic conceptions of action. For Nussbaum emotion has less to do with detachment than selection: combining the proper feeling and thoughts for the occasion or situation at hand. Our emotions accompany and inform the judgments we make about the objects we desire and the actions we take to obtain them.

Nussbaum offers four important insights about the emotional quality of the kinds of judgments we make when planning.

1. *Emotions Do not Push but Pull Us*. They direct our attention to objects. Our fears, hopes and anger focus on someone or something. The kind of object we conceive in turn shapes the kind of emotion. As a child we fear the onset of the storm. And as the storm crashes down upon us we wail and weep as we imagine a lightening strike taking our life. We may in time learn to feel less fear as we acquire new knowledge about storms informing us about the improbability of such a strike. As we acquire this knowledge

we may need courage at first to act upon our new understanding. Reducing the emotional attachment of fear and storms may require some practice to replace fear with other feelings such as indifference or wonder. When people learn about a new redevelopment plan that introduces a change they may react with fear about the uncertain consequences this change may produce. But if they learn how the relevant benefits outweigh the costs the feelings change from fretful resistance to hopeful optimism. The work by Peter Marris (1996) among planning scholars elaborates how this works using insights from psychoanalytic and phenomenological theory.

Humans enjoy the additional ability to evoke such emotional responses within our own imaginations. We re-enact the earlier emotional response to an object. I feel fear recalling the memory of the storm. The emotions not only fuel memory, but direct and shape the attention we give to the content. However, these counterfactual accounts include more than the slivers of cognitive psychological function studied so closely by social psychologists – they include the quality of emotional responses that people rely upon to evaluate beliefs. John Forester (1999) uses Nussbaum to show how the conduct of plan deliberation can be improved in challenging emotional disputes as participants learn to recognize their emotional commitments as a source of mutual insight.

2. *Emotions Engage Us Intentionally; they draw us into an interpretation of the object that shapes our response internally and expressively.* The range of emotional response to the same object can vary with this emotional response. I am fearful of the power of the storm, but hopeful that it will provide needed water in a time of drought. Emotions include cognitive features that give meaning to our experience and actions.

Damasio offers a more clinical explanation of such object stimulated response. The emotional response

> begins with an appraisal-evaluation phase, starting with the detection of an emotionally competent stimulus ... The radical excision of the appraisal phase should obscure rather than illuminate the real value of emotions: their largely intelligent connection between the emotionally competent stimulus and the set of reactions that can alter our body function and our thinking so profoundly (Damasio 2003, pp.53–54).

Damasio's more technical language emphasizes the adaptive value of emotions that shape human perception and judgment. Our emotional responses lead rather than follow cognitive reflection and inquiry. Instead of casting emotion as an impediment to thought, this view recognizes emotions as an inescapable accompaniment to human thought. We can and do learn to use emotional responses to improve or to undermine the quality and effectiveness of cognitive judgments and other actions. Feelings not only betray our thoughts but provide a stimulus for innovative judgment and action under stress.

3. *The Emotions Shape How We Think About the World.* If I believe the storm reflects God's wrath for my recent anger, then I may feel a mixture of guilt and fear with the onset of the storm. Our beliefs can shift with a change in emotion. As I experience the joys of secular living, I lose my sense of guilt and fear before to a wrathful God. My feelings of fearful attachment diminish, replaced by feelings of confidence tied to people and customs. I can also learn new beliefs that change the meaning of my commitments. Replacing belief in God with beliefs about the hydrological cycles on earth may displace feelings of guilt and fear with feelings of wonder and even joy at the power and beauty of the storm. No matter if I change my belief or feeling, their joint effect on intentions and judgment, changes my relationship with the world. As people sincerely adopt a plan, they use it to provide an emotional as well as cognitive framework for assessing progress, effort or accomplishment. Many kinds of feeling may accompany the making, carrying out and accomplishment of a plan; differences that shape the relevance and success of the plan. People may understand the cognitive value of a plan, but if they do not feel a sense of ownership or possession that fuels their intention to follow the plan, then the plan does not work. For instance, Leonie Sandercock (2002, 2004) makes the case for a more robust planning enterprise as she includes stories of the dispossessed to evoke a compassion that is strong enough to challenge conventional attachments to planning membership.

4. *Finally, the Intentional Beliefs that Inform Emotions Find Value in Objects.* Whether or not we feel anything depends on the importance of the object for us. The value refers to my specific prospects for what Nussbaum calls 'flourishing'. Emotions represent crucial aspects for our own cognitive and moral development. The value of the object may also be related to the needs of others through compassion and empathy. I recognize that what makes it possible for me to feel free will also offer the same value for others who are similarly disposed, but not as well provisioned. Emotional intensity varies with the comprehension and clarity of belief and its effects for me or for others for whom similar effects yield similar results. As competent professionals make a comprehensive plan they not only include all the important logical parts of the community but attend to the feelings and beliefs different people hold about those parts and their combination. They conduct citizen participation not only to ensure fairness of representation, but to solicit knowledge about the meaning of the plan among a diverse assortment of people offering a diverse range of responses (Churchill 2003).

Damasio and Nussbaum teach us that the plans we make will not prove attractive or useful to individuals without offering both emotional and cognitive meaning. If we believe their arguments, then we need develop planning analysis that pays more attention to both aspects of planning judgment. But how would this work?

Planning Research and Emotions

Case study planning research can include narratives about planning issues and activities that describe the emotions and feelings of individuals and groups of individuals (Baum 1983, 1997; Forester 1999; Marris 1996; Throgmorton 1996). Narrative accounts do more than report the emotions and feelings of individuals involved in the action; they anticipate and evokes an emotional response from the readers (Cole 1990). The reader not only learns about the outrage of a protagonist planner in the face of a betrayal, but feels something as well – indifference perhaps, but more likely suspicion, empathy or even some mixture. These case accounts avoid the analytic separation of rational and emotional dimensions of judgment, describing their integration in the context of practical judgments.

I have studied planners in the US for decades, conducting interviews and observing them in meetings, offering testimony, conversing with colleagues, advising clients, conducting site visits, interpreting regulations and more. In studying what they said and did, I recorded actions and emotions in detailed narrative reports. The two cases that follow draw from these original reports collected in the early 1990s. The narratives use Damasio and Nussbaum's ideas to illustrate how emotions shape the judgments planners make as they compose and offer advice.[4]

The Site Visit: Implementing the Zoning Code

Michael De Soto heads the community development department of an aging inner suburb of a US Midwest metropolis. He takes pride in his professional role, a suit and tie guy among a blue collar staff less artfully adorned. Michael visits with Adriana Hernandez who claims her neighbor's new fence violates code. As we traveled to the site Michael filled me in on some local history. Adriana had for years tended a large garden on the lot next to her single-family home before the current owner constructed a duplex. Adriana resents the loss of the garden and the increased density, even though the construction met the R-2 zoning requirements. Adriana has filed many complaints with municipal agencies about the new duplex residents and the landlord. Most notable was her success using municipal code enforcement to force her neighbor to remove a fence that encroached on her property line by just one inch. This did little to inspire good will. The landlord has just completed installing a new fence and Adriana has called Michael out to conduct an inspection – hoping to force removal once again. Michael speculates that the intensity of the antagonism may be complicated by the fact that the Hernandez's are the only Mexicans in white ethnic neighborhood. Adriana's resentment may flow not only from her selfish disappointment but a sense of injustice.

Adriana mutters a gruff greeting standing stiff and awkward, guarding the threshold to her house sandwiched between half open screen door and front door. Michael responds in Spanish, the stiffness flees she smiles and both doors open wide. She tells the story of the first fence and then sheepishly admits that she knows the new fence meets the code. She checked herself. It seems she wants Michael to advise her on the location of a new back gate she hopes to construct. As we follow her out back Michael looks at me whimsically wincing acknowledgement at her cleverness. It takes only a few moments to take the measurements and satisfy her worry. *Gracias* all round.

As we turn to leave, Michael spies an elderly man repairing automobiles in his garage. Their eyes meet, and the man motions us to approach. "I saw you at the meeting last night," he says. Michael responds with an affirmative nod. "You do community development, right?" Michael responds, "Yes." Pointing to the jumble of cars in his garage the elderly repair man raises his voice to make a point, "I have owned my home here for more than 30 years and repairing cars here since 1961, it's a grandfathered use!" Michael, responding softly, agrees. Reassured the elderly man paused and then voicing indignation reported,

> I tried to speak last night, but the mayor cut me off. He would not listen to me. I think you City employees do a good job, but not the mayor. I voted for him, but not any more. He doesn't even live in town. He lives in *Rich* Town.

As he spoke, the man would step forward aggressively and then rock backward like a boxer. Michael obliged stepping back and forth offering sympathy in sync. A litany of complaints followed starting with neighborhood matters and then escalating to more global municipal issues.

> They were gonna fix the street lights her and the City Council removed them from the list of eligible projects. Then they took the money and used it for street improvements in the Jungle (a racist euphemism for a dense residential subdivision in the municipality inhabited mainly by Mexicans)!

Michael abruptly stopped his rhythmic rocking and the elderly man stumbled to a halt. The bond of sympathy had snapped. Both knew it. Michael offered an account of the redistribution describing the efficiency and justice of the Council decision. The elderly man stood rooted, inert, hands to his side indifferent to every word Michael spoke. Clipped goodbyes and we left.

Michael makes moral judgments that include attention to his own feelings and the feelings of others. The unexceptional routine planning activity included a range of feeling. He shows empathy for Adriana's exaggerated encroachment claims speaking Spanish as he listens to her concerns. She responds generously to this little ethnic gift and drops the persona of aggrieved neighbor, taking the opportunity to seek practical advice on location of a backyard gate. Michael extends a sympathetic ear to the complaints of the elderly neighbor and then deflects the unexpected racial remarks using an impartial persona to accompany his policy story about redistributive justice. The psychological and cognitive aspects of judgment blend together (Bailey 1983).[5]

The Prison Plan: Recommending a Facility Location

Valerie makes plans for state prisons. She works for a national consultant that provides prison planning expertise. Prison planning and construction was a booming industry in the US at the time I conducted this interview. Valerie describes her work for a national consultant. Her firm contracts with State prison boards studying the suitability of eligible counties for new prison development and recommending sites at the conclusion of the study. Valerie, barely out of her twenties, has angular cheekbones and porcelain skin, blue eyes and long thick eyebrows emphasizing thick bangs. Other than a silver barrette she wears no other jewelry or makeup. She looks like a demure first grade teacher, not a prison planner. She tells me how she plans for prisons.

> I'm not sure there is a good way to plan for prisons. The demand for the employment prisons provide greatly exceeds the supply. There are lots of places to choose from and little time to conduct a thorough assessment ... I do a lot more than is required. All you need do is visit a handful or prospective sites, attend a local meeting, take notes and offer priorities. But I spend a lot of time and effort collecting and assessing the needs and desires of each place.
>
> I am willing to admit that I don't know things. Most of my colleagues won't. I try and learn. I put myself in the place of the local residents and officials. I try and get an accurate sense of their feelings about the prison and its consequences for them. The prison is full of bad people. Would I want to live near one? No, I wouldn't. But there is more to the decision than just that risk. The prison brings jobs and economic development. You don't have to identify your community with the prison.
>
> I point out to residents fearful about the prison that they already turn a blind eye to undesirable activities, buildings, etc. ... in their community. You can learn to do the same with the prison. But I ask myself, "Could I really not notice it everyday?" I have a hard time answering yes. I try avoiding this question, but when someone puts it to me I'm honest. I say no.
>
> At first, I thought that if I lied to people it wouldn't make that big a difference. But I could never bring myself to do it. When I went on my first site visit I traveled with a colleague who lied. He would say whatever he thought the audience wanted to hear. He said things like "It will not be that bad." and "The governor will think you're an important place. You'll get political attention." He wanted the residents to believe that the prison itself was a good thing. I believe the people left a lot more afraid than when they first came. Many seemed resigned and defeated. They felt the coming of the prison was inevitable. They lost the sense that their participation mattered.

At least with honesty residents will trust you and listen to what you say. Partly they have no other choice but to trust me since I'm their main opportunity to make their participation count. But they also trust me because I speak sincerely and honestly. I tell them that what they say matters and then I make every effort to take what they say into account – use it in setting priorities. Many of my colleagues leave work whistling, carefree. I carry this stuff home. I spend 60 hour weeks thinking about the people. What is best for them? Am I exceeding my authority? Did I leave something important out? Maybe I should do something more?

I make these huge charts on my walls at home and divide them into parts, one for each county. Then I paste all the information I've collected: demographics, economic stuff, reports, notes and pictures. I include the fears and hopes of residents. I read each one and compare the information weighing good and bad consequences for each county. What people say matters most to me, I think.

I delay making final recommendations because I always feel doubts. I'm never really sure. I get scared that I am recommending a choice that won't really prove beneficial. Once a final choice is made I leave feeling bad that choices B, C, D, and E didn't get the prison. Getting to know the places and people in detail meant that I feel the frustration of not helping the places that deserve a prison but didn't get one.

Valerie does not envision feelings as the enemy of reflection, but a cognitive and moral resource that she uses to guide her planning judgments. She not only recognizes the effects of her own doubts, fears and frustration; but uses empathy and sympathy to both publicly and professionally assess and communicate the feelings of others. Her plan assessment scheme combines aspects of multi-attribute analysis informed by an emotional overlay that draws upon the passionate testimony of residents most likely to endure the consequences of the plan. The analytic methodologist will find it hard to grant validity to such an eclectic practical synthesis. No analyst can reliably recast Valerie's judgment; but such criticism overlooks the critical analyst's own passion for reliability tests untainted by emotional attachments. Such tests have value in research settings where the assumptions do not impose too costly a burden. They may prove too restrictive when making plans for prisons. Valerie puts her planning judgments to a public test before an audience that appraises them morally, emotionally and politically. She claims objectivity based less on detached rational analysis and more on a passionately fair minded, empathic judgment.

Both stories tell us about specific people and events, yet, the practical moral paradoxes in each case exhibit qualities that planners everywhere might recognize. I had both planners offering good advice; one giving advice attending to the feelings of each person the other offering advice using subtle emotional assessment to weigh the cognitive merits of complex alternatives.

The skeptical reader might raise questions about the validity of my reports or the quality of my characterization, but the episodes provide insight about how feelings matter in planning judgment. The knowledge we obtain from these accounts provides evidence against the view that planning and planners should focus mainly on rational theory, skill and method; or that practical know how, moral character or emotional maturity bear no intrinsic relation to planning judgment. Reading these episodes draws attention to the complexity of our everyday action and the important role emotions play helping us cope with complexity. We cannot, however, grasp an emotion like we grasp a concept. We learn to adjust and modify emotional responses in the context of making practical judgments about specific planning issues and proposals. We acquire sensitivity to emotional effects as we learn to recognize the quality of the emotions and feelings that influence practical judgments in a wide variety of specific contexts and instances.

This type of case study does not provide an effective tool for grasping systematic relationships between institutional conditions or organizational practices and emotional responses. However, it need not preclude such inquiry and it may even help analysts recognize the merits of conducting such research. If we cannot escape emotions as we make plans, we need to learn how they shape expectations and judgment in more valid and useful ways that will improve both planning insight and action.

Conclusion: Beyond Objectivity and Sensitivity

As we make plans we draw upon our own emotional resources, but we also create an object that we hope will shape the emotional response of others (Bagozzi & Pieters 1998; Lerner & Keltner 2000). We can consider this response instrumentally much as advertisers and public relations people do. We organize the objects of persuasion in ways that actively subvert emotional intelligence – manipulating images and text to project beliefs that will provoke a predictable emotional response.[6] We do not want to inspire a response but compel or trigger one. Professional planners can use their sensitivity to emotional response to organize planning messages that will elicit the desired response. This strategy represents what Nussbaum would consider a cynical disregard for the moral quality of social emotions like compassion and empathy (Pullman & Gross 2004; Manna & Smith 2004; Menon 2000).

But professionals may also craft plans to shape the emotional response of relevant stakeholders by focusing on beliefs that inform different expectations about the future. Each person responds to a plan uniquely, but the act of making a plan with others invites people to make that plan their own by investing it with practical intentions oriented toward accomplishing different future goals. This is what analyst Lew Hopkins describes as vision in his analysis of plan making, but it might also include policy, strategy or agenda (Hopkins 2001). Hopkins emphasizes the cognitive and logical aspects; but the practical use of any strategy involves judgments that draw upon emotional dispositions and feelings (Schwarz 2000; Kahneman & Lovallo 1993; Bailey 1983).

How we do this matters and emotions play an important role. For instance, we may present fearful images of impending disaster that seek to undermine public confidence in current practices (Markman et al. 1993). The plan presents images and evidence to show how future consequences will damage property resembling the property possessed by the audience. The evocative portrayal of future effects evokes fear that can motivate people to consider remedies to avoid these destructive results. But if the images exaggerate the effects beyond the limits of available cognitive evidence then persuasion becomes manipulation (McMullen 1997). If the images are used to channel fear into a desire for a specific alternative without allowing for, much less fostering, deliberation about potential options then we need to restore the proper balance. Recognizing the proper balance requires reframing our ideas about planning in a way that include both logical and emotional aspects in the same account (Nussbaum 2003). We have inherited from the social sciences and the design arts conventions that separate the two aspects as independent. But in the practical art and craft of planning both remain stubbornly linked as we reflect and act.

Analysts who expect planners to offer 'objective' results about potential consequences that evoke neither feeling nor intentions may inspire indifference rather than understanding. People ignore the analysis because they do not grasp the importance and relevance of the consequences so portrayed. Later, after the flood has destroyed their property, the residents complain. "You did not warn us." Responding defensively the planners respond, "We gave you the results of the analysis. The risk was clearly described." The owners counter, "But the risk for us was not laid out." The planners insist. "We invited you to study the data and draw your own conclusions. The risk values in the data included probability estimates." The fury of the owners will likely grow in this fictitious exchange that illustrates how accuracy is less the issue than concern for the meaning of the information – the combination of emotional attachment and cognitive assessment that shapes judgments about the risk of specific consequences (Marris 1996). Had the planners directed their attention to the risks and then framed the meaning of these risks for different stakeholders; the after-the-fact interrogation might focus less on what was left out ("You planners failed to warn us.") and more on the fit between planning objectives and future consequences ("What went wrong with our mitigation efforts?") (Kahneman & Lovallo 1993).

Many professional planners tacitly and cleverly use emotional intelligence to inform judgments about the application of plans or evaluations about the selection and representation of information and ideas in making plans. The cases of Valerie and Michael illustrate this fact. Planning analysts also use emotional intelligence when they author case studies, policy reports, advisory memos, editorials or other persuasive documents. They write narratives and arguments that employ and describe emotions animating the actions people take, the territory (physical and institutional) they inhabit, the policies in place (or not) and ensuing effects (real or imagined) (Forester 2004; Throgmorton 2003; Mandelbaum 2000; Hoch 1994). But there are many aspects of the practical art of planning that we do not understand because analysts have overlooked how emotions and feelings shape the plans people make individually as urban dwellers or urban planners (LeBaron 2002). The planning field possesses a bountiful case study literature that tells us much about the political, social, economic, geographic and historical meaning of planning and plans. Analysts need to spend more time and effort studying the role emotions play shaping judgments in each of these aspects of planning. This essay tapped only a small portion of the vast research literature on the relationships among emotions, judgment and action. Three planning areas especially merit the study of emotions: creation, communication and evaluation. How do emotions shape the imaginative art of plan making? What role do emotions play in shaping the different aspects of communication used to inform and persuade people about proposed plans? How do emotions shape the expectations and criteria used to judge the merits of planning methods, experience and outcomes? The pragmatist approach recognizes the relevance and value of emotional intelligence professionals use as they make plans. The following chapters shows what this can and should mean for spatial planning practice.

Notes

1 Note that the assumptions associated with cognition among social psychologists is less demanding than among those psychologists studying cognitive psychology of planning.
2 Pollock writes as a heretic among those studying normative decision theory using models of optimality. Instead of embracing Simon's satsificing strategy, he embraces planning. We make plans to organize how we judge and choose among alternatives as we make decisions.
3 "First came the machinery for producing reactions to an object or event, directed at the object or at the circumstances – the machinery of emotion. Second came the machinery for producing a brain map and then a mental image, an idea, for the reactions and for the resulting state of the organism – a machinery of feeling … Eventually, in a fruitful combination with past memories, imagination, and reasoning, feelings led to the emergence of foresight and the possibility of creating novel, non stereotypical responses" (Damasio 2003 p.80).
4 The method is described in the author's book, citation omitted to protect the integrity of peer review.
5 F.G. Bailey (1983) argues that we manage our passions using a 'colony of selves'; what I refer to as personae. Michael, in Bailey's terms shifts from a moral to a civic persona – from an attachment of solidarity to publicity.
6 Plato's Socrates recognized the threat by the Sophists in similar fashion. The dialectical method was designed to thwart the sort of direct emotional appeals made by orators indifferent to a truth based in cognitive judgment. Of course not all sophists were con artists or the sort of dupes that Plato sometimes creates in the *Dialogues*. My point is to emphasize that the pursuit of truth emerged in the dialectical exchange as an antagonism between the inherent distortions that emotions allow and the purity of ideas unencumbered by such corporal limitations.

References

Bagozzi, R. P. and Pieters, R. (1998). Goal-directed emotions. *Cognition and Emotion*, 12, 1–12.

Bailey, F. G. (1983). *The Tactical Uses of Passion: An Essay on Power, Reason, and Reality*. Ithaca, NY: Cornell University Press.

Baum, H. (1983). *Planners and Public Expectations*. New York: Schenkman.

Baum, H. (1997). *The Organization of Hope: Communities Planning Themselves*. Albany NY: SUNY Press.

Boninger, D. S., Gleicher, F. and Strathman, A. J. (1994). Counterfactual thinking: From what might have been to what may be. *Journal of Personality and Social Psychology*, 67, 297–307.

Burgess, P., Simons, J., Coates, L. and Channon, S. (2005). The search for specific planning processes. In R. Morris and G. Ward (Eds.), *The Cognitive Psychology of Planning* (pp. 199–227). New York: Psychology Press.

Churchill, S. (2003). Resilience, not resistance. *City*, 7, 349–360.

Cole, R. (1990). *The Call of Stories: Teaching and the Moral Imagination*. New York: Mariner Books.

Damasio, A. (2003). *Looking for Spinoza: Joy, Sorrow, and the Feeling Brain*. New York: Harcourt Brace.

Edwards, D. and Potter, J. (1992). *Discursive Psychology*. Newbury Park, CA: Sage Publications.

Elster, J. (1996). Rationality and the emotions. *The Economic Journal*, 106, 1386–1397.

Faludi, A. (1973). *Planning Theory*. New York: Pergamon.

Forester, J. (1999). *The Deliberative Practitioner: Encouraging Participatory Planning Processes*. Cambridge, MA: MIT Press.

Forester, J. (2004). Planning and mediation, participation and posturing: What's a democratic planner to do? *Interaction*, 17, 1–2.

Forgas, J. P. (1990). Affective influences on individual and group judgments. *European Journal of Social Psychology*, 20, 441–453.

Forgas, J. P. and Smith, C. A. (2003). Affect and emotion. In M. A. Hogg and J. Cooper (Eds), *The SAGE Handbook of Social Psychology* (pp. 161–189). Thousand Oaks, CA: Sage Publications.

Frijda, H. H. (1986). *The Emotions*. Cambridge, UK: Cambridge University Press.

Goldie, P. (2005). Imagination and the distorting power of emotion. *Journal of Consciousness Studies*, 12(8), 127–139.

Hayes-Roth, B. and Hayes-Roth, F. (1979). A cognitive model of planning. *Cognitive Science*, 3, 275–310.

Hoch, C. (1994). *What Planners Do: Power, Politics and Persuasion*. Chicago: Planners Press.

Hopkins, L. (2001). *Urban Development: The Logic of Making Plans*. Washington, D.C.: Island Press.

Houston, D. A. and Fazio, R. H. (1989). Biased processing as a function of attitude accessibility: Making objective judgments subjectively. *Social Cognition*, 7, 51–66.

Izard, C. E. (1991). Perspectives on emotions in psychotherapy. In J. D. Safran and L. S. Greenberg (Eds.), *Emotion, Psychotherapy, and Change* (pp. 280–289). New York: Guilford.

Kahneman, D. and Lovallo, D. (1993). Timid choices and bold forecasts: A cognitive perspective on risk taking. *Management Science*, 39, 17–31.
LeBaron, M. (2002). *Bridging Troubled Waters: Conflict Resolution from the Heart*. San Francisco, CA: Jossey Bass.
Lerner, J. S. and Keltner, D. (2000). Beyond valence: Toward a model of emotion-specific influences on judgement and choice. *Cognition and Emotion*, 14, 473–493.
Mandelbaum, S. (2000). *Open Moral Communities*. Cambridge, MA: MIT Press.
Manna, D. R. and Smith, A. D. (2004). Exploring the need for emotional intelligence and awareness among sales representatives. *Marketing Intelligence & Planning*, 22, 66–83.
Markman, K. D., Gavanski, I., Sherman, S. J. and McMullen, M. N. (1993). The mental simulation of better and worse possible worlds. *Journal of Experimental Social Psychology*, 29, 87–109.
Marris, P. (1996). *The Politics of Uncertainty*. New York: Routledge.
McMullen, M. N. (1997). Affective contrast and assimilation in counterfactual thinking. *Journal of Experimental Social Psychology*, 33, 77–100.
Menon, K. (2000). Ensuring greater satisfaction by engineering salesperson response to customer emotions. *Journal of Retailing*, 76(3), 285–307.
Miller, G. A., Galanter, E. and Pribram, K. H. (1960). *Plans and the Structure of Behavior*. New York: Holt, Reinhart & Winston.
Morris, R. and Ward, G. (2005). *The Cognitive Psychology of Planning*. New York: Psychology Press.
Newell, A. and Simon, H. A. (1972). *Human Problem Solving*. Englewood Cliffs, NJ: Prentice Hall.
Nussbaum, M. (2003). *Upheavals of Thought: The Intelligence of Emotions*. New York: Cambridge University Press.
Ormerod, P. (2005). Complexity and the limits to knowledge. *Futures*, 37(7), 721–728.
Pollock, J. (2004). Plans and decisions. *Theory and Decision*, 57, 79–107.
Pullman, M. E. and Gross, M. A. (2004). Ability of experience design elements to elicit emotions and loyalty behaviors. *Decision Sciences*, 35, 551–578.
Roese, N. J. and Olson, J. M. (1995). *What Might Have Been: The Social Psychology of Counterfactual Thinking*. Mahwah, NJ: Lawrence Erlbaum Associates.
Rolls, E. T. (2000). On the brain and emotion. *Behavioral and Brain Sciences*, 23(2), 219–228.
Sandercock, L. (2002). Difference, fear, and habitus: A political economy of urban fears. In J. Hillier (Ed.), *Habitus: A Sense of Place* (pp. 219–234). Aldershot: Ashgate.
Sandercock, L. (2004). Out of the closet: The importance of stories and storytelling in planning practice. In B. Stifteland V. Watson (Eds.), *Dialogues in Urban and Regional Planning*. London: Routledge.
Schwarz, N. (2000). Emotion, cognition, and decision making. *Cognition and Emotion*, 14, 433–440.
Shafir, E. (1993). Choosing versus rejecting: Why some options are both better and worse than others. *Memory & Cognition*, 21, 546–556.
Simon, H. (1982). *Models of Bounded Rationality*, Vols. 1 and 2. Cambridge, MA: MIT Press.
Throgmorton, J. (1996). *Planning as Persuasive Storytelling: The Rhetorical Construction of Chicago's Electrical Future*. Chicago: University of Chicago Press.

Throgmorton, J. (2003). Planning as persuasive storytelling in a global-scale web of relationships. *Planning Theory*, 2(2), 125–152.
Ward, G. and Allport, D. A. (1997). Planning and problem solving using the 5-disk Tower of London task. *Quarterly Journal of Experimental Psychology*, 50, 49–78.
Ward, G. and Morris, R. (2005). Introduction to the psychology of planning. In R. Morris and G. Ward (Eds.), *The Cognitive Psychology of Planning*. New York: Psychology Press.

Part II

3 Integrating the Planning Field, Movement and Discipline
Planning Theory for Practice

The American Planning Association (APA) sponsors a membership survey every 10 years or so to assess what professional planners do and know. The APA uses the results to amend and validate questions for the national American Institute of Certified Planners (AICP) exam. In 2007 more than ninety five percent (of nearly 5,000 respondents) reported learning planning theory, mostly at planning schools. When asked about the importance of this knowledge for current professional work most ranked it on par (2.2 out of 4.0) with economic forecasting, hazard mitigation, waterfront planning or institutional planning. Professionals report using their most valued knowledge within the context of specialized areas of competence: development review, zoning administration, urban design, neighbourhood development, coastal zone management, affordable housing and more. Theory for these practitioners represents a kind of specialised knowledge useful on some occasion, but not relevant for daily use on the job (Hoch 2010).

Richard Klosterman (2011) completed a fourth survey of planning theory course syllabi from instructors at US planning schools. Comparing the reading assignment citations spanning three decades he found a modest minority of faculty staff using the same textbook essay collections, but mostly instructors relied on unique readings. The popularity of specialised knowledge among practitioners appears to hold true for planning theory instructors as well. Planning theory ideas for spatial planning do not show signs of convergence. This poses a problem as professionals seek knowledge to plan for complex spatial settlements across the globe. What can be done to encourage theoretical understanding that fosters integrative understanding for professional practice?

In this chapter I group the diverse contributions to planning knowledge into three discourse arenas linking each of three planning domains. I argue that the planning theory enterprise offers robust knowledge within these arenas, but that this success makes theoretical convergence for all domains unlikely. Instead of seeking integration of discourse about theory and method like the now discredited rational model planning analysts might focus instead on comparing and studying how people practice and teach the craft of plan making. Convergence depends on the practical steps colleagues take to learn and judge how and what plan makers do. This shifts the goal of planning theory from establishing an intellectual foundation for planning to foster better ideas for plan making. This shift does not displace or replace the fruitful explosion of planning knowledge binding field, movement and discipline together. We can and should build practical pathways for convergence even as we foster the scope and depth of specialized knowledge in diverse discourse arenas.

Field, Movement and Discipline

I want to argue that we distinguish planning theory ideas into three arenas formed between each of three spatial planning domains: 'field', 'movement' and 'discipline' (Figure 3.1). The spatial planning field includes purposeful efforts to anticipate, influence and cope with urbanization and its effects. Professional planners contribute to the field; but the plans of firms, governments, non-profit agencies, civic associations, community groups and countless individuals account for most of the practical advice used to make and maintain urban settlements across the globe. The planning movement refers to collective efforts to develop and promote the practice of spatial planning as a legitimate and useful organised practice and profession. Various social, political and civic associations and their members contribute to the movement. Professional associations like the Royal Town Planning Institute and the American Planning Association represent prominent but not exclusive planning movement institutions. The planning discipline describes efforts to study and teach spatial planning on the job, in the profession and at the university. Disciplinary knowledge consists of ideas and tools that people use to do spatial planning and theories that guide and justify their use.

Movement and Field

Most planning theory ideas published in edited books such as the Healey and Hillier (2008) opus and journals like *Planning Theory* explore the relationship between the planning field and movement. Analysts offer focused theoretical arguments that emphasise a specific dimension of the field:

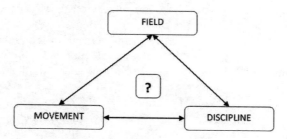

Figure 3.1 Planning theory domains.

environmental sustainability (Beatley, 2005); social justice (Fainstein, 2009); new urbanism (Talen, 2005); and, many more. These works tap into the policy reform tradition that animates planning movements developing theory to explain and interpret movement institutions and activity in the light of select knowledge from the planning field. Other works focus on specific cases or places using a selection of institutions or activity from the planning field offering critique (Hall, 1982) or celebration (Landry, 2000). Professional and civic associations sponsor publications that include exemplary case studies, surveys and interpretations of current and past practice tied to popular cultural beliefs and emerging public policy.

Field and Discipline

Planning theory linking ideas from the field with ideas in the discipline often focuses on the tools and methods that advance knowledge about complex spatial problems. Analysts develop planning tools to grasp and comprehend complex problems from the planning field in geography, economics, history, sociology, architecture and other disciplinary journals. The increasing specialisation of disciplinary knowledge fuels the multiplicity of discovery and application. Equipped with new tools and disciplinary ideas analysts slice up and recombine the planning field into problems susceptible to purposeful resolution.

Movement and Discipline

Plans include purpose as a resource for improvement. Planning theory can move people using disciplinary ideas to project contours of possibility and movement ideas to promote strategies for decision. Professional planning journals like *Town Planning Review* and the *Journal of the American Planning Association* nurture and promote work that rigorously evaluates the claims for a professional planning idea, explores the impact of a new planning tool for professional uptake or reviews the evidence for competing policy ideas guiding planning intervention. As more aspects of modern life involve purposeful collective efforts to prepare for the future the arena expands for the disciplined invention and evaluation of planning institutions and activity.

No Unified Theory for Spatial Planning

The contest among planning ideas within each arena stimulates learning and debate (hence the question mark in Figure 3.1). What counts as theory within each arena does not lend itself to agreement among those involved. My distinction among arenas highlights how those of us curious about planning theory divide up our intellectual work. I did this not to impose a fixed order, but offer a coherent framework to account for why planning theorists find it difficult to invent a theory that cuts across and combines all the domains within a single arena.

John Friedmann and now Patsy Healey provide masterful synthetic work that strives to bridge ideas from the field, movement and discipline of spatial planning (Friedmann 1973, 1987; Healey 2007, 2010). Politically progressive and sensitive to the interplay among intellectual traditions each take special care to locate their work at the edge of intellectual and political discourse about spatial planning. They hope to inspire the planning movement and the field using disciplinary ideas. Others like Alexander (1992), Faludi (1986) and Archibugi (2010) emphasise a synthesis of ideas that focus more on planning ideas tied to planning institutions and professional traditions. They want to develop planning methods using disciplined field knowledge to improve planning movement institutions and activity. The contest for a theory of planning across these domains will likely never end with one grand theory achieving intellectual hegemony. Hillier and Healey (2010) struggle with this dilemma addressing the desire for some coherent set of shared planning ideas and end up celebrating the current diversity leaving unification or integration to others.

Academic Discipline and Planning Craft

The planning theory enterprise emerged with the growth of the planning academy. Theory provides a powerful source of legitimacy for the planning discipline within the academic culture of the modern university where most planning schools exist. Planning academics seldom come from the ranks of planning practitioners and earn promotion and stature demonstrating intellectual acumen as disciplinary scholar or researcher. The variety of theoretical vocabularies and ideas reflects these differences. Recent debates using political economy, communicative action, post modernity and many other sources of intellectual inspiration signal a lively and interesting conversation among analysts, but these debates tend to cycle and subside in the literature without generating ideas for uptake among members of the planning movement, profession and field. The analysts themselves sometimes face difficulty reading one another's work as parallel tributaries of precedent and citation prove daunting to travel. Practitioners rarely read the work of planning scholars because specialized 'shop talk' insists that readers scale a mountain of challenging and unfamiliar concepts to view the theoretical landscape.

Once upon a time in the early 1970s it seemed that rationality could bind the field, movement and discipline of spatial planning together in a model of inquiry and practice. Compelling critiques by political economists and critical theorists quickly dispatched the hegemony of this hopeful if naïve model of rationality. Practitioners in the US have learned to pay lip service to the critiques, but often revive versions of the rational model to frame comprehensive plans. Ironically, the rational model still succeeds as a rhetorical protocol even as it fails as meaningful theoretical guide. Practitioners have learned to expect theory to provide a kind of justification for the judgments they take. Planning educators and theorists share some responsibility for this.

Planning Education

I served six years (2005–2011) on the North American Planning Accreditation Board (PAB): two years as chair. Studying and reviewing the practice of planning education for some 71 schools sensitised me to the rules and conventions that planning academics use to organize and justify how they educate professional students. The experience taught me to ask the question: "How do planning schools deliver a coherent planning degree with multi-disciplinary faculty teaching, a diverse student clientele a wide range of planning ideas and skills?" What did I conclude? The source of coherence within schools flows mainly from a commitment to planning practice rather than a shared theory. How each school organises and supports education for practice varies, but rarely as much as differences in education for theory and method. A small school in a rural land grant university and a large school in a coastal metropolis can each meet the thresholds for accreditation criteria, but the range and depth of knowledge and skill by the larger school will dwarf the smaller. Yet regardless of these differences as students in each school learn to do planning the educational trajectories across schools converge. The wisdom of practical judgment for professional practice does not necessarily improve with additional knowledge about theory and method.

Consider the differences in disciplinary affiliation, institutional location and professional association among the growing number of planning schools across the globe. Where do planning academics find common ground? I am not optimistic that we can find solidarity across the theoretical arenas spanning the three planning domains I described earlier in this essay. As someone who criticised the rational model I remain suspicious of claims for theoretical and methodological convergence. As a planning intellectual I am excited and stimulated by the flow of competing ideas and the promise of invention and innovation in theory and method, but as a planning educator I am more prudent and cautious; worried about issues of care, competence and relevance as I advise student efforts to make plans for a specific clientele in a complex place. The practical craft of plan making requires learning that uses theory and method, but tacitly without attribution to distract from the artistry of composition.

Where Theory and Practice Converge

Like other modern academic specialists planning theorists write for each other, but I think the community of planning theory scholars has a responsibility to attend to the practical enterprise of planning robustly considered. Such attention means subjecting the theoretical conversation about planning to demands for practical relevance, provisional adaptability and critical inventiveness. This happens as analysts organise new journals and prepare books for students in planning schools and professionals in the field. A more ambitious challenge, however, the one I am making, urges theorists to do scholarship that studies and refines the craft of planning and plan making. Many others have traveled this route. Donald Schon (1983) focused on practice. John Forester (1999, 2009) has made the practical critical. The work of Patsy Healey has been an inspiration (see Healey & Underwood 1978), later assessment by Campbell and Marshall (2005) and the recent (Healey & Upton 2010). See also Watson (2002) and Lauria and Wagner (2006).

In School

The scholars of the planning academy cannot and should not sacrifice the elegance and power of their ideas before some common abstract doctrine, no matter how generously and creatively conceived. No need to cool the theoretical and methodological jets that rely on disciplinary fuel, but planning academics from across the globe can find a common ground for mutual understanding if we focus on the pathway people travel as they make spatial plans – a pathway planning schools everywhere provide. Studio learning provides a powerful precedent for such convergence, even if specific design traditions do not. Borrowing the studio idea means learning planning by working together to make plans and do planning (much more than architecture or landscape). Instructors show how rather than explain why.

Different kinds of disciplinary ideas and methods get used as tools for making or crafting process and product. How this practical integration works among participants facing similar situations in different places will not fit one disciplinary frame. The integrity of the project distils the experience of plan making as the proper source of knowledge. The joint activity of learning and creating the plan subordinates disciplinary ideas and methods to the situational demands for relevant practical judgment. Instead of relegating plan making studios, workshops, internships and projects to secondary status as derivative learning activities where practitioners apply method or test theory; these learning activities become the central focus – the culmination and achievement of planning education. We learn to plan through practice. We learn to discipline practice through theory. Practice and theory converge as we make plans.

At Work

Planners (professional and otherwise) offer useful advice in their various occupational settings and specialized roles responding actively to problematic situations. Everyday planners across the globe study the location and layers of interaction that shape settlements. They identify and analyse relevant spatial relationships using current facts and theories to represent and interpret purposes for a place. These plans describe and evaluate alternative options cast imaginatively into the future. Local planning lore takes shape in cases, exemplars, principles and rules of thumb passed on through networks of professional and craft association. National and regional conferences and meetings provide formal opportunities for stylised show and tell; but stripped of context and craft the cases and stories appear superficial and contrived – often packaged comically in the rhetoric of a popular theory.

I think we need discipline planning practice with theory, but the theory needs to include those involved in the craft of plan making (sponsors, professionals, stakeholders and other clientele). I agree with the criticism that Franco Archibugi (2008) makes about planning theory, that current theorists study knowledge about planning, but do not create knowledge for planning. But instead of pursuing his impossible dream (or nightmare) of a universal planning method, I want to attract these disciplined theorists to study more carefully and insightfully what planners do; both as stakeholders for craft and audience for critique. Practitioners use ideas to make plans, but they do so in an undisciplined practical fashion shaped by the demands of culture and context (Hoch 2009; Davoudi 2009). I think we can tap the diversity of theoretical method and insight as theorists learn to adapt their ideas to fit and inform the undisciplined demands for practice.

I think we already do this kind of integration at the local retail level. Theory and practice converge among professionals, stakeholders and academics in plan making efforts all the time all over the world. We possess a wealth of local practical knowledge and experience increasingly at our electronic finger tips. The formation of planning associations for professional planners and planning academics across the world has provided institutional frameworks for joint face to face conferences, meetings, workshops and events (Stiftel 2009). Figuring out how to socialize these different resources and episodes for convergence into intellectual resources at the wholesale level remains a theoretical challenge worth pursuing.[1]

Conclusion for Spatial Planning

Andrew Abbott in his sociological study of professions treats these special occupational domains as products of complex social negotiation and conflict. Casting spatial planning at the intersection of social movement reform, disciplinary norms and the vast field of practice heeds this advice. The urban planning profession exhibits a provisional fluid identity precisely because it embraces these dynamic currents of belief. The APA and AICP promote the discipline even as they occasionally tap streams of moral critique or planning efforts undertaken by other actors and agents. Offering these distinctions provides a framework for grasping the complexity.

The pragmatist approach does not require that ideas for spatial planning provide a foundation or justification for planning practice. Trying to fit planning activity into a too narrow rationality sacrifices relevance for predictability; blueprint conformity for provisional resilience. Seeking a unified common vision underwritten by a broad consensus mistakes temporary agreement for lasting doctrine. The pragmatist does not elevate theory beyond the grasp of practical judgment but seeks to understand how different kinds of knowledge and experience might be used to comprehend and respond to current and imagined situations. This conception treats plan making as a cognitive and practical communicative activity. We make plans to inform intentions about what actions to take. Plans do not govern even as they shape what those who govern can and might do.

The multitude of planning ideas enriches the discipline, but not if we do not take steps to integrate these ideas with the varieties of practice at play in the field, movement and discipline of spatial planning. We scholars do this in many ways as we convene conferences, organize journals and otherwise stimulate our inquiry. The planning theory enterprise can be enlivened as we turn attention to using the ideas pitched by our scholars to understand what these mean for practice. I have tried to show how this can work. We can do theory not only by conceiving new ideas but showing how ideas inform the understanding of practice in ways that invite comparison and debate beyond the confines of a disciplinary specialty.

Spatial planners should take time to try out these ideas searching for complementarity as well as difference. Practitioners do this kind of appropriation all the time by selectively combining policies, regulations, designs, innovations and other forms of planning activity that they find useful for their own work. Such practical synthesis fits the demands of professional work and of course my own pragmatist conception of the discipline. But I think it offers a more fruitful role for theory. This pragmatist approach does not treat theories as deep foundations justifying specific planning ideas, but as ideas offering useful if competing, contested and complementary insights about socially and spatially complex planning relationships. Truth tests in such inquiry are not arbitrary, but sensitive to contextual fit that includes environmental and cultural relationships. Theory does not work like the sun, but more like a flashlight.

Note

1 Bernd Scholl at ETH Zurich (the Swiss Federal Institute of Technology) has convened a group of colleagues to figure out how to foster planning education that takes its focus from an integration of practical planning. This small group of academics has worked since 2009 developing a vocabulary for planning education that converges around practice without diminishing disciplinary inputs.

References

Alexander, E. R. (1992). *Approaches to Planning: Introducing Current Planning Theories, Concepts and Issues*. Amsterdam: Gordon & Breach.

Archibugi, F. (2008). *Planning Theory: From the Political Debate to the Methodological Reconstruction*. New York: Springer.

Beatley, T. (2005). *Native to Nowhere: Sustaining Home and Community in a Global Age*. Washington, D.C.: Island Press.

Campbell, H. and Marshall, R. (2005). Professionalism and planning in Britain. *Town Planning Review*, 76, 191–214.

Davoudi, S. (2009). Planning and interdisciplinarity. Paper presented at the AESOP Heads of School Seminar, Lille, 28 March.
Fainstein, S. (2009). *The Just City*. Ithaca, NY: Cornell University Press.
Faludi, A. (1973). *Planning Theory*. Oxford: Pergamon Press.
Faludi, A. (1986). *Critical Rationalism and Planning Methodology*. London: Pion.
Forester, J. (1999). *The Deliberative Practitioner*. Boston, MA: MIT Press.
Forester, J. (2009). *Dealing with Differences: Dramas of Mediating Public Disputes*. Cambridge, MA: Oxford University Press.
Friedmann, J. (1973). *Re-tracking America: A Theory of Transactive Planning*. New York: Anchor Press.
Friedmann, J. (1987). *Planning in the Public Domain*: Princeton, NJ: Princeton University Press.
Hall, P. (1982). *Great Planning Disasters*. Berkeley: University of California Press.
Healey, P. (2007). *Urban Complexity and Spatial Strategies: Towards a Relational Planning for our Times*. London: Routledge.
Healey, P. (2010). *Making Better Places: The Planning Project in the Twenty-first Century*. Basingstoke: Palgrave Macmillan.
Healey, P. and Hillier, J. (2008). *Critical Essays in Planning Theory*, Vol. 1: *Foundations of the Planning Enterprise*; Vol. 2: *Political Economy, Diversity and Pragmatism*; Vol. 3: *Contemporary Movements in Planning Theory*. Aldershot: Ashgate.
Healey, P. and Underwood, J. (1978). Professional ideals and planning practice: A report on research into planners' ideas in practice in London Borough planning departments. *Progress in Planning*, 9, 73–127.
Healey, P. and Upton, R. (2010). *Crossing Borders: International Exchange and Planning Practices*. London: Routledge.
Hillier, J. and Healey, P. (2010). *The Ashgate Research Companion to Planning Theory*. Farnham: Ashgate.
Hoch, C. (2009). Planning craft: How planners compose plans. *Planning Theory*, 8, 219–241.
Hoch, C. (2010). What knowledge does planning education contribute to practice? Paper presented at the ACSP Annual Conference, New Orleans, 7 October.
Klosterman, R. E. (2011). Planning theory education: A thirty-year review. *Journal of Planning Education and Research*, 31(3), 319–331.
Landry, C. (2000). *The Creative City, A Toolkit for Urban Innovators*. London: Earthscan.
Lauria, M. and Wagner, J. A. (2006). What can we learn from empirical studies of planning theory? A comparative case analysis of extant literature. *Journal of Planning Education and Research*, 25, 364–381.
Schon, D. (1983). *The Reflective Practitioner: How Professionals Think in Action*. New York: Free Press.
Stiftel, B. (2009). Planning the paths of planning schools. Paper presented at the Symposium on the Future of Planning Education, Adelaide, South Australia, 13 February.
Talen, E. (2005). *New Urbanism and American Planning: The Conflict of Cultures*. New York: Routledge.
Watson, V. (2002). Do we learn from planning practice? The contribution of the practice movement to planning theory. *Journal of Planning Education and Research*, 22, 178–187.

4   Anticipating Complex Spatial Change

Introduction

The study of complexity has caught up with the sorts of problems that professional spatial planning set out to solve. The utopian schemes for urban new towns on the periphery of industrial cities and plans for regional development imagined continuing complexity [usually with an organic metaphor] successfully challenged by those who believed plans should tame and subject complexity to a predictable order. As research on complexity unfolds it turns out that many of the tools and techniques of the social sciences from the 1950s and 60s grafted onto planning methods appear less attractive. The rational precision of econometric analysis, social surveys, urban models and many other not so quick and dirty tools has not made complex urban relationships more predictable – except in those cases where powerful institutions imposed a uniform master plan – and then only for a while, before people in its grip could find ways to undermine the disciplined uniformity. The proliferation of specialized analytic knowledge yields useful insights, but mainly within disciplinary domains or areas where patterns of linearity and continuity make such inquiry fruitful. Spatial analysts know more about how select urban elements and relations change, but little about how whole urban districts and regions ebb and flow (Batty & Torrens 2001). Most importantly planning scholars now realize with our growing understanding of complexity that our attachment to disciplinary ties may lead us to overlook sources of conceptual coherence and practical innovation that can tap multiple sources of disciplinary insight. We need become undisciplined in our understanding of urban plans.[1]

In this chapter I argue that we should not envision planning as a rational synthesis of social science insight placed in the service of the public interest, but at once a more pervasive and modest activity. As Keiran Donaghy and Lew Hopkins warn we should be wary of efforts to offer spatial plans to master and predict complex changes. They argue that we should search for coherence across different conceptions of planning and plan making efforts (Donaghy & Hopkins 2006). Donaghy and Hopkins make room for planners promoting spatial plans, economists studying markets, collective social choice theorists and deliberative analysts. Some critics insist that such an embrace needs to distinguish between plan making and institution building – especially across scale (Salet 2018b; Healey 2007; Alexander 2005; Saeger 2002). They believe efforts to conduct deliberative planning need be tempered with greater sensitivity and attention to the demands of institutional practice and design.

I want to address this critique by focusing on the relationship between planning and institutions. I briefly describe how Lew Hopkins (2001), Elinor Ostrom (1990, 1994, 2002) and my own conceptions of plan making conceive institutional design and plan making respond to the complexity described by Hopkins (2001). I distinguish how rules work to guide human choices and how plans work to form intentions. How might we use coherence to integrate ideas about institutional design with ideas about plan making? I apply the ideas about institutional design and plan making to interpret the case of a state planning mandate.

I believe the critics comments prove less distressing as we shift attention away from the assumptions of the respective disciplinary boundaries and focus on practical judgment. It seems unlikely to me that we can ever convince one another to adopt the assumptions of another field or discipline as a pre-requisite for joint comprehension. But we might improve the prospects for mutual insight and learning as we analyze how each approach the same case. We routinely read and learn from cases in just this way. I am trying to suggest that this form of comprehension offers a resource that when cast in a pragmatic light provides a resource for the kind of coherence Donaghy and Hopkins recommend as well as the sort of integration described by Salet (2018a).

Plan Making and Complexity

Hopkins on Urban Complexity

Unlike linear conceptions of system equilibrium that inform models of metropolitan development, complexity theory focuses on systems that produce order within and among networks of nonlinear relations. These systems do not exhibit predictable patterns of continuity nor are they completely random or chaotic. The agents of a complex system anticipate the consequences of change by selectively adjusting familiar patterns of response. The system may evolve over generations of tacit selective response or through purposeful learning by intelligent agents.

Lew Hopkins focuses on urban development and identifies four different sources of complexity that describe the sorts of change susceptible to deliberate urban planning: interdependence, indivisibility, irreversibility and uncertainty. Hopkins argues that professional planners may confuse planning with predictable control. In his view plans offer information about purpose and intention that others can use as they adjust and compose their own plans within highly interactive real estate markets or political contests.

Some argue that plans offer a too simple snap shot of a more complex interaction. Hopkins argues that we use a variety of plans to inform and guide our interactions. In his work (Hopkins 2001; Donaghy & Hopkins 2006) he argues that we should not seek to displace, simplify or distill the many plans different stakeholders use to guide urban development decisions within a single comprehensive vision. Rather professionals should serve a coherent web of plans.

Hopkins distinguishes between the authority of decisions as a quality that flows from institutional relationships (e.g., the state, the market) and the authority that flows from the deliberate formulation of plans. Plans work cognitively to help us represent and comprehend future decisions and their imagined consequences. We make plans within the context of institutional settings that shape selection and composition of planning options. The head of household, supervisor at work, minister in the church or mayor at city hall might insist that we only plan for a narrow band of future decisions and exclude options unfavorable to his or her purposes. The professional planner needs to understand and anticipate these institutional relationships as part of how plans are made and used.

Ostrom on Institutional Design for Local Common Goods

Elinor Ostrom studies common pool resource goods, the kind often describe as social dilemmas or the tragedy of the commons. She recognizes social, economic and environmental interdependence across scale and the difficulty this poses for conducting analysis and conceiving effective institutional change. As a social scientist she wants to build a body of general research findings, yet her practical interest in reducing human suffering and environmental waste keeps her focused on those relationships at the intermediate scale where the disruptions to market efficiency prove most limited and prospects for institutional innovation and redesign most promising. Her work proves especially useful in this case because the commons good problems play such a prominent role in urban development.

Common goods problems are often described as dilemmas (e.g., the prisoner's dilemma), but Ostrom argues that they are not as intractable or as inevitable as conventional belief maintains. People learn over time to develop joint strategies for coordinating their individual use of a common good. Ostrom (1990) studied what people did who manage a common good over hundreds of years. She identifies the following 'design principles' for governing:

> Clear boundaries (rights of use and resource boundaries clearly defined)
> Adaptive congruence between appropriation rules and provision rules
> People affected by the operational rules participate in modifying the rules
> Monitors who audit use include appropriators accountable to other appropriators

Graduated sanctions applied to rule breakers based on context and consequences
Conflict resolution: inexpensive, flexible, deliberation among parties
External authority accepts legitimacy of commons' governance does not interfere.

(p.90)

Ostrom envisions a self-generating order formed in response to the boundaries of the common good. She describes common goods whose users develop institutional rules and conventions to balance provision and appropriation. The provision of the common good cannot flow from instrumental market exchange [although participants do plenty of calculations and adopt heuristic models that estimate the impacts of individual actions] reaching equilibrium but relies upon institutional rules that bind together individual self-interest and social trust with specific features of the shared good that participants can monitor to ensure the fair allocation and efficient renewal (e.g., water or fish). Markets are not well suited to coordinating use of common goods.

Urban Collective Goods and Common Goods

In his theoretical review of urban development planning analyst Lew Hopkins (2001) treats market allocation as the 'natural' system for urban land development. But he argues that the market for urban development does not produce equilibria because temporal and spatial conditions generate impediments. The urban system is complex and unpredictable in ways that violate the rules for efficient markets. Hopkins identifies four sources of complexity that accompany urban development: indivisibility, irreversibility, uncertainty and interdependence. Hopkins' account of urban land development complexity has features similar to the characteristics of common pool resources described by Ostrom: indivisibility (subtractability), irreversibility (temporal exclusivity), uncertainty (cognitive limits) and interdependence (spatial exclusivity). We make urban plans as agendas, designs, visions, policies and strategies to coordinate the use of urban resources for specific places and clientele identifying and anticipating the relevant interaction among these features.

The many complex effects of urban development require adjustment across increments of time – adjustments informed by monitoring, feedback and adaptation informed by the behavior of others in response to plan related rules, sanctions and innovations. The self-organizing institutions that Ostrom describes become the agents and clients for plan making. The common pool resource concept provides a way to grasp what the 'comprehensive' refers to in comprehensive planning. We do not plan for everything, but for those attributes of local collective goods that diverse actors tap in common as specific subsets of urban agents (organizations, groups and individuals). Instead of using a market driven model of equilibrium tied to the exchange of private goods adopt an ecological model; one that focuses less exclusively on individual competitive gains and more on cumulative individual adjustment within adaptive systems that combine competition and coordination – a mix of reciprocity and coercion. This distinction provides a way to conceive the intermediate goods that compose the many spatial and physical features of built settlements: goods that animate institutional life in all its many spatial manifestations.

Combining Ostrom and Hopkins' ideas reframes expectations about what counts as a plan, how we collectively agree to adopt a plan and how we might evaluate the efficacy of the adopted plan as a guide. Instead of imagining a plan as a kind of blueprint offering a predictable sequence or pattern of linear deterministic relationships – the image of a comprehensive state plan – consider spatial plans as practical provisional agreements about how to act together anticipating the consequences of future relevant interactions. Anticipation informs how diverse purposeful actors approach the future based on a comparison of different possible, plausible future interaction effects (e.g., scenarios). Planning provides provisional advice about what to do next having selected a destination along the horizon. How do people use institutions to do this at intermediate and higher scales?

Institutions and Planning

Wilem Salet (2018a) in his masterful study of planning institutions critiques the still prevalent practice of treating institutions and organizations as agents that make plans to reduce uncertainty. The relational complexity of modern places defies such efforts. Spatial planning requires that professionals learn to recognize the multiplicity of agents shaping any specific situation. This includes an understanding of institutional and organizational standing as well as the interests, beliefs and feelings of those people imagining future consequences and those likely to experience them. Delegating spatial planning to a single administrative agency or department cannot handle the demands of relational complexity. Salet casts institutions as the product of earlier action that takes shape as norms, while he imagines planning as I do – a pragmatic approach to practical problem solving. The formation of habits provides a useful way to address how the legacy of prior actions become norms susceptible to ongoing adaptation.

Conventional moral philosophizing and social science analysis strive to identify general principles independent of practical context. A pragmatic orientation treats principles as conceptual tools to cope with specific problems. These problems emerge in specific times and places shaped by complex environmental and social relationships. We start inquiry selecting and focusing attention on a problem within a practical situation. Principles and rules previously learned as habits and routines guide our perception and judgment about those that no longer work. We learn our institutions and they learn from us.

Habits

Philosopher Todd Lekan (2003) argues that we can best understand how we do institutional inquiry if we adopt the concept of habits: patterns of response to changing conditions that focus behavior and attention in useful ways. These patterns include socially shared combinations of thought, feeling and behavior. We comprehend habits in relation to other habits as well as in relation to the situations where we put them to use. Lekan helps us understand that the small 'p' plans we make to shape our intentions that guide deliberations with others draw upon habits that already tie us into larger institutional and environmental settings. We do not encounter conventions, rules, obstacles and the like as solo agents, but as social actors who already combine a selection of habits that inform our attitude and expectations.[2]

Lekan argues that practical judgment involves more than fitting means to ends that exist independently in some fixed, external domain. He identifies three qualities of practical life that make such a view of practical reasoning unrealistic and misleading. First, we do not follow rules like a computer runs a program but draw upon *practical know how* that we have learned from others. We learn to speak before we learn about grammar. We learn to cook before we learn to read a cookbook and follow a recipe. We learn to tell the truth and lie before we learn the sixth commandment. Skilled expertise does not require action based on following rules, but know-how that meets the demands of specific situations. Second, practical life changes as we learn to solve or live with novel problems. The conventions change and with these the very meaning of practical judgment. Expertise refers to the skill at anticipating and adjusting to these changes in ways that still gets the job done. These new innovative responses then feedback and change the craft offering variations on current conventional responses. The American Planning Association ironically tries to capture such activity as best practices. Copying innovations regardless of context poses serious risks. Third, practical life involves complexities that cannot be reduced to a set of precepts. We need beliefs that can change to meet the demands of a changing world.

This dynamic conception of habit reaches forward and outward to find the meaning of action within a comparative assessment of the habits people bring with them to specific situations. This conception allows us to consider moral beliefs, technical beliefs, political beliefs and social beliefs contributing to habits that offer more or less functionally useful responses to changing situations. To say that we are creatures of habit does not mean that we fall blindly into inherited routines, but that the ideas and reasons we use to cope with the diverse situations we encounter come to us as habits. We learn them by practicing them in different contexts where they prove useful.

For Lekan we make plans to represent new patterns of association that promise to resolve the problem when and where our habits break down. We use plans to take us from confusing unfinished situations to comprehensible situations. "In a sense, action plans are attempts to recontextualize conduct by framing a situation in terms of new possibilities" (Leakin 2003, p.33). Lekan's conception helps us grasp the small 'p' plans we each compose imagining choices about what we might do to solve a problem. The sort individuals use to make good on promises made to themselves and peers. The features will remain as we travel across scale but modified by the demands of increased complexity.

Plans

The everyday planning we do anticipates and coordinates future behavior with others. We may plan a battle or a wedding. We deliberately prepare for a contest or a social union. We may change plans sometime between initiating and acting upon the plan. The plan may fail to accomplish the purpose we expect, but the plan still works as advice. We used it to guide our action. Planning always takes place in specific cultural and institutional contexts and situations, and plans will be shaped by these influences. We can act without plans as we follow habits, social customs, rules, roles and other learned routines that trigger sequences of behavior. We plan when routines get disrupted, as we face problems not solved by current rules and customs.

Small 'p' plans coordinate activity among people who can meet in groups that allow for deliberative give and take. Articulating a mutually agreeable joint intention provides the focus for many interpretive accounts of planning rationality (Forester 1999a; Innes & Booher 1999a, 1999b; Healey 2007). Small scale interaction can also involve competitive strategic behaviors, the sort described by game theory and studied by behavioral economists (/Seabright 2004; Ariely 2008, Webster 2005). These approaches often treat planning as exogenous because not the product of individual interaction, but the imposition of social or political authority. I believe that research in cognitive science and social psychology shows us that both interpretive and strategic judgments rely upon plans (see Chapter 2).

As actors choose and act, they stop planning. Plans do not decide, they inform. Plans do not act, they advise. Making plans is a kind of action, but the action of reflective imagination and deliberation about future consequences. We make plans to prepare for an uncertain future that has attracted our attention and concern. We do not need to presume rationality guides our plan making. Rationality depends on the plans we already make before taking any deliberate action. When we reflect on a problem and conceive a choice or action that we might take we form our intentions and make choice possible. When we describe different conceptions of rational choice we add on more elaborate and precise descriptions of how we make the choices we do according to certain beliefs about logic, reasons, argument and the like. Conceptions of rationality leverage many cognitive skills, including planning that may generate more powerful and encompassing ideas.

This pragmatic recasting of rationality sidesteps the displacement of action that the embrace of scientific rationality insists when firmly embraced. As we study planning across scale we need not adopt rationality as guide or justification but consider pragmatic criteria to judge what planning does to help us cope with complexity.

Plans for Urban Problems Rely on Coherence and Coordination

Pragmatic attention to the scaling up of plan making includes institutional rules and conventions, prior organizational decisions and consequences, local environmental conditions and the goals and actions of relevant clientele considered together as a specific planning context. Both the subject and object of planning activity increase in complexity with size because the situation that describes the context for relevant planning problems includes more interactive relationships. We can plan our individual trip along a busy expressway route and local arterials from home to work, but we face difficulty conceiving how to plan the flow of daily trips along the same expressway given the large number of routes. In some cases, the problem difficulty increases because we do not understand important relationships that contribute to the problem or do not know how to use our conceptual tools well enough to imagine and conceive a solution. We adopt strategies to simplify the complicated combination of parts into separate smaller problems. We presume that we can later combine solutions for the different parts of a complicated problem into a coherent plan for the whole. In many urban cases the problem consists of many intersecting layers and dimensions of interaction across scale that cannot be decomposed. In these cases, the interaction effects create interdependencies and uncertainties that we cannot know. Complexity describes those relationships that reproduce ordered effects across scale. Interaction among different agents generates patterns of coherent order that emerge as a system of relationships even as the encompassing situation changes. How do we prepare plans that can address this complexity (Alexander 2005)?[3]

Coherence

Donaghy and Hopkins compare how very different theoretical conceptions explain or justify planning for complexity: comprehensive plans, collective choice, markets and communication.[4] They urge us to adopt a more robust tolerance for a multiplicity of theoretical outlooks as we make and study plans. They show how we can coherently adapt these outlooks when we consider planning. We can learn about freight transportation plans for the region along with plans for public education reform and affordable housing even if in doing so we find no consistent interplay among the different proposals. Plans that offer inconsistent and conflicting representations for the same region need not be unified hierarchically by a single regional government (i.e., rational comprehensive plan). Donaghy and Hopkins adopt a tolerant outlook that seeks order in relations of similarity based on contextual meaning and practical usefulness. Relevance displaces consistency and nested hierarchy as the conceptual resource for generating and using the web (Verma 1998). How might we conceive of coherence playing such a central role in releasing the grip of disciplinary attachments and shifting our attachment to contextual meaning?

Hopkins recognizes that many organizations, groups and institutions make plans. Many plans intersect and overlap for a neighborhood, municipality or region. These include a multitude of private plans by owners, investors and developers as well as a host of local government agency plans. (I classify this multitude of plans as a vast field of plans in Chapter 3). No single agency can create a plan to usefully encompass and organize the complex interplay of the plans at play in the field. Like Salet, Hopkins recognizes that spatial plans do not govern complexity, but seek to complement, coordinate and enhance relations among plans underway. How might this work?

Coordination

I turn to the work of Elinor Ostrom at an intermediate scale of social goods. She uses the concept of coordination to describe the activities that people use to modify their social appropriation of a common pooled resource or modify the social provision of the resource. She and her colleagues initially used game theory to model coordination presupposing rational individualism and equilibrium over many trials. They found that game theory models predicted endless defection whereas empirical research uncovered coordination and cooperation. Irrigation and fishery users trapped by exchange rules fueled by individual self-interest and competition exhausted the common good. Changing the rules to allow for purposeful coordination communicated and sanctioned collaboratively allowed for solutions to the seemingly inevitable tragedy of the commons. Individuals learned to respond adaptively to common good assignment and provision difficulties. But they do so in specific contexts. How do they learn to do this?

Ostrom, Gardner and Walker (1994) argue that successful common good users avoid the tragedy of self-defeating competitive over use by creating institutional relationships tied to plans.

> Arriving at a joint plan of action for a series of future interactions, individuals may have in their repertoire of heuristics simple sharing rules backed up by a presumption that others will use something like a measured response. If, in addition, individuals have learned how a monitoring and sanctioning system enhances the likelihood that agreements will be sustained (i.e., trust for the worthy and sanction for the unworthy), they are capable of setting up and operating their own enforcement mechanisms.

Clever planning builds upon the efficacy of current practices and then offers innovations that will enhance the efficacy of those practices. The plans include institutional expectations informed by trust and the threat of coercive sanction. The plans represent institutional activities that members can use to inform their individual compliance. The plans advise, but do not decide. Each person uses the plan as an institutional member.

Ostrom recognizes the value of small 'p' planning as the activity people use to coordinate self-governance of a common good. When members of a common interest development teach new members the rules for governing the common good they learn to adopt a provisional plan. The plan works as each agrees to follow the plan pending the participation of others. The contextual features of each set of rule agreements make the patterns of interdependence clear and the practical sanctions feasible. The kind of work that Hopkins (2001) do on representation and Innes and Booher (1999b) and Booher and Innes (2002) do on collaboration provide useful insights about planning for action situations enabling participants to imagine future relationships across scale that do not lose their relevance for local practice. Plans flesh out provisional designs for future effects of common good utilization linking new goals within old ways. Institutional rules and incentives can draw upon the knowledge and direction plans offer but cannot substitute for such foresight. The details of the plan include both substantive knowledge about individual member resource use tied to a complex environmental setting as well as procedural beliefs, rules and practices tied to complex social agreements.

Plan Making and Institution Making Together

Ostrom's concern to comprehend and explain the complex ways that people manage common goods led her to abandon models of economic behavior that did not allow for forms of learning and reciprocity that fell outside the assumptions about rationality. Rational self interested competitors will not honor common pool resources but exhaust them. Ironically, attachment to this belief invites external government authority to impose limits on use. But central authority increases inefficiency and a loss of freedom as coercion reduces individual discretion (Ostrom 1994, p.219).

Ostrom studies how participants in collective good management communicate with each other over time considering the context and the consequences of different sharing arrangements. These participants create, test and amend rules and regulations for using common goods. They combine different types of reciprocity (taking turns, sharing, first come first served) with different kinds of trust (mutual vulnerability, limited liability, assurance schemes, social investment). Participants monitor and sanction violations of reciprocity and trust.

As Ostrom moves away from an effort to predict and attempt to describe and catalog how people adapt, that is, develop heuristics to help guide how they manage the use of a common good she adopts a pragmatic outlook that links instrumental results with the relevance of social purpose. People do, as Forester (1989) using Habermas shows, anticipate and rely upon sincerity, truthfulness, legitimacy and clarity when they communicate. When they plan together people do this paying close attention to the specific institutional rules and customs that link their individual purposes in a coordinated plan for the use of a common good.

As we apply the insights about common goods to urban problems, we can identify important institutional linkages between the practical deliberation that Forester (1999), Innes and Booher (1999b) and Booher and Innes (2002) write about and the kind of institutional design that Ostrom describes. Paying attention to the appropriation and provision of urban land as a common resource emphasizes institutional design efforts to anticipate and counter the damaging effects of externalities and assignment problems as these emerge in response to interdependence, uncertainty and indivisibility. But the efficacy of the design relies on how well those who manage the resource and experience the effects collaborate in making the plans work over time. There need be no theoretical or conceptual gap between deliberation and institutional design; but rather a complex set of institutional, political, economic and cultural barriers to making and sustaining democratic plans. These intersect in planning situations that foster specific problems and invite specific solutions offering few general lessons for practice.

Case Example: Illinois Affordable Housing Plan Mandate

How might the ideas from Hopkins and Ostrom contribute to understanding a specific spatial planning case that includes both institutional design and plan making. I use a study that I conducted about the implementation of state mandated municipal plans in Illinois. My pragmatic orientation shaped the inquiry, but not for a planning theory audience – but an audience of local officials. The brief that follows is cribbed from my analysis of how local municipalities in the Chicago metropolitan area respond to a state mandate to make plans (Hoch 2007b).

The State Plan Mandate

The State legislature of Illinois passed the Affordable Housing Planning and Appeal Act (IAHPA) in 2003. The Act required municipalities and counties without at least 10 percent of their housing stock classified affordable to make and adopt an affordable housing plan by April 2005. The legislation defined four plan requirements:

1 Count the number of units needed to meet the 10 percent requirement.
2 Identify land and structures available for development as affordable housing.
3 Identify and adopt incentives to attract affordable housing development.

4   Adopt one of the following goals:

   Make 15 percent of new housing development affordable
   Achieve a three percent increase in total affordable housing units
   Provide enough affordable housing to reach 10 percent of total units.

The Municipal Plans

According to the State affordable housing formula 49 of 272 municipalities in the Chicago Metropolitan Region failed to meet the 10 percent requirement. Thirty six of the 49 municipalities submitted plans to the Illinois Housing Development Authority. I read theses and evaluated their quality for each of four questions: compliance, consistency, relevance and commitment. Compliance consisted of a checklist of requirements spelled out in the statute (full, partial and non-compliant). The consistency test compared the logical fit among the required parts of the plan and how well the parts taken together as a whole to fit the purpose of the mandate. Relevance focused on the coherent fit between plan proposals and local municipal context and conditions. Plans that included any description about how, where and when affordable housing would be solicited, permitted, subsidized and built were high in relevance, while those that made no mention of specific changes to local policy, practice or geography were not. Commitment included written acknowledgment of local responsibility to provide affordable housing (high) or willingness to meet the target (low).

Many plans included plans for more planning. The most common proposal set out a timetable for a series of plan making activities focusing on affordable housing (9). All but a handful followed a bare bones legal format that echoed the statute. The plans offered relevant advice when identifying potentially suitable sites for affordable housing (14). But the most eloquent portions described the rural and pastoral character of each locale and how the fragile limits of the current infrastructure would be gravely taxed by the imposition of inappropriately sited affordable housing. The plans offered careful analysis of local conditions to document compliance (the state estimates were wrong), justify home rule (the state has no jurisdiction) and otherwise defend the existing land use arrangements. The most cynical proposed annexing a large 140 acre federally subsidized elderly residential complex to satisfy local compliance.

Only five of the documents described how changes in local housing policy objectives and regulations could foster affordable housing on local sites. Most plans included short abstract bullet lists of regulatory, administrative and fiscal incentives. The commitment to current land use was vivid – the commitment to affordable housing vague. The rationale for hardship was unique and compelling – the policies and regulations fostering affordable housing derived and dreamy.

Outcome

Five years after the mandate and two years after the submission of plans little had happened. A few municipalities had taken some modest steps to amend their zoning regulations to allow for mixed use housing. One exceptional municipality has adopted a rich assortment of regulatory and fiscal incentives to foster increased provision of affordable housing with some modest results. The state commission has been appointed, but no affordable housing developer has sought development approval from a noncompliant municipality been denied and appealed. How might Hopkins and Ostrom interpret these findings about an effort to institutionalize local housing plans as a remedy for longstanding municipal segregation by household income?

Analysis: Institutional Design and Plan Making Deliberation

Hopkins would direct our attention away from the state mandate by reminding us that there are many other planners besides municipalities shaping urban development. Regional housing markets include many more important actors than municipal officials. The plans created by these actors need be taken into account. Hopkins would then point out the mistake made by the legislators as they crafted the law, the mistake that a centrally imposed standard (the 10 percent) would accomplish the goal of increasing the geographic heterogeneity of housing value across the metropolitan region. The policy plan does not adequately recognize the layers of interdependence and uncertainty that shape the decision making by municipal officials. Threatening to take away local zoning authority generates perverse counter strategies as local officials seek to reduce another source of uncertainty. The mandate inspired cynical plans that met the consistency requirement without seriously undertaking the important steps needed to plan for increasing the amount and availability of affordable housing.

Hopkins would frame the problem of affordability by describing the intersecting systems of housing provision that contribute to the current regional housing market. The plan making activities of developers, lenders, realtors, lawyers, owners, renters, taxpayers, elected officials and professional planners together compose a very complex web indeed. The mandate framers did not appreciate this complexity and the difficulties comprehending how a top down plan would work to obtain compliance across imagined slices of interdependent decision making. Hopkins would urge reframing the study of the housing affordability problem as a kind of coordination problem rather than a hierarchical allocation problem.

Ostrom would celebrate the polycentric promise of so many independently elected self-governing municipalities. The state mandate, however, hardly helps because it sets both an arbitrary 10 percent limit and does not rely upon local authorities to sanction one another. Ostrom would recognize the common good features of urban catchments created by the provision of regional infrastructure. The extent to which the value of local collective goods is capitalized unevenly for housing prices among municipalities may reflect an assignment problem. This assignment problem occurs because the rules designed for the creation of municipalities does not include provisions for the geographic interdependence of municipalities as neighbors within metropolitan regions and does not recognize their joint reliance upon regional infrastructure systems. Ostrom's research makes clear that if the provision and appropriation of common good resources is not monitored by the users with sanctions for those tempted to take too much, the result will be uneven use. Large portions of well served urban land lie vacant while other areas become elite playgrounds increasingly subjected to congestion and over development (e.g., infill McMansions).

Following Ostrom analysts should break the region into interdependent subsets of municipalities bound together by joint reliance on transportation and utility systems that all need and use, but none can dominate and exploit. In fact such analysts would quickly find that associations of suburban mayors and managers have already emerged in response to such interdependencies, but mainly to coordinate access to collective toll goods (e.g., police and fire service reciprocity) rather than common goods (e.g., water management and housing mix). The uneven cost distribution imposed by the inefficient appropriation of collective resource by a small number of well positioned and provisioned municipalities makes it difficult to obtain voluntary reductions. Furthermore, the indirect nature of the appropriation and legitimacy of municipal status makes it difficult to know how to obtain efficient and fair coordination of housing mix. Ostrom would warn that the inequalities are likely to increase despite the mandate.

Integrating both we might ask how to jump start a coordination strategy rather than pursuing implementation of the mandate? Innes and Booher (1999a) focus on the complex social and institutional purposes, rules and beliefs that bring different stakeholders together to form a specific problem situation. Instead of imposing a single plan or insisting upon unilateral legal authority, they invite the many different stakeholders to a planning situation or dispute fostered by complex interdependence to learn from their differences seeking agreement through collaboration.

The pragmatic mix of both approaches would have professional planners build on the civic activity already underway by regional civic associations and use the information about housing market coordination breakdowns to demonstrate the interdependent features of regional housing and labor market changes. Ask local leadership and stakeholders to review and approve indicators of rent seeking or privileged assignment among municipalities within each sub region; or even better indicators of municipal efficiency and responsibility. Invite local public officials from sub-clusters of local municipalities to meet and discuss strategies for negotiating joint housing provision agreements across municipal boundaries. Keep expectations modest because local officials from the most prosperous enclaves can defect from the conversation. Entrepreneurial developers need be part of the conversation arguing for more sustainable higher density housing configurations. Include residents and other stakeholders often not included in these sorts of deliberations to learn and anticipate unexpected effects.

As local municipal officials learn to accept the new inequality indicators, they may recognize how municipally enhanced housing provision foster collective costs that filter down a hierarchy of prosperity eventually concentrating in impoverished municipalities. Routine meetings among sub regional clusters of municipal officials can highlight interaction effects that demonstrate how municipal autonomy does not protect places from jointly generated risk of decline – a risk increased by a failure to coordinate housing market regulations. Foster experimental provisional agreements to adopt and test together new local plans of housing provision and regulation that involve local officials, developers, investors, owners and taxpayers. As new rules are tested and housing market coordination among municipalities becomes routine, the plan will give way to occasional meetings to resolve disputes. A new sub regional housing coordination institution would emerge to manage this collective good.

Conclusion

This chapter explored the institutional design for plan making at an intermediate scale; from the planning situation conceived among actors to the planning situation shaped by custom and laws. The thread of inquiry focused on how plans work within institutions and in relation to efforts to create and manage institutions. I selected ideas from authors writing in different disciplines about planning issues. But instead of treating planning as an application of their respective disciplinary knowledge, I search instead for elements of planning coherence within each disciplined inquiry as it relates to planning and plan making. Paying attention to matters of practical judgment directs attention toward the consequences of the ideas for specific problem situations. Instead of arguing about disciplinary differences at the outset of inquiry (even in our own minds) we can focus instead on searching for analogies and distinctions that improve the coherence of the judgments we make about problematic situations and accompanying plans. We become more pragmatic and less analytic in outlook.

The integration illustrates how different disciplinary ideas can work together to illuminate the relationships between institutional change and plan making. The demands for coherence are not as exacting as the requirements for disciplinary consistency. We can in practical situations imagine many combinations of plausible plans and feasible institutional adaptations. Had I adopted a disciplinary focus to this comparison I would have focused on the different conceptions of social action and planning that each analyst draws upon. Instead of traveling upstream to their disciplinary beliefs I adapted their ideas to this case by keeping attention focused downstream toward the consequences their ideas about institutions might have for planning effectiveness.

I agree with planning theorists Donaghy and Hopkins as they turn our attention to the study of how people make plans and put them to use anticipating and coping with urban development problems. But I translated their advice about theoretical coherence into the domain of practical judgment. If we learn to rely on our disciplinary knowledge less as an epistemic guide and more as a conceptual tool, we might find greater opportunity for practical collaboration. The coherence we use to make practical judgments can provide a resource for plan making about collective goods at the urban scale. Such collaborations are commonplace and useful among analysts, practitioners and reflective activists facing every kind of urban problem. Planning scholars and professional often overlook the relevance and meaning in many instances of such learning because we rely upon a misdirected search for disciplinary consistency or planning integrity. But careful attention to how professionals make plans reveals a more promising and exciting prospect. Professionals deploy their imaginations as they make plans just like everyone else, but they use a wider set of disciplinary tools to compose what the future might hold. This makes all the difference.

Notes

1 The planning profession has always combined the knowledge and practice from other professions and disciplines. My rhetorical hyperbole warns us about the pursuit of disciplinary orthodoxy for the planning field.
2 The concept of habit contrasts with the concept of role. Role often has a dramatic and functional meaning. We play a role within a scripted social setting. The functional meaning emphasizes the routine features of a social activity that prompts conformity by those who participate. The dramatic aspect refers to the interpretive aspects adopted by an actor and the functional aspect to the underlying continuity of shared expectation. In both cases the concept of role exists independently of the actor – it is scripted like a play. Habit combines both aspects, but esmphasizes authorship by the person. It emphasizes the intersection of what a person does in a specific instance with an interactively produced sequence of such doing.
3 Alexander identifies design at three scales: Macro, meso and micro. Macro includes national constitution design or multinational development projects; meso includes the vast array of neighborhood development corporations, common interest developments, special purpose authorities and more; the micro includes intra organizational rules defining work teams, division of labor arrangements and game playing conventions. In this essay I focus on the middle range. Alexander agrees with Friedmann (1987) when he argues that planning translates ideas into action envisioning institutional design as part of that translation. I believe plans form intentions that may include institutional design, but also practical actions that include moral commitments and social promises.
4 Donaghy and Hopkins distinguish explanation and justification as they classify these issue domains: plans, organizations, process and collective choice. The selection treats 'plans' as an issue area we can explain or justify – a kind of knowledge and not a kind of practical judgment. I use plans as part of practical judgment and treat this focus on plans as specialized and derivative.

References

Alexander, E. (2005). Institutional transformation and planning: From institutionalization theory to institutional design. *Planning Theory*, 4(3), 209–233.
Ariely, D. (2008). *Predictably Irrational: The Hidden Forces That Shape Our Decisions*. New York: HarperCollins.
Batty, M. and Torrens, P. M. (2001). Modeling complexity: The limits to prediction. Centre for Advanced Spatial Analysis (CASA) Working Paper Series. London: University College London.
Booher, D. E. and Innes, J. E. (2002). Network power in collaborative planning. *Journal of Planning Education and Research*, 21, 221–236
Donaghy, K. and Hopkins, L. (2006). Particularist, non-positivist and coherentist theories of planning are possible and even desirable. *Planning Theory*, 5(2), 173–202.
Forester, J. (1989). *Planning in the Face of Power*. Berkeley: University of California Press.
Forester, J. (1999). *The Deliberative Practitioner*. Cambridge: MIT Press.
Friedmann, J. (1987). *Planning in the Public Domain: From Knowledge to Action*. Princeton, NJ: Princeton University Press.
Healey, P. (2007). *Urban Complexity and Spatial Strategies: Towards a Relational Planning for Our Times*. London: Routledge.
Hopkins, L. (2001). *Urban Development: The Logic of Making Plans*. Washington, D.C.: Island Press.
Innes, J. and Booher, D. (1999a) Consensus building as role playing and bricolage: Toward a theory of collaborative planning. *Journal of the American Planning Association*, 65(1), 9–26.
Innes, J. and Booher, D. (1999b). Metropolitan development as a complex system: A new approach to sustainability. *Economic Development Quarterly*, 13(2), 141–156.
Lekan, T. (2003). *Making Morality: Pragmatist Reconstruction in Ethical Theory*. Nashville, TN: Vanderbilt University Press.
Ostrom, E. (1990). *Governing the Commons: The Evolution of Institutions for Collective Action*. Cambridge, MA: Cambridge University Press.
Ostrom, E., Gardner, R. and Walker, J. (1994). *Rules, Games and Common-pool Resources*. Ann Arbor: University of Michigan.
Saeger, T. (2002). *Democratic Planning and Social Choice Dilemmas: Prelude to Institutional Planning Theory*. Burlington, VT: Ashgate.
Salet, W. (2018a). *Public Norms and Aspirations: The Turn to Institutions in Action*. London: Routledge.
Salet, W. (2018b). Institutions in action. In W. Salet (Ed.), *The Routledge Handbook of Institutions and Planning in Action* (pp. 3–23). London: Routledge.
Seabright, P. (2004). *The Company of Strangers: A Natural History of Economic Life*. Princeton, NJ: Princeton University Press.
Verma, N. (1998). *Similarities, Connections and Systems*. New York: Lexington.
Webster, C. J. (2005). Editorial: Diversifying the institutions of local planning. *Economic Affairs*, 25(4), 4–10.

5 Planning Imagination: Utopia, Scenario and Plan

Introduction

In this chapter I explore three popular concepts used to imagine the purposeful response to the future for a place: utopia, scenario and plan. I argue that viewed pragmatically the challenging vision of Utopia does not differ fundamentally from the insights offered in scenarios and plans. Each offer imaginative advice assessing the future as a prelude for action. Paying attention to this continuity invites plan makers (professionals as well as other stakeholders) to integrate the demands of utopia as part of the expectation for practical planning rather than an exceptional exercise that ignores the relevance of current opportunities and constraints.

Planning theorists want to include practical judgment at the center of planning, but they tend to privilege knowledge over action. As much as I have learned from both Patsy Healey (2010) and John Friedmann (2011) I think both lead us astray as they urge us to believe that planning turns knowledge into action; that knowing utopian ideals will inspire aspirations for a new way of life that fit these ideals. I will make the case in this article that a pragmatic approach does not rely on this gap. The claim that we need a strong utopian vision to provide a compelling attachment to a desirable future place sets off alarms for the pragmatist who rejects that ideas compel consent. The pragmatist account treats utopias as imagined places where specific ways of life reconcile current problems while suspending the commitments to many current constraints. Utopias, scenarios and plans all do inspirational work along the same cognitive path. The moral changes and policy improvements described in the stories and arguments that compose each become less demanding and more feasible moving from utopia to plan. All remain relevant because tied to practical concerns about the differences imagined changes might make to current ways of life.

Can Pragmatism Be Utopian?

Pragmatism can seem anachronistic and uninspired. The attraction of utopian inspired vision and explicit moral doctrines seems so much more attractive

(Bauman 1976; Eaton 2002). Planning theorists use the concept of utopia to describe a kind of place detached from the gritty unpleasant features of the current scene – a place that reconciles social conflicts within an imagined spatial order. When John Friedmann focused on the good city many decades ago and more recently (Friedmann 2000) in a response to Manuel Castells he conceives utopia as a radical departure from current conventions and possibilities. The utopian vision must preclude the pragmatic approach with its presumptive attention to context and purpose. How could a pragmatist imagine a radical alternative without making it fit into the limited bounds of current norms and purposes?

I want to show how the pragmatic approach can allow for and embrace the radical rupture of utopia without abandoning the practical demands of the problems at hand. This requires recognizing the crucial insight of the pragmatic approach, that we humans already use planning as an inescapable resource for any judgment we take for problem solving or future gazing. The conceptual contrast comes from a common misunderstanding of pragmatism as a kind of rational instrumentalism – a version of utilitarianism that inspires the sort of social engineering that confidently calculates future benefits for alternative plans. Another critique casts pragmatists as liberal incrementalists deeply wedded to feasible compromise at the lowest common denominator of political agreement. Still others treat the pragmatic approach as process focused and abstract, unable to offer specific advice about what to do.

I think the pragmatic approach can encourage people to inhabit visionary temptations as citizens, students and professionals imagining new forms of civic life and practical virtue. As people learn about the moral and cultural details of cases and places that imaginatively resolve pressing problems they can find room for action and change. The pragmatist spatial planner will communicate the utopian place in imaginative stories or in critical discourse, interpretation and debate. Communicate with empathy and solidarity (what difference will this make for your future?), if not fidelity (where will you fit in this future world?), offering alternatives that challenge the tradition of existing trends and current constraints. On this account utopia loses status as a compelling vision becoming instead especially detailed conception of a future place at one end of a long continuum of practical possibilities. The pragmatist does not want to hand off popular consent to a vision conceived by someone else, no matter how perfect the vision may seem.

Three Concepts Used to Envision the Future

Utopia

Planning theorists use the concept of utopia to describe a future place that reconciles current social, political, and economic problems within a single spatial community. The imagined space for settlement describes current problematic relationships as forms and types of activity and accomplishment that replace familiar problems with new ways of life. These ways of life consist of detailed relationships represented in the utopian landscape and narrative as successful and fulfilling. The details of the imagined garden, village, town or city replace social competition with cooperation, exploitation with justice, squalor with beauty, selfishness with generosity and so much more. The utopian place has a long lineage.

Utopia envisions how purposeful changes flow from compliance with inclusive doctrines. Utopias describe landscapes where diverse human inclinations, impulses, desires and unfinished edges find closure and significance. The Old Testament Genesis story of Eden proclaims the innocence of Adam and Eve before they ate from the tree of knowledge. They inhabit a garden that fulfills their needs. Neither of them experiences uncertainty, scarcity or conflict. The Genesis story of Judaism, Christianity and Islam describes Adam and Eve's life in a garden landscape; a place that supports the union of the human family with a single powerful God who designed both people and place. These human creatures had it all. Life was perfect. But they cast it aside by violating the one prohibition that God had set – do not eat fruit from the tree of knowledge. This original sin unleashed the inclinations and desires that fuel human curiosity, trouble making and ultimately death. Satan tempted Eve to try the fruit, but this could only work because Eve could choose to disobey God. The devil's clever temptations awaken a dormant autonomy. The exercise of choice destroys the perfect union leaving future generations vulnerable to death. The return to paradise in heaven will require an act of God.

Once, long ago, I was trained as a scripture scholar. I learned the art of hermeneutics as I struggled to discern what portion of a scriptural text was genuinely inspired revelation and what portion the product of human intention and interpretation. This effort to disclose the kernel of inspired truth remains a central pre-occupation in epistemological analysis that treats language and culture as delivery systems for some grander meaning beyond human authorship. Utopia aspires to this kind authenticity suspended beyond the reach of human fallibility and corruptibility. Utopia imposes a moral horizon that anticipates and delivers perfection.

On this account the audience does not discover utopia. The author fashions a future landscape that consists of layers of meaning the audience inhabits vicariously as a way of life. Utopia invites the audience to journey to an ideal place leaving behind the current troubling details of the present. Unlike self-improvement literature that details all manner of individual strategies we each might adopt to command a tumultuous environment; utopias envision social life in a place whose inhabitants already combine many ambitious goals showing how they should work together in unison. Utopian details inspire interest and hope as the audience can witness in these the consequences of animating ideals.

Utopias work their motivational magic not only through literary, philosophical or theoretical means; but as images that bind human expectations to a vision of future. Despite the record of failure, utopia persists as an attractive option, clothing ideals in familiar yet unblemished landscapes. The snapshot of the composed order for a perfect place ironically taps and fuels discontent with the present even as prospects for inhabiting such a place seemingly remain unlikely. In modern industrial and postindustrial times architecture remains especially susceptible to the attraction of utopia because the artistry of physical design attends to the salient layers of built space. The artistic rendering of a purposefully designed place includes not only those formal elements of composition that answer to beauty (the elegant geometry of the lines), but also combines the social and cultural meanings within the visual scene, landscape, park, garden or other imagined place. The designed image attracts viewer attention and commitment. The final rendering offers a complete vision as all the earlier versions sketched and compromised disappear before and beneath it (Eaton 2002; Rosenau 1983).

I briefly compare two analysts from different scholarly traditions within planning theory who adopt vivid and compelling arguments for pursuing utopian ideals imagining the outcomes such efforts will produce for the places people live: John Friedmann and Emily Talen. Friedmann develops his conception of future urban outcomes at the societal scale. He traces his guiding ideals to societal movements for social justice in light of changing forms of urbanization. The geographic features of place do not animate his conception of imagined social outcomes, but channel and shape the conditions for their emergence. For instance, in his future people obtain adequate housing security as the system for social and economic provision changes to reduce inequality across social divides and geographic places (Friedmann 2011).

Talen (2005) imagines future places emerging from the spatial arrangement of urban spaces. The guiding ideals combine conceptions of urbanism tied to professional movements in design and planning for places. The geographic configuration of space contributes importantly to imagined outcomes. For example, the proper combination of density, mix of use and street configuration reduces travel times and costs as it fosters local social cohesion.

Despite their difference in approach both authors imagine ideal future outcomes for places that anticipate a shift in political and institutional governance. The knowledge and focus for each varies in scale and form; but they converge in projecting expectations that not only describe ideal outcomes, but authorize them. Both argue for ideals strong enough to govern how places and people interact in the future. Ironically, neither author exhibits single minded doctrinal fidelity to the ideals they describe. Each in their related scholarship study the complexity of institutional planning and how current ideas undermine hopes for the ideals they champion.

Scenario

Scenarios like Utopias rely on narrative, but the purposes in the plot reflect the expectations of scripted stakeholders for each future. Scenarios offer plausible comparable options that project and evaluate interaction effects tied to specific expectations and assumptions about a future time and place. The compressed version is a proverb, the longer version a vignette or short story (Zapata 2007).

Storytelling and the narratives that the telling inspires animates the future with characters involved in plots susceptible to modification and reversal. Most of us experience life as a journey generating memories fueled by the language and culture we each inhabit. As we cast our glance backward we author our past selectively to make sense of current practice. If we failed a friend or betrayed a promise we might revise what we regret offering a counterfactual account. If only I had offered assistance or kept my word, I might have avoided the consequences that fuel my anguish. The explosion of research on human cognition and memory provides empirical grounds for the tacit scenario building each conduct as we reconsider and revise prior judgments. As we recognize the active role, we each play shaping our joint destiny we may reconsider our responsibility for past events. The inertia of familiar habits and conventions diminishes this sensibility. Counterfactual accounts revising memories of prior events can prepare us to respond to future events. Vivid disciplined storytelling about the future can offer prototypes for living together in a place that complement or trump the precedent of prior arrangements (Mandelbaum 1991; Albrechts 2005; Bruner 2002; Throgmorton 1996).

The creation of scenarios combines the selection of several causal attributes that frame the contours of change for a place, for instance, climate change and economic prosperity. The authors then conceive and project the goals of a local clientele as different plots that describe what might be done in the future to cope with the change. Comparing the scenarios that result informs the judgments that the clientele take now to prepare for an uncertain local future (Hopkins & Zapata 2007). Instead of seeking a story that will ground our future in a perfect place, spatial planners use scenarios to selectively compose and compare alternatives to inform current choice about what to do to prepare now for the imagined future.

The scenario concept was adapted by planners seeking to remedy the limits that accompanied the application of rational scientific methods to decision making within modern global corporations. Herman Kahn borrowed the concept of a plot summary for a novel or play to describe the narrative account of future consequences for alternative organization decision paths (Kahn & Weiner 1967). Scenario plans combine simulations used by generals, engineers and managers to compare the effects of possible strategies with the complexity of social meaning and choice. Among spatial planners, scenarios offer plausible accounts of future events tied to current choices about cause and purpose. The narratives invite users to compare how changes entailed by different causal and moral assumptions combine to shape the contours channeling consequences for select actors. The collaborative scenario invites the participation of current stakeholders reviewing assumptions and crafting the plot interactively. Instead of seeking the best scenario as a guide for practice, participants learn to compare several scenarios obtaining improved insight about the complex interaction effects of their guiding assumptions within competing narratives.

Scenarios describe possible futures not necessarily desirable or predictable ones. They describe the process of change for a place as a contingent narrative whose imagined outcomes tell us more about current beliefs and unexpected interactions than setting a clear path for action. Lew Hopkins puts it this way:

> Expanding the use of scenarios from simple preference selection among multiple scenarios to creating and maintaining multiple plausible narratives about the uncertain future allows planners to explore the range of possibilities scenario planning offers. Spatial planners can employ scenarios as a way of discovering unknown or poorly understood interrelationships or use scenarios to engage broader public input into planning processes. Planners can make use of scenarios to help differing interest or social groups understand one another's experiences in a particular place and their concerns and ideas about the future (Hopkins & Zapata 2007, p.12).

Scenario offers a much less morally ambitious concept for judging the future than utopia. First, their users must adopt the outlook of the analyst for whom stories lose their bonds with doctrine and belief. We do not inhabit the scenario we create but create stories that help us compare what kinds of world we might make and then inhabit. Second, the scenarios do not rely upon a sensitive grasp of cultural history and literary style; but a critical comprehension of relevant assumptions about change and the ability to animate these assumptions using narrative conventions to explore plausible effects related to the context at hand. The scenario maker must create each narrative fairly and transparently. The discipline of detached comparison requires that the author recognize the contingency of their own beliefs and possess detachment of judgment needed to craft the episodes and outcomes that faithfully portray the beliefs of others.

Since most scenario makers are neither novelists nor play writes, spatial planners make scenarios in settings that include diverse stakeholders representing different interests pursuing multiple goals. The drafting of comparable episodes includes the input of a diverse audience who can competently critique and revise drafts to improve plausibility and reduce bias. Sharing and comparing stories improves cognitive grip, emotional attachment and so elaborates the meanings different futures may offer.

Spatial planners use scenarios to enliven imagined counterfactual story plots that study how different strategies might resolve anticipated uncertainties for the future of a place. The scenario allows the professionals and participating stakeholders to explore different responses to the complex conditions and causes that threaten current habits, conventions and purposes. What differences in future housing provision availability and spatial pattern might emerge for different changes in the relationship between energy costs and population migration for the region? But scenarios may also be used to imagine how people adopting explicit normative principles and goals might respond to forecast conditions and causes. If we adopt an equity approach to housing provision what differences will this make given the conditions we anticipate for the region (Holway et al. 2012)? Either way the users interpret the differences across narratives to consider how current decisions might generate better outcomes for the forecast future.

Plan

Plans provide options we compose and compare how consequences might ensue for each. The urgent push of desire, the rational tug of belief or any problem that disrupts habit and convention stimulates planning. Plans encompass both a wider range of activity and looser set of constraints than utopias or scenarios. Narrative episodes and spatial patterns emerge in plans as shorthand tied to conceptual inquiry describing the origins of a place and then setting out alternative strategies, policies or designs to shape intentions toward the future at hand.

Most spatial plans prepared by professionals *describe* goals and existing conditions at the outset. Then the plan includes some *appraisal* of these conditions in relation to sponsor and client objectives. Next come proposals for the future; alternatives that the plan audience *compares* before making a decision: plausible imaginative simulations of future consequences and effects. Finally, the plan *concludes* with a recommendation or less decisive proposal guiding the decision of the sponsors and clientele. These conclusions may describe specific policies, programs or actions that stakeholders to a plan may adopt to make good on the decision they take. The plan works if the sponsors and stakeholders take some of the advice using it to change purpose and goals into practical intentions. Implementation turns intentions into commitments as stakeholders make decisions and adopt strategies to fit the context of a specific situation and place. If they enjoy time and money, they might assess the meaning of a policy, program or action by simulating strategies and testing the sensitivity of the consequences for each. Often stakeholders must act without the benefit of simulation. The plan may still offer good advice for its sponsors and clientele even if these stakeholders never find the means to implement it (Hoch 2012). This sounds familiar to the planning theory audience.

The rational model with all its well documented flaws abstracted this cognitive activity from the context of learning and use (Dalton 1986; Baum 1996). The revival of pragmatism among planning theorists rejected this rationalization (Healey 2009). Pragmatically speaking, spatial planners do not need a theory about planning to justify what they do. Planning does not require epistemic justification based on method and rationality – but a practical (i.e., politically savvy, culturally aware, socially astute, etc.) justification that offers credible, plausible and useful beliefs about the world as it is and how purposeful change may matter. Spatial planners use a diverse assortment of techniques and tools for manipulating information about complex urban systems and behavior. The tools need be properly calibrated and reviewed, but practically rather than theoretically. The population projection, the economic forecast, the land use suitability assessment, and other similar studies do not uncover the truth of the city but provide ordered relationships that plausibly frame future conditions – frames that rely upon judgments that combine future expectations, prior assumptions and current observations. Plans order urban complexity in ways that inform the choices we make about current polices, practices and behavior. Spatial planners compose these frames with specific audiences in mind. That is how spatial planners can interpret the meaning of the goals and plausibly relate these to the contextual conditions of a specific situation. Spatial planners do not make the plan for a universal, godlike audience, but specific audiences. As they compose judgments that frame future conditions, spatial planners anticipate the responses to these forecast changes and use knowledge of these estimated and imagined interaction effects to modify expectations, assumptions and observations. The objectivity of spatial planning comes from the quality of this composition rather than any imagined capacity to form judgments exclusive of a specific audience (van Dijk 2011; Hoch 2007).

Professional plans offer robust, but modest useful advice. The plans may as Hopkins (2001) describes be as simple as a project agenda or as complicated as a comprehensive regional environmental strategy. The plans help stakeholders assess options relative to current practice and the available competing arguments and assessments. The plans offer provisional support for a judgment about what to do for the future. As stakeholders accept a version of the plan and intend to follow the advice their focus shifts from deliberation toward commitment and decision. The decision maker may mention the plan as a reason for the choice, but the choice and the ensuing action does not rely upon the plan as cause but merely a guide. Changing purposes and conditions may lead stakeholders to ignore the plan, revise it or oppose it. The plan does not shape action, but intention.

Pragmatic Integration

The powerful grip of rational expectations still leads spatial planners and stakeholders to expect a linear progression in plan making from percept, through concept composing options susceptible to optimal choice. The authors of each kind of imagined place do conceive purpose and context in a deliberate and reflective fashion. They possess and deploy rational conventions to structure utopian details, plot scenarios and envision plans. But the audience (sponsors, clientele and public stakeholders) for the advice inhabits the complex contours of expectation and routine within a specific institutional nexus. For the pragmatist each audience creates its own utopia, scenario and plan within the historic contours of culture and place.

How people listen and adapt advice flows through the layers of institutional habit and convention they each learned. Annette Kim (2011a) notes how our attention gets shaped by the expectations we form in relation to what others do and say. Furthermore, this happens less from deliberate discussion and more from visual impressions and emotional empathy. We imagine our own future deeply tied to social meanings about the relationships that matter to each of us. Kim lays out the research agenda: "The challenge will be to disentangle socially contingent factors from neurological functioning and understand how they interact … Given the recent criticisms of planning theory, this research agenda should connect these social, cognitive processes to material, spatial impacts" (Kim 2011b, p.335).

Taking this insight, we may compare each concept in relation to a different kind of social cognition pragmatically conceived. Utopia offers a heroic conception of social change. The utopian vision shows us how radically different goals we envision adhere in the detailed image describing specific relationships and their effects for a future place. The cognitive judgment relies upon the coherent fit among the many parts within a unified order. The psychological impact might work like the insight described by Gestalt psychology – an alternating perceptual shift between the outline image of a vase to the empty space between facing human profiles. In effect, the utopian vision skips incremental developmental change encouraging a sharp break from the past – a conversion experience that builds a new way of life on a foundation of assumptions and norms rather than experience and tradition (Cooper 2011).

Utopias, scenarios and plans each include narrative and argument organized to persuade readers and viewers to consider changing their ways in the future. All three selectively conceive complex relationships (architecture, morality, economy, politics and society) within placed based community. The sheer multiplicity of relations convinces us that the alternate place could prove capacious enough to complete unfinished business, tie together loose threads, bind up old wounds and otherwise banish the vulnerability of death. They each describe future changes to illustrate the consequences of specific doctrines, practices and purposes.

A pragmatist approach enables scholars to recognize the allure of an ideal place and to imagine the favorable interactive effects, but with a mix of irony and hope that remains unwilling to project consent for future generations. Foucault's great contribution was to show us how enlightenment optimization not only sheds light into the dark corners of ignorance, but how these norms exact new forms of self-inflicted social compliance and order (Foucault 1972; Hoch 1988). Other planning theorists have adapted his insights composing a post structural pragmatism. See for instance the essay by Beunen, Assche and Duineveld (2013) analyzing how conservation discourse relies on the performance of culturally embedded conflicting narratives and not the reflection of timeless norms. The pragmatist recognizes the vitality and power of imaginatively conceiving social and physical outcomes for a future place. But these outcomes should not seek to inculcate the ideal as a doctrine compelling consent. The images for the place need be prepared for an audience whose inquiry will test the ideal and assess its merits for their own expectations. Utopia for the pragmatist loses any privileged authority and describes what we do as we conceive the future for a place in enough detail to assess what living there might mean for resolving some of the purposes and problems currently at hand. Even if we manage to build such a place, we will face new problems. The pragmatist embraces the edification that radical visions inspire, but without imposing the conceptual grip of perfection or a firm foundation. There is no substitute for practice.

Proponents of strong doctrinal norms for the future design of places disparage pragmatic conceptions of planning as unimaginative, incremental and conservative. This flows mainly from a narrow and misleading conception of pragmatism that treats current practice as uncritically normative. Pragmatism focuses exclusively on maintaining the continuity of incremental good an outlook that distracts the believer from considering the prospects of more expansive and critical ends (Fainstein 2010; Hillier 2011).

But pragmatism includes a wide and robust set of thinkers who care deeply about the sorts of long term improvements that the planning enterprise evokes (Forester 1999; Innes & Booher 2010; Harper & Stein 2006; Healey 2009, 2010). The pragmatists like their contemporary postmodern brethren are suspicious of 'just so' stories about the future that offer tame picturesque places without continuity and conflict. Unlike the Hegelian and Kantian idealists whose students would seek social harmony through practice tied to concepts in action; pragmatists borrowed the intuitive grasp of cognitive action but naturalized it using Darwin's insights about evolution. They broke from the classic philosophical belief that we are rational animals and emphasized that we are learning animals that invent rational tools subject to recall and revision based on practical use (Garrison 1999). We will learn from prior mistakes and problems by resisting the longing for closure recasting fate as an invitation to freedom (Gunder & Hillier 2003). Pragmatists agree that we cannot tame complexity and should beware the elusive promise that we can do so. But they also believe planers should focus on practical judgments and the actions people take to cope with complexity. That means attending to what science teaches us about expectations and causes. We can use this knowledge to improve how we comprehend and make judgments about imagined futures for specific people and places. We combine moral sensitivity, social craft, technical artistry and political savvy as we make professional judgments about future changes and effects. The pragmatist approach can use conceptions of utopia, scenario and plan to improve how spatial plans bridge local expectation and global fate for diverse clientele inhabiting unique institutional and geographic locales.

How might we use these concepts to guide our own judgments as spatial planners envisioning the future for civic and public institutions? First consider research on expectations that shows how our emotions direct attention, fuel desire and guide judgment together with cognitive efforts that deliberately frame, analyze and value imagined options as intentions susceptible to choice. The complexity of practical human judgment makes clarity of purpose and intention less a matter of vision and more a matter of action (Sandercock 2003; Hoch 2006). Bias and desire direct attention and judgment even as purpose and goals require reflection using forethought that takes these into account (Kahneman 2011; Rogoff 1990). The practical details of each type of imagined future can include the irony of political agonism (Mouffe 1999, 2007) and the allure of unconscious desire (Allmendinger & Gunder 2005; Baum 2010). How do utopia, scenario and plan integrate feelings and purpose as people conceive the future for a place?

Second consider research about the causes and patterns of modern settlement and competing claims about their epistemic grip and normative clout. The increasing multiplicity of disciplinary methods and moral goods makes it unlikely that anyone can comprehend the field, much less offer a unified synthesis (Mandelbaum 2000). Analysts studying patterns and cause labor within familiar disciplinary and moral turf using their ideas to conceive the forces for change whether tied to structure, agency or some combination. The emphasis on different kinds of cause, different frameworks for moral interpretation and competing orientations within each offers diverse accounts of change – but no way to reconcile and choose among these. How do utopia, scenario and plan help resolve the composition and choice of causal order and change for the future of a place?

Utopias Offer a Good Place

When spatial planners and planning scholars conceive utopias to tame the complexity of social, economic and political life within complete places, they offer assurance and security as they stretch the bounds of human imagination and effort. The pragmatist is wary of utopias less by their power to excite the imagination, and more by their disregard for the inherent limits of human fallibility and corruptibility while overlooking the surprising resilience of human imagination and creativity. The pragmatist constructs utopias when confronted with cynical disregard for the future tied to doctrinal narrowness, unimaginative abstraction, listless indifference or external repression. Utopian visions awaken the possibility of individual fulfillment through new forms of civic sociability within a place. Utopias reawaken the possibility for hope in the future. Fainstein (2005) makes the case for this effort using the intellectual resources of political economy; as does John Friedmann (2011) as he envisions conditions for a good city resting on four pillars: paid work, social provision, affordable housing and healthcare. But the ideals they describe imagine audience inspiration and conversion independent of context and practical judgment.

Utopian conceptions of the future viewed pragmatically imagine interaction effects tied to dramatic changes in the habits of daily living. This does not require audience commitment to a singular moral system of doctrinal belief. A pragmatic tolerance for cosmopolitan diversity of social norms relies on an increasingly inclusive and shared infrastructure of democratic civility. The meaning of these contours flows not from generic rules, but conventions tied to specific practices and habits that combine differences into a rich plurality of interactive social outcomes. The contested development of liberal social and political institutions provides a range of local contexts for place focused plans. Utopia describes a way of life that reproduces the shared infrastructures that generate new values and foster individual meaning. Utopia in this view will be imperfect and contested even as it resolves current problems (Pinder 2010). Utopia describes desirable details of new ways of life at the horizon we never reach, but towards which we aspire as we imagine (and even practice) recasting old habits into new.

Scenarios Tell Useful Stories

Scenarios capture the interplay between interpretation and complexity offering imaginary reconciliation for the futures envisioned in stories. They help plan making stakeholders create and compare alternative responses to the future together framing the plot. Imaginatively inhabiting the story enables the users to comprehend the emotional and cognitive meaning of the place. Each participant taps the narrative to assess the simulated impact for important purposes and strategies. Scenarios do not provide details of a purposefully detailed alternative way of life, but selective comparisons explicitly tied to assumptions and arguments about causes and consequences as currently conceived.

Pragmatically, scenarios offer narratives stakeholders can compare to capture the meaning and significance of changes that currently haunt their imagined futures albeit in abstract and elusive ways. These stories help people tied to a place to remember that seemingly inevitable trends or immovable structures remain susceptible to their collective purposes and actions. Each person makes choices that rely upon the inspiration and guidance of stories in memory that motivate and animate the choice. Pragmatically, scenarios draw upon this familiar narrative form of comprehension. While utopia explores the meaning of pursuing dramatically different purposes reconciling differences within an integrated narrative, scenarios provide narratives that test differences among alternative divergent stories. Utopia edifies like a novel, while scenarios function more like proverbs.

Scenarios are not merely tools for tapping human storytelling to reduce strategic uncertainty for a place facing a complex future. For the pragmatist complexity takes shape as a resource for survival and flourishing; as problems susceptible to action. Scenarios put flesh on the bones of arguments that forecast changes in complex behavior and ensuing interaction effects. The narratives help us frame, compose and select better options than we would otherwise relying on tradition, ideals or argument alone. Storytelling binds past and future together in ways that improve the quality of practical choice and so address complexity without sacrificing social meaning (Van Hulst 2012).

Plans Inform Intentions for the Future

Spatial planners make plans for people deeply constrained by political demands and other changing conditions. Plans help set problems and conceive choices in ways diverse stakeholders can comprehend and use to assess future actions and consequences. Plans inform intentions toward some future action. The cultural interpretation of plan ideas profoundly shapes the meaning of the ideas people use to make policies, rules, projects, proposals, programs, incentives and other collective action strategies that can traverse the complicated institutional landscapes for towns, cities and regions. Unlike social norms or laws that constrain us as we learn their meaning and so help govern a place; plans help us review and compare the meaning of different expectations for the future of a place. This imaginative reconsideration requires that people suspend attachments to familiar practices and beliefs so as to compare these against others as practical alternatives. This detachment does not distance people from the practical details of a place or the many competing moral purposes and political interests. It means that for stakeholders to plan they must experience and recognize doubts, curiosity, desires and expectations that disrupt current habits and conventions that currently govern the place they inhabit. The confidence and commitment that assured our compliance with law and custom now shifts to the plan making as stakeholders consider what options might resolve the problem for the place. The decision to choose one solution among the many considered does not flow from the planning, but from the intentions of the stakeholders who used the plan to conceive and compare choices.

Collaborative planning seeks to include stakeholders in the plan making so that the participants comprehend the meaning of optional decisions for the purposes and circumstances at hand. The deliberation among the community of stakeholders making the plan helps set or frame the problem to include differences in purpose and interpretation. For the pragmatist the plan works if someone adopts it as a guide for judgment. The choice of an option and the ensuing action includes personal, social, institutional and environmental influences. So if the actions achieve consequences that solve problems than the public clientele rarely mention the plan. Plans do not decide or act, people do. People take credit for good outcomes emphasizing the virtue, integrity and wisdom of their decision making. Good plans become psychologically invisible until the next problem.[1] Ironically, if future events turn out badly, sponsors and clients often blame the plan and spatial planners regardless of evidence for blame. It may be that the plan included error and misleading goals, but accurate and relevant plans may become scapegoats for bad leadership and poor decisions (Baum 1999).

The pragmatist approach places expectations and knowledge along continua that invites planning stakeholders to adapt the advice they compose about an uncertain future to the circumstances and conditions that emerge. Faced with the calamity of ambitious modernist inspired inner-city public housing high rise projects HUD planners in the 1990s adopt a utopian urbanism tempered with more modest ideas and expectations (Vale 2002; Goetz 2013). The award winning regional plan for Chicago uses scenarios to highlight the advantages of infill mixed use development even as ensuing project and infrastructure ideas offer only modest adjustments to current practice (CMAP 2040). Instead of critiquing these sorts of efforts from the heights of moral perfection or optimal rationality, the pragmatist focuses on increments of successful adaptation. Harper and Stein (2006) describe how deploying a wide reflective equilibrium the pragmatist can conceive increments that coherently bind together the imagined possibility with practical opportunity. But this approach allows for a wide range of strategies. For instance, consider the tight tentative assessment of plans in the context of historical comparison (Ryan 2011) or the expansive assessment of collaborative efforts (Innes & Booher 2010).

Conclusion

The pragmatist does not believe we can craft a utopia, scenario or plan for a place without already imagining and deploying the active imagination we each use to conceive and compare options for practical attention and judgment. As we anticipate and prepare for the future of a place we combine our expectations and knowledge to conceive the imagined place. We make plans to guide deliberate comparisons about what options to choose. The plan helps us settle on the option clients intend to choose and use. I think planning practitioners professional and otherwise do well enough if the plans they make guide and form the intention of their collaborators and clientele; especially as utopian visions and scenarios improve the moral reach and relevance of the advice. If people and institutions take advice, but do not act upon it, stakeholders should not feel their plan failed. Plans advise. They do not compel, but counsel. The research on planning practice can and should explore how spatial planners of every sort mobilize and adapt these concepts as Albrechts (2005), Healey (2010) and van Hulst (2012) do as they explore how spatial planners and plans imagine futures as guides for practical judgment.

I used plan in this chapter to describe the advice people learn to imagine and use as they encounter problems in their daily lives: where should we meet, when do I arrive, what route do I take, how should I travel and who will come with me? Mostly people learn to rely on habit, but reflective comparison of options provides part of the crucial architecture for practical judgments about the future. This pervasive planning fuels the varieties of plans professionals, public officials, civic activists, organizational leaders, local stakeholders and others conceive and make as they attend to the future for a specific place. The collective purposeful efforts to deliberately and publicly prepare and consider options for the future of a place can create a utopia, scenario or plan. But all three remain tied to the practical art of planning that people everywhere use to cope with problems and prepare better for an uncertain future.

This continuity makes sense because I decouple planning from rationality. Rationality (with all its variety of meanings) need not accompany or support planning although it may. Planning contributes cognitive and conceptual support for the development of rationality (Hoch 2007). Professional and other spatial planners can and do use all sorts of rational distinctions, tools and insights as they make plans for places. As spatial planners and planning scholars turn to practical plan making we should deploy the thin liberal virtues of prudence and tolerance to practical judgments about congestion, density, pollution and the homeless to frame the complex goals and causal interplay that shapes the situations where sponsors and public clientele seek advice. Planning practitioners offer advice about a specific situation and the problems it poses for practical judgment and action. The spatial planner helps people compare and consider options. The proposals should be specific and tied to context. The audience should be recognized and engaged. This may include compelling accounts of future outcomes that participants' desire embedded as stories susceptible to challenge and amendment. But the conceptual and imaginative reach of these arguments and tales need not provide foundation for belief. That belief remains open to practical experimentation achieving together the purposes we intend to pursue. The flourishing that John Friedmann embraces in his conception of the good society provides an apt description of the sort of effects that the authors of utopias, scenarios and plans hope their advice will inspire; cultural and institutional evolution that builds upon the natural kind that produced *Homo-sapiens*. The pragmatist concentrates on the journey more than the destination because the destination will change as we learn how to flourish. Of course we may not.

Note

1 The stereotype of plans gathering dust on a shelf blinds us to this common psychological practice.

References

Albrechts, L. (2005). Creativity as a drive for change. *Planning Theory*, 4, 247–269.
Allmendinger, P. and Gunder, M. (2005). Applying Lacanian insight and a dash of Derridean deconstruction to planning's "dark side". *Planning Theory*, 4(1), 87–112.
Baum, H. S. (1996). Why the rational paradigm persists: Tales from the field. *Journal of Planning Education and Research*, 15, 127–135.
Baum, H. S. (1999). Forgetting to plan. *Journal of Planning Education and Research*, 19, 101–113.
Baum, H. S. (2010). Planning and the problem of evil. *Planning Theory*, 10(2), 103–123.
Bauman, Z. (1976). *Socialism: The Active Utopia*. London: Allen & Unwin.
Beunen, R., Assche, K. V. and Duineveld, M. (2013). Performing failure in conservation policy: The implementation of European Union directives in the Netherlands. *Land Policy*, 31, 280–288.

Bruner, J. (2002). *Making Stories: Law, Literature, Life*. New York: Farrar, Straus and Giroux.
Cooper, M. (2011). Rhetorical agency as emergent and enacted. *College Composition and Communication*, 62(3), 420–449.
Dalton, L. (1986). Why the rational model persists: The resistance of professional education and practice to alternative forms of planning. *Journal of Planning Education & Research*, 5, 147–153.
Eaton, R. (2002). *Ideal Cities: Utopianism and the (Un)Built Environment*. London: Thames & Hudson.
Fainstein, S. (2005). Planning theory and the city. *Journal of Planning Education and Research*, 25, 121–130.
Fainstein, S. (2010). *The Just City*. Ithaca, NY: Cornell University Press.
Forester, J. (1999). *The Deliberative Practitioner*. Cambridge, MA: MIT Press.
Foucault, M. (1972). *The Archaeology of Knowledge*, translated by A. M. Sheridan Smith. New York: Pantheon.
Friedmann, J. (2000). The good city: In defense of utopian thinking. *International Journal of Urban & Regional Research*, 24(2), 460–472.
Friedmann, J. (2011). *Insurgencies: Essays in Planning Theory*. London: Routledge.
Garrison, J. (1999). John Dewey's theory of practical reason. *Educational Philosophy and Theory*, 31(3), 291–312.
Goetz, E. G. (2013). *New Deal Ruins: Race, Economic Justice & Public Housing*. Ithaca, NY: Cornell University Press.
Gunder, M. and Hillier, J. (2003). Planning fantasies? An exploration of a potential Lacanian framework for understanding development assessment planning. *Planning Theory*, 2(3), 225–248.
Harper, T. L. and Stein, S. M. (2006). *Dialogical Planning in a Fragmented Society*. New Brunswick, NJ: Center for Urban Policy Research.
Healey, P. (2009). The pragmatic tradition in planning thought. *Journal of Planning Education & Research*, 28, 277–292.
Healey, P. (2010). *Making Better Places*. London: Routledge.
Hillier, J. (2011). Strategic navigation across multiple planes: Towards a Deleuzean-inspired methodology for strategic spatial planning. *The Town Planning Review*, 82(5), 503–528.
Hoch, C. J. (1988). A pragmatic inquiry about planning and power. *Society*, 26(1), 27–35.
Hoch, C. J. (2006). Emotions and planning. *Planning Theory and Practice*, 7(4), 367–382.
Hoch, C. J. (2007). Making plans: Representation and intention. *Planning Theory*, 6(1), 15–35.
Hoch, C. J. (2012). Making plans. In *Urban Planning Handbook*, edited by R. Weber and R. Crane (pp. 241–258). New York: Oxford University Press.
Holway, J., Gabbe, C. J., Hebbert, F., Lally, J., Matthews, R. and Quay, R. (2012). *Opening Access to Scenario Planning Tools*. Cambridge, MA: Lincoln Land Institute.
Hopkins, L. D. (2001). *Urban Development: The Logic of Making Plans*. Washington D.C.: Island Press.
Hopkins, L. D. and Zapata, M. A. (2007). *Engaging the Future*. Cambridge, MA: Lincoln Land Institute.
Innes, J. and Booher, D. (2010). *Planning with Complexity: An Introduction to Collaborative Rationality for Public Policy*. New York: Routledge.
Kahn, H. and Weiner, A. (1967). *The Year 2000: A Framework for Speculation on the Next Thirty-three Years*. New York: Macmillan.

Kahneman, D. (2011). *Thinking, Fast and Slow*. New York: Farrar, Straus and Giroux.

Kim, A. M. (2011a). Talking back: The role of narratives in Vietnam's recent land compensation changes. *Urban Studies*, 48(3), 493–508.

Kim, A. M. (2011b). Unimaginable Change: Future directions in planning practice and research about institutional reform. *Journal of the American Planning Association*, 77(4), 328–337.

Mandelbaum, S. (1991). Telling stories. *Journal of Planning Education and Research*, 10, 209–214.

Mandelbaum, S. (2000). *Open Moral Communities*. Cambridge, MA: MIT Press.

Mouffe, C. (1999). Deliberative democracy or agonistic pluralism. *Social Research*, 66(3), 745–758.

Mouffe, C. (2007). *Deconstruction and Pragmatism*. London: Taylor & Francis.

Pinder, D. (2010). Necessary dreaming: Uses of utopia in urban planning. In J. Hillier and P. Healey (Eds.), *The Ashgate Companion to Planning Theory: Conceptual Challenges for Spatial Planning* (pp. 343–366). Burlington, VT: Ashgate.

Rogoff, B. (1990). *Apprenticeship in Thinking: Cognitive Development in Social Context*. New York: Oxford University Press.

Rousenau, H. (1983). *The Ideal City: Its Architectural Evolution in Europe*, 3rd edn. London: Methuen.

Ryan, B. (2011). Reading through a plan. *Journal of the American Planning Association*, 77(4), 309–327.

Sandercock, L. (2003). Out of the closet: The power of story in planning. *Planning Theory and Practice*, 4(1), 11–28.

Talen, E. (2005). *New Urbanism and American Planning: The Conflict of Cultures*. New York: Routledge.

Throgmorton, J. (1996). *Planning as Persuasive Storytelling*. Chicago: University of Chicago Press.

Vale, L. J. (2002). *Reclaiming Public Housing: A Half Century of Struggle in Three Public Neighborhoods*. Cambridge, MA: Harvard University Press.

van Dijk, T. (2011). Imagining future places: How designs co-constitute what is, and thus influence what will be. *Planning Theory*, 10(2), 124–143.

Van Hulst, M. (2012). Storytelling, a model of and a model for planning. *Planning Theory*, 11(3), 299–318.

Zapata, M. A. (2007). Person-oriented narratives: Extensions on scenario planning for multicultural and multi-vocal communities. In L. D. Hopkins and M. A. Zapata (Eds.), *Engaging the Future: Forecasts, Scenarios, Plans and Projects* (pp. 261–282). Cambridge, MA: Lincoln Land Institute.

Part III

6 Crafting Plans

Introduction

Seymour Mandelbaum (2000) argues that we can read the same plan as a policy brief, a story or a design and so learn how the plan fails or succeeds as persuasive written discourse. He reads plans critically to learn how to write them more credibly. Lew Hopkins (2001) argues that we make plans to represent the current decisions we should make based on comparison with other current and future decisions. Mandelbaum analyzes the plan rhetorically and Hopkins analyzes the plan logically. Both acknowledge the role plans play helping us cope with complexity; Mandelbaum the complexities of social and political intentions, Hopkins the complexities representing collective decisions: interdependence, irreversibility, indivisibility and uncertainty. My effort combines ideas from both. My intention is not to prove something, but to persuade the reader that these distinctions might prove useful first, showing that plan makers integrate both, second that they do so in different ways and third, that these differences might be combined in ways that offer more useful practical judgments about how to structure the intersecting filaments in Donaghy and Hopkins' (2006) web of plans.

In earlier essays I argue that seeking rational plans sets up misleading expectations for what we need know to make plans. We humans early on learn what I describe as small 'p' planning ability. We use planning to contribute to practical judgments about future action with others. Our plans turn desires and interests into intentions. Many of these take shape under routine conditions (e.g., commuting) and others under random conditions (e.g., gambling). Most fall between. The most relevant kinds for urban planning focus on complex coordination and communication with others – conditions that invite adaptive response (Hoch 2002, 2007). We prepare large 'P' plans to anticipate and cope with this complexity when we plan for urban development and encompassing ecologies.

How do urban planners compose plans for complex urban settings? How do they combine logically ordered, analytically astute coordination with rhetorically persuasive, socially savvy communication? When we compose urban plans, I argue that we rely upon one or more compositional frameworks: precedent, protocol or prototype. We adopt one or more of these frameworks to guide how we organize complex urban relationships into a comprehensible and useful representation. The composition of the plan may draw upon the ideas and practices of prior plans (precedent) or adopt existing conventions or rules promoted by competent authorities (protocol). The composition may include formal mandates or informal customs as a guide for action (policy). The composition may introduce imaginative and inventive new ways to tame complexity (prototype). Such innovation may draw upon the artistry of a gifted designer or the savvy of a strategically inventive policy analyst.

I consider these frameworks using a pragmatic outlook that treats plans as products of practical judgment sensitive to context and consequences. This outlook treats conflicts, ambiguities, disruptions or disturbances in the continuity of complex urban activity as issues deserving planning attention. The kind of plan we choose to make reflects the interplay between these practical pragmatic concerns and the framework(s) used to compose it (Hoch 1984, 1994). Plans offer meaningful advice in the context of specific situations. I use examples to illustrate how each style of composition binds representation and intention together to tame complex situations – what I term compositional frames. The comparisons illustrate how differences in composition shape the meaning and use of the plan for specific situations.

Logical Representation and Rhetorical Interpretation Making Plans

Before taking the linguistic turn planning analysts often treated logical scientific analysis as superior to rhetorical analysis. Analysts believed that logical order reflected an underlying reality. Rhetoric proved less compelling because tied to the contingent dimensions of purpose – history and audience. As analysts recognized the inescapable rhetorical features of human inquiry, logic lost this prominence appearing more instrumental and contingent. Instead of uncovering a timeless foundational order independent of human purpose and history, creating logical representations remains closely tied to practical cognitive judgments shaped by context and culture (Lee 1973). This does not diminish the power of logic to improve the accuracy and validity of reasoning but places this power in the service of less transcendental hopes. Rhetoric lost its secondary status as superficial illustration for underlying logical truth. Both may now be considered together as partners in human judgment. I use Hopkins to give voice to the logic of representation and Mandelbaum to do the same for interpretation. I believe plans put representations to use forming intentions that help us tame complex situations (Hoch 2007).

Interpretation

According to Seymour Mandelbaum we often justify the arguments we make in our plans by appeal to universal principles or communal norms. He exhibits little confidence in either the invention or discovery of transcendent guidance and adopts a communitarian outlook that insists we rely on familiar concepts of community to frame planning deliberation. Our intentions take shape within social communities of three types: the deep solidarity of religion and kinship, the thin contracts of the marketplace and negotiated settlements among competing moral claims.

> He warns us not to extend the expectations of solidarity and contract too far into the public arena of contested collective choice. We should rely instead upon a respect for a kind of deliberation that enjoins and engages competing claims for public attention and collective choice. We should adopt the conception of open moral communities (Hoch 2006a, p.128).[1]

Mandelbaum (2000) does not trust the pursuit of a systemic rational plan – a complete formal order. He adopts a pluralistic embrace of complexity that enjoins us to foster open moral communities that can forge understanding and agreements across complex divides. We cannot settle good intentions beforehand once and for all. We must foster modest incomplete unions on the go. Plans need be provisional to respect the differences that make life worth living.

Mandelbaum identifies two complementary sensibilities that nurture his conception of open communities: a belief in the efficacy of overlapping communities and a willingness to use public interpretation to navigate the passageways among them. People holding different views can sustain an ongoing conversation with a semblance of order because they speak ambiguously and avoid "tightly disciplined choices between alternative cities of the mind" (Mandelbaum 2000, p.141). Mandelbaum criticizes shifting from one definition to another in an endless contest held together by the false belief that a 'real' unity lurks in the wings. We need learn instead how to sustain the ambiguity as a resource for exploring differences and finding what these differences mean in more practical and immediate relationships. We need believe in a myth of open moral communities.

Representation

Lew Hopkins (2001) studies the logic of plan making with a clear awareness of the meaning of such logic for a planning audience. The conceptual order he describes speaks to an audience of professional planners interested in using plans to improve settlements. The logic he envisions takes shape within a context of professional practice (although like Mandelbaum he imagines many kinds of people and organizations making plans – not just professional planners). What do planners face making plans? They face problems. What sort of problems? Problems related to the features of urban development that escape the expectations and practices of ideal market conditions: indivisibility, interdependence, irreversibility and uncertainty. Complexity emerges as inescapable relationships that challenge our ability to adapt. Hopkins relies upon an underlying evolutionary and developmental conception of order to conceive how professionals make plans. Table 6.1 describes the four kinds of urban complexity in relation to differences between temporal and spatial conditions susceptible to adaptation and those that are not (Hoch 2007).

The purpose laden context of professional planning gives historic and spatial meaning to the logical distinctions Hopkins makes. Take the concept of indivisibility. The history of land development in the US documents how vast expanses of territory became millions of parcels to be sold and taxed. The legacy of this development includes thousands of local jurisdictions across the urban landscape set apart by geographic and legal boundaries that rarely respect the physical features and contours of the underlying territory. The boundary makers cluster and rationalize the increasing number of territorial segments parcel splitters produce. Hopkins hopes to tame this cadastral subdivision by arguing that planning knowledge recognizes the underlying territorial indivisibility that boundary makers and parcel splitters treat as so much geographic putty. Parcels in a flood plain share vulnerability to inundation. The land coverage in each parcel has a cumulative territorial effect for all parcels in the underlying flood plain. The water entering the plain has less open soil surface to absorb it, so flood levels rise faster and higher. Describing indivisibility as a kind of logic abstracts from the historic conditions of land development and attempts to draw upon a larger and more inclusive rationality to persuade boundary makers and parcel splitters to mend their ways. But what compels rational consent to the logic, I think, has less to do with a deductive order than the utility of the concept in describing the collective consequences of parcel level decisions within a shared geographic territory. The scope and intensity of the sharing shape the meaning of the indivisibility rather than the other way around.

The meaning of the plan for the participants flows from how well the plan coordinates their respective uses along multiple dimensions (instrumental, social, etc.) while meeting their individual expectations over time. People learn to anticipate how to adapt to complex situations by creating plans. Hopkins identifies five kinds of tools that people use to make urban plans: agendas, policies, vision, design and strategy. Each offers a distinct way to organize cognitive assessments of decisions about the future as part of a plan.

In a more recent paper Hopkins teams up with colleague Kieran Donaghy (2006) to propose a theoretical account of plan making. They keep intact a

Table 6.1 Urban complexity conditions and adaptability.

Conditions	Urban System Adaptability	
	Pliable	Rigid
Space	Interdependence	Indivisible
Time	Uncertainty	Irreversible

consequentialist outlook – that we should treat plans as practical schemes focused on outcomes that improve how people cope with complexity. They contrast the still common place expectation that plans offer rational comprehensive (e.g., complete) blueprints for taming urban complexity against their belief that we need compare many different plans to form a coherent practical understanding of urban complexity. Hopkins and Donaghy argue that planning analysts and planners should abandon the quest for consistent order in a single plan (a correspondence between plan and reality) and embrace the ambiguity of a coherent order among many plans. The comprehensive approach tries to eliminate complexity with a too simple order and in so doing hides or distorts the unavoidable complexity of urban development. Hopkins and Donaghy treat planning as a practical activity tied to situations. There is no need for a general plan. The fantasy of completeness distorts the provisional practicality of plans. Adaptability should replace predictability. Instead of one integrated plan eliminating complexity, many plans working together can anticipate and cope with complexity. In this respect the authors share Mandelbaum's sensibility to openness.

Instead of searching for systematic hierarchical order within a plan, they envision intersecting fibers of meaning forming a web that offers coherent conceptual connections among many plans. Hopkins and Donaghy compare how very different theoretical conceptions explain or justify planning for complexity: comprehensive plans (Kelley & Becker 2000), collective choice (Saeger 2002), markets (Webster & Lai 2003) and communication (Innes 1996; Forester 1999). They urge us to adopt a more robust tolerance for a multiplicity of theoretical outlooks as we make and study plans. We can learn about freight transportation plans for the region along with plans for public education reform and affordable housing even if in doing so we find no consistent interplay among the different proposals. Plans that offer inconsistent and conflicting representations for the same region need not be unified hierarchically. Hopkins and Donaghy adopt a pragmatic outlook that seeks order in relations of similarity based on contextual meaning and practical usefulness. Relevance displaces consistency and nested hierarchy as the conceptual resource for generating and using the web of coherence (Verma 1998).

Although Hopkins and Donaghy acknowledge the inherently practical nature of planning, they focus their attention on second order cognitive reflection describing how coherence works among explanations and justification about planning issues. This makes it difficult to tell how a coherence approach will help us grasp the meaning of any one plan within an encompassing web of coherence.[2] They help us to understand that searching for coherence can obtain cognitive insight from multiple plans, but do not show us how we accomplish coherence. Hopkins and Zapata (2007) offer useful examples in their book detailing scenarios, plans and projects. I believe we need use the distinction not only for theoretical judgment but more practical judgment. In their account coherence remains an abstract epistemic act detached from the kind of judgments that plans inspire and guide. How do we use coherence to improve how well we anticipate and cope with urban complexity?

I focus on the kind of theory plan makers use to craft plans – theory that draws upon both ideas about what I call small 'p' planning in individual and interpersonal settings and ideas about the behavior (explanations) and actions (justification) of large 'P' planning in more complex social and organizational settings. I have argued elsewhere for a conception of planning tied to practical reasoning. Here I want to describe how we use plans to inform practical judgments – how plans combine causes and reasons as coherent guides for practical action (Hoch 2007).

Planning Conduct and Habits: Small 'p' Planning

In order to grasp how we make plans it may help to first consider how individuals make practical judgments. We use plans to shape the intentions that take shape as preferences and priorities that guide our judgments about deliberate choices. As we make these choices, we take action. Most of the time, however, we operate without paying attention to what comes next. We follow habits and behave. We do not plan or compose. We plan when we encounter problems that do not fit reliable and predictable routines. We plan when we need decide what to choose.

We do not usually attend to the complex layers of relationship that make up our daily routines but rely upon habits to guide our behavior (Gronow 2011).[3] These routine behaviors become action when we attend to changes that disrupt the routine and find ourselves considering not only what we need do to restore the routine, but even reconsider the taken for granted norms and associated purposes. We listen to others obtaining new ideas and information about different purposes and improved practice. We craft small 'p' plans at these moments. We may encounter problems with our behavior as others resist or ensuing consequences disappoint. We might take action impulsively or reactively with little reflection. But as we reflect on our action and consider how we attend to changes in relationship to the future activity of others we make plans. We do more than plan as we take action, but planning offers important value because it anticipates future joint activity by comparing optional actions and imagined consequences before we choose. Planning informs deliberation by offering vicarious review of shared or collective outcomes in an imagined future. We might deliberate with ourselves or include others at the scale of dyads, work groups or teams.[4]

How do we use what we already know and believe to deliberately change habits that no longer work? Philosopher Paul Thagard (2001) dissatisfied with rational decision-making adopts a coherence approach to practical reasoning. The rational approach popular among planning analysts relies on deductive inference and the conventions of calculation – formal cognitive assumptions and rules that do not capture the kinds of practical steps people take when making a judgment or a decision in complex settings. Thagard argues that individuals rely on coherence rather than calculation (e.g., utility) or deduction (e.g., logical consistency) to make useful plans.

Thagard uses experiments to compares conventional rational and coherence criteria as subjects make practical judgments about future choices. Most choose based on how information hangs together (or not) around each option. Thagard describes how subjects create patterns that bind together bits of information about each choice generating constraint satisfaction. He describes how the strands in Hopkins and Donaghy's web of coherence take shape in a fashion analogous to the way neural networks that grow in the brain.[5]

How might this work? I adapt the following example from Robert Burton (2008). The online book seller Amazon.com uses software that tracks the books you select online assigning weights to search behaviors (view citation, explore contents, save in cart, purchase) for each book. The software program uses your book selections to calculate a combination of networks linking your book choices as a mathematical model that selects additional books for your view from the data base. The more you visit and use the Amazon software the more you improve the coherence of your artificial network model improving the quality of fit between what the model automatically selects for your review and your reading preferences. The outcome relies upon interaction among the increasingly larger network. "One cannot extract a piece of the network for independent observation any more than you can pull out a single strand of a Persian rug and infer what the rug's pattern might be" (Burton 2008, p.48).

Thagard combines cognitive science and philosophy to elaborate the principles of coherence he argues individuals use to make practical judgments about future choices. He envisions a framework with minimum assumptions that responds to the complex conditions of practical judgment for choice. He adopts a coherence based versus correspondence based conception of truth. Plan making plays a crucial role. Deliberate choices involve planned judgments.

Thagard uses computational models and empirical examples to show how the small 'p' planning judgments, the kind we make as individuals about specific practical problems rely on principles of practical coherence rather than reasoned calculation and logic.[6] Additionally, practical judgments use emotions and cognition. Our appraisal of the relevant elements for any choice draw upon feelings associated with these elements. Our intuitive sense of fit includes the impact of emotional attachments combined with cognitive assessments (Hoch 2006b; Thagard 2007).

Practical reasoning focuses on the cognitive dimensions of choice that we use to represent how different reasons shape our choices. But reason alone does not capture the synthetic and intuitive dimensions of the plans we make inferring the most satisfactory choice (satisficing). Thagard uses neural network analysis to describe how interactive patterns of association among action goal plans cluster into meaningful selections from across a vast information field. Instead of reasoning in linear fashion as we read text, practical judgment relies more on the evaluation we make reading a map or comprehending a picture. So the plans we use to make judgments rely on cognitive and emotional capacities whose coherent interaction in practical action guide our choice. But how does such coherence work as we compose plans for urban settlements?

Plans for Communities and Institutions: Large 'P' planning

We use different planning tools to carry our small 'p' planning conduct forward into community and institutional relationships tied to more encompassing urban environments. These complex social relations require attention to greater social and environmental complexity. This complexity complicates comprehension among diverse actors holding different purposes in shifting contexts. As we attend to neighborhoods, corporations, public works departments or state legislatures the tacit skill of individual planning conduct no longer proves an adequate guide for coordination. Our large 'P' plans build on small 'p' planning conduct: the large 'P' plans attend to joint purpose, assess the context for actions associated with that purpose, identify plausible future actions and joint effects in context and finally, propose specific sets of action. However, large 'P' plan coordination rarely follows the tacit and predictable social interaction (interpersonal adjustment and correction) made possible by intimate and familiar deliberation. The large 'P' plan serves as a tool for the conduct of joint coordination among many diverse groups interacting in overlapping and intersecting institutions.[7] But how do we compose these plans?

How We Compose Plans

When we compose plans for urban settlements we prepare representations that inform and shape the intentions of different individuals, organizations, communities, jurisdictions and institutions directed toward an imagined future. For more than fifty years planners have adopted versions of the rational model to organize planning composition. Planning theorists have spent decades criticizing the impossibility of meeting its requirements. Meanwhile tens of thousands of professionals, stakeholders, officials, clients and citizens use the model to make plans without ever meeting the requirements for rationality. What were these planners doing? How do we account for the value of the plans they made?

Instead of salvaging the rational model (or celebrating a return to architectural design ideals tied closely to physical improvements) I adapt the coherence framework for practical judgment described by Thagard (2001) and Donaghy and Hopkins (2006). Practical judgment includes three distinct phases: appraisal, comparison and decision. The elapsed time for a judgment may vary from milliseconds for an instinctual reflex to years; but the distinctions describe how plans work to inform practical judgment across temporal and spatial scale. These differences reflect the varieties of use that accompany practical judgment for large 'P' planning problems.[8]

Appraisal

There are many distinctions about the way we appraise a complex situation. Sometime we focus on what people bring to a judgment: an attitude, belief or viewpoint. Other uses emphasize what we do to select. Do we evaluate, reckon or interpret? Still other uses describe how our selections foster discretion, refinement and taste. These subtle differences in use reflect the prominence of appraisal in human social life. Appraisal includes individual emotional responses as well as social beliefs and conventions. The plan maker focuses on select urban relationships representing choices within a framework informed by theory and purpose for a specific context.

Comparison

We may in considering judgment emphasize the reflective phase. The emergence of any problem feeds on the difference between untroubled continuity and unexpected disruption. Judgment may respond to these disruptions using analysis, observation and rationality rather than impulse, reflex or habit. Rash judgments not only lack discretion, but careful comparison. The plan maker uses different emotional and cognitive tools to test coherence among a limited set of feasible alternatives.

Appraisal and comparison accompany and complement one another as distinct moments of judgment cycling through iterations of assessment. The street vendors on the commercial corridor at first take appear threats to retail storeowners. Removal seems the appropriate response. But analyzing the economic impact of vending in other corridors where vending persists uncovers complementary growth in sales. Closer comparison of the mix of periodic and permanent retail goods providers uncovers a range of agglomeration effects for different combinations. Plans represent cycles like these as different options available for choice.

Selection

Judgments also bring matters to a close. These may be conclusions imposed by authority (verdict or decree), reasoning (deduction) or negotiation (reconcile or settle). We make judgments within a social and institutional context. We draw upon organized institutions, conventions and traditions to authorize and guide how we conduct each phase of judgment. Each proves more useful and robust in different contexts. We plan differently in a legal context than a family context; at a small scale versus a large scale and so on. The rational model represented an important, but very specialized distillation of these more basic features of judgment (e.g., logical and analytical transparency that allow for precise calculation). The vast richness of human knowledge about practical judgment and the infinite variety of situations for judgment emphasizes the foolishness in retaining an attachment to a too narrow model of rational analysis as a guide for plan making.

Plans inform intent. Plans offer advice about a choice. Plans help us decide. Urban plans do this by helping frame practical judgments about the pursuit of multiple purposes in changing locales. But how do we formulate the selective sets of goals and actions that compose the different alternatives? I turn next to the concept of framing to describe how planners create plans. This framing activity produces filaments of practical meaning that taken together compose a coherent web of planning ideas and proposals. As we appraise, compare and conclude what plan to take we frame our future actions.

Framing Urban Plans

Planning analysts have used the concept of framing to describe how plans work to shape judgments about urban development. Framing selects and integrates cognitive parts within an encompassing visual gestalt (Lakoff & Johnson 1980; Lakoff 2006). The spatial metaphor selects and orders patterns of association used in practical judgment.[9] When Schon and Rein (1994) describe 'framing' they use the picture framing metaphor – a uniform physical boundary around an image. The conception of the field and ground features of visual recognition studied by Gestalt psychologists comes to mind. Our inherited and learned perceptual functions lead us to recognize the contrasting features of visual framing that assign priority to the elements of the field and blur the features that compose the surrounding ground. The ground, however, provides the context upon which the image takes shape. The distinction draws upon the tacit ways we perceive and comprehend spatial relationships (Lakoff & Johnson 1980).

Framing also draws upon the activity of selection used by a photographer, painter and viewer. The image makers set the context and organize the image within it. Framing includes more than circumscribing a completed painting (or cropping a photograph) but composing a specific image on a canvas surface. The incremental adjustments taken to select and organize the application of paint to brush and brush to canvas frame the image. This use emphasizes the selective perception and judgment of painting – composing – as the relationship relevant to the practice of planning. How do we describe the aspects of composition that contribute to the final painting? We cannot describe how the intuitive artistry of the composer generates a beautiful and compelling image. But we can identify the effects the image produces – the differences it makes for viewers.

As we identify these qualities we can map the parallels between composing a painting and composing a plan. This kind of learning takes place within specific contexts of use. We learn the meaning of concepts in the practical efforts to give form to our desires and beliefs about a question or problem within that context. We cannot learn to paint without learning to compose.[10]

This distinctly pragmatic approach conceives plans as a response to problems; disruptions in the complex network of routines and processes that coordinate the interdependent layers of interaction that make urban settlements possible. Plans anticipate these disruptions even as they cannot predict or prevent them. Plans help us form practical intentions we can use to prepare for the future. We can appraise, compare and choose alternative action-goal sets that make good on that intent. The plans represent problematic relationships using representations that we can use to appraise, compare and recommend as a guide for future decisions.

Planning Situation, Complexity and Planning Craft

We make plans to respond to situations – practical settings that describe relevant contextual features in relation to human purpose and action. How we describe a situation shapes how we anticipate and cope with these features. Professional planners learn to craft planning situations that frame and focus the representation and interpretation of plans (Hoch 2007). We can consider the situation for its validity and faithfulness to other earlier descriptions that proved useful. We map the selective features from past onto the current moment of reflection adding or subtracting elements or relations in so far as these follow the order set in place by the earlier description. We might decide and act without reference to an earlier description, and so learn anew by trial and error. But the evolutionary biologists and sociologists tell us that humans developed brains that allow us to remember (or learn from other people) patterns and structures of relations that provide concepts we can use to anticipate and prepare for future events (Minsky 1988, 2006; Tomasello 2008, 2014). Pretty much all of what we call civilization has relied upon our human capacity to learn and use what we learn to change our world in ways that makes our lives less uncertain and insecure.

Instead of casting representation and interpretation into two separate and antagonistic categories; I am arguing that the insights of a pragmatic outlook and research from cognitive science suggest that both are distinct features of practical judgment. The separation of substance from process in the quest to explain makes little sense as a guide for making plans. I am taking special effort to sustain the distinction of each feature as a resource for plan making; but it is how we combine both that shapes the validity and meaning of a specific plan. The craft of plan making uses practical judgment.

Representation

We make plans to represent for ourselves selected relationships as a planning situation. The plan usually describes expected changes in these relationships tracing possible, probable or plausible effects for the relevant plan stakeholders or audience. The plan maker describes a set of relationships (e.

g., temporal changes and spatial patterns) that taken together represent a context for future change and action. The planner relies upon prior knowledge to prepare the description – knowledge that draws on a wide range of facts and ideas about urban change. Representation involves selective abstraction. The planner describes only a portion of the many interactive relationships that coexist. But these different parts are held together using a planning frame to guide and organize the different phases of judgment (appraise, compare and decide). Spatial planners search for the most coherent combination of urban relationships to compose plan alternatives.

Interpretation

The selection of these relationships and the organization of the representation rely upon an interpretation of purpose and context. What the plan maker selects and how the plan maker represents the relationships flows from an appraisal of purpose. The plan stakeholders (planners, clients, sponsors) may hold different beliefs, desires and preferences leading each to formulate and propose different purposes. The plan maker need find ways to identify and include these different purposes in the plan. The democratic planner listens and learns the viewpoints of the plan audience and so uses the values and beliefs of these people to frame the representation of the planning situation. (Strategic plans may be sensitive to the purposes of others, but mainly to anticipate and pre-empt the strategies they might use on the battle field or the market place.) But sometimes the purposes prove too numerous or too conflicting to allow for meaningful inclusion. The purposes need be selectively filtered to make completion of a plan feasible and useful. The students of plan negotiation, mediation and dispute resolution offer one avenue of inquiry exploring how planners distill differences into practical forms of indifference, compromise or agreement (Susskind 1987; Susskind & Ozzawa 1984; Shunneli, Kaufman, & Ozzawa 2008). The action focused analysts offer complementary ideas and evidence about mutual learning, collaboration and deliberation (Innes & Booher 2004; Forester 1999). Organizational and institutional analysts study the incentives, rules and conventions that people use to democratically orchestrate and advance interests and beliefs as useful plans for purposeful advance (Alexander 2001, 2005; Faludi 2000; Fischer 2003; Saeger 2002; Saeger & Ravulum 2004; Webster & Lai 2003).

Composition:
Representational Interpretive Combo

The plan takes shape over several iterations of appraisal and comparison. The planning situation changes as efforts to include different purposes modify attention, emphasis and meaning. The representation includes not only facts and flows, but expectations and interests - worries and hopes.

Feelings and emotions tacitly and explicitly shape judgments about what relations to consider and how to respond.

The interaction between representation and interpretation varies with respect to the levels of representational and goal complexity within a planning situation. Urban planning does not impose order on complexity but responds to the challenges of complexity by offering ways to tame and even domesticate complexity within different planning situations. Table 6.2 provides a conceptual framework identifying different orientations urban planners adopt in response to four kinds of planning situations classified by levels of representational and interpretive complexity. Leaving aside the pursuit of epistemic certainty shifts attention to contextually sensitive modes of judgment that turn knowledge about change and interpretation about purpose into practical intentions. The cells describe orientations that plan makers should practically adopt in response to different combinations of complexity. The table works as a heuristic tool for matching orientation to situations. The table does not offer a classification or typology for explanation.

Protocol: Routine practice for low complexity

We adopt protocols to guide our plans when facing urban situations consisting of predictable relationships that planners, sponsors and clientele comprehend in familiar terms. Analysts often describe such situations as technical implying that efforts to anticipate future change will produce familiar and agreeable options. But adopting a protocol relies on important social and political agreements that only seem unimportant because not subject to attention getting disagreement. Most plan making activity works using protocols because the institutional and organizational settings professional planners inhabit generate predictable cycles of plan preparation and reporting. State and local governments sponsor most urban plan making in the US and so set the terms for the emergence of plan making protocols. States may authorize consistency and uniformity of official urban plan elements. The American Planning Association may play a role designing 'model' legislation and seek to promote adoption nationwide. Adoption of

Table 6.2 Practical plan making.

Orientation	Interpretation of Plan Goals		
Representation of spatial relationships	Complexity	High	Low
	High	Prototype (problem seeking)	Precedent (problem prevention)
	Low	Policy (problem solving)	Protocol (problem setting)

different protocols shapes how planners working in different organizational and occupational settings make plans.

The diagram in Figure 6.1 comes from the California General Plan Guidelines (State of California 2017, p.21); a book filled with check lists and criteria for making a plan to fit the protocol adopted as state law. Consistency tied to the principles and guidelines described in the protocol centers on compliance. The relevant context for this plan making protocol includes the intergovernmental organizational field of government agencies and the various laws and regulations that authorize different plan components. The fragmented overlap and conflicting interaction among agencies pose a threat to this orientation. The orderly nested hierarchy of bureaucratic organization becomes a model for plan making expectations. This

Figure 6.1 Diagram for local government plan making in California.

works if the responses to urban complexity by planners and plan clientele cohere. Such coherence occurs when urban changes are predictable and expectations hang together.

Treating plans as a kind of protocol greatly expands the reach of planning ideas among the staff working in public agencies and planning consultancies. Breadth of dispersion usually comes at the expense of contextual sensitivity and relevance. The protocols prove useful for helping people recognize they can take systematic practical steps to prepare for future urban development. The criteria work well where people agree about goals and face familiar changes in urban relationships. For instance: Anticipating cycles of change tied to routine organizational interactions such as budget allocations for capital improvements, or regulatory reviews for development approvals or impacts. Anticipating changes in the capacity of a natural system based on variations in use (e.g., water and air) as well as adopting models for estimating the effects of population growth and migration on urban systems (e.g., utility use, housing demand, land absorption).

Analysts studying the impacts of plans often adopt consistency as an indicator of plan success (Berke & French 1994). The protocol not only shapes beliefs about how to plan, but what counts as a useful plan. Empirical tests often turn up more complex results. Municipalities and neighborhoods may adopt plan making protocols to comply with state regulations, but ignore those plans as a guide for urban development decisions (Pendall 2001; Hoch 2007).[11]

Precedent

Planning professionals often develop plans that offer vivid and successful advice for some portion of urban complexity. Planners facing complex urban relationships copy a prior response that offers the promise of proven results. These proven plan ideas provide practical models for adoption and emulation as local government, consultants and other agencies seek familiar yet sophisticated precedents for making their own plans. Professionals use precedent to improve the legitimacy and popularity of a plan making precedent (e.g., the mall, the super block and now mixed use development) often overlooking the crucial relevance of contextual fit. Hopkins (2001) critiques this approach in so far as it ignores the complexity of urban development – imposing a too abstract model from the past on a complex present. Burnham's *Plan of Chicago* adopted the form and scale of residential development from early 20th century Paris and Vienna to fill out images of plaza and parkway improvements. See Figure 6.2. The precedents did not fit the complex context of housing development in a gritty industrial metropolis.

Precedent does offer access to a rich archive of prior human experience and creativity. Consider how planers use the historic confluence of three street grids to provide precedent for the identification of a San Francisco (2002) neighborhood. In Figure 6.3 the San Francisco planners use the intersection of three street grid forms to emphasize the importance of current transportation and

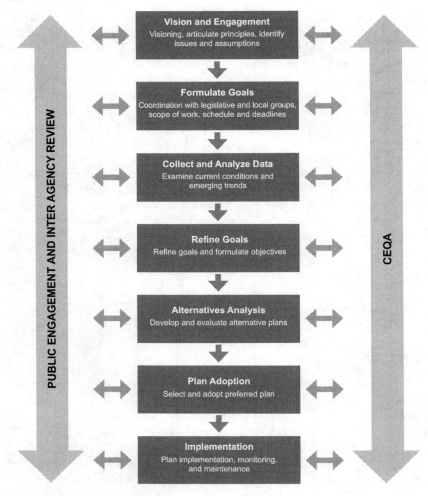

Figure 6.2 Burnham used misleading residential precedent based on styles popular in European cities like Paris and Vienna (Burnham & Bennett 1909, p.100).

land use density relationships for a neighborhood plan (San Francisco Planning Department 2018). Popular and familiar precedent that distracts planners and their clientele from crucial contextual features needs more critical attention.

Prototype

Prototypes invent combinations of ideas about complex urban relationships that anticipate and help resolve contested interpretations. These combinations of insight might flow from reliance on different epistemic approaches, for instance an analytic model versus a comparative case study approach; different

Crafting Plans 101

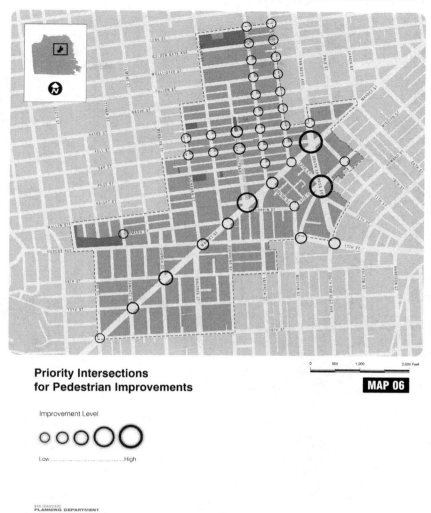

Figure 6.3 The confluence of grids at Octavia Hill in San Francisco.

ideological or moral approaches, for example liberal versus conservative; different disciplinary approaches, for instance engineering versus social science and so on. The range of concepts, beliefs and methods used to describe and analyze urban relationships yields a variety of contextually distinct representations for the same time period and locale. Planning professionals since the inception of the modern profession have embraced a multi-disciplinary effort to compose alternatives that plan clientele can use to grab hold of salient crosscutting features that promise to tame complexity.

Professionals use representational cleverness to anticipate and reconcile the interaction among complex urban relationships simulating diverse interpretations. These innovations may emphasize tools such as GIS visualization and planning support tools (e.g., What if or Community Viz), institutional innovations like performance zoning or currently form based zoning or urban development plans that offer unprecedented proposals for urban improvements. We tend to think of such innovations as products that others can adopt as precedents (e.g., the mall). But most innovations consist of combinations of relationships tied closely to a specific context. The vast case literature that informs planning describes and interprets these local plan making efforts to others.

The consultants for the San Jose urban renewal plan created reader profiles at the beginning of their report identifying the audience stakeholders (San Jose Redevelopment Department 2001) (Figure 6.4). The profiles advise each audience about the plan features of most interest. The planners write different clientele into the report as readers whose interpretation the authors anticipate and invite. This innovation invites different stakeholders to read the plan more like a newspaper or cookbook than a single report.

Policy

Planners adopt a policy approach to plan making when they face diverse interpretations about framing and solving familiar urban problems. In this situation most stakeholders agree about the features of complexity associated with the problem (e.g., traffic), but disagree about what policies to adopt to solve it. Planners often use models to simulate complex urban

A New Hire at a Valley Firm…		**a new hire**
Looking for a cool place to live		Turn to the Recommendations by Area (Ch3, by area) and consider the extraordinary life and vitality planned for places such as digital Broadway on Santa Clara Street, new food, shopping and entertainment on 1st and 2nd Streets and total development plans for a new lively neighborhood around the Diridon train station.
Tired of the travel demands and delays of suburban living		Review the full range of public transportation options you will get downtown (Ch 3, by system): from new rail and light rail service, to convenient downtown shuttles, and eventual BART access to the region.
Searching for the heart of Silicon Valley		Flip through "Strategy 2000" and stop in any chapter to get confirmation of downtown San Jose as the heart of the Valley – the crossroads of the internet, the place to be for growing international businesses, the setting in which to live and grow and work together.

Figure 6.4 The San Jose urban renewal plan offers a stakeholder guide.

relationships and then invite plan sponsors and stakeholders to select policy inputs, weight parameters and evaluate outputs for model simulations that estimate future policy outcomes. These may be spreadsheet models calculating cost benefit ratios for development projects, GIS models estimating and allocating residential development activity by geographic area, transportation models calculating future mode split and environmental models that estimate and locate externalities. The model provides a test bed for assessing different policies within a shared framework – a framework reflected in the assumptions any model need take for granted (and that the stakeholders accept). Planners may imagine different future outcomes based on the attention and input of different stakeholder expectations. This approach describes differences of purpose and meaning illustrated in alternative scenarios. The scenarios include usually include strategies for recognizing and reconciling these differences among the stakeholders.

The narrative distilled in Figure 6.5 from the planning scenario development workshops represents a divided future, a problem projected forward and expanded, but as a warning to inspire current action. The scripts represent problems as contributions to policy arguments and discussion about what to do now to prepare for different kinds of plausible futures. The imagined futures can also be represented using tables, charts and maps visually illustrating future outcomes that different stakeholders can use to inform deliberations. The narrative does not supply a visual blueprint for how to live nor does is propose a specific set of norms or rules to guide behavior. The text invites the reader to imagine a future that will inform arguments about what sorts of policies to adopt in a specific local situation – an argument informed by interaction effects that focus attention on salient (the axes of the two by two table), but not definitive relationships. Relevance and plausibility play a more prominent role than reliability and probability in guiding judgment (Hopkins & Zapata 2007).

Conclusion

When we craft spatial plans well, we allow for the uncertainty and ambiguity generated by the interaction of representation and interpretation. Complete or final agreement about the relevant representation and goals rarely exists, and then for only a short time because people and cities change. Any prospects for useful plans require that the audience use the plan to comprehend different sets of goals within selective representations of contextual complexity. People need to comprehend the plan and use it to form their intentions toward the future. Plans offer provisional accounts of future outcomes that users intend to accomplish by changing the relationships represented in the current urban situation.

We make plans to guide collective action using some form of deliberation. But such deliberation occurs in organizational and institutional settings that influence how interests, needs and goals influence deliberations. In the best of circumstances we describe the conduct of such deliberation as a kind of

San Joaquin Scenario

San Joaquin: At the San Joaquin Valley workshop participants brainstormed a long list of key factors and environmental forces. They prioritized the list to identify a few clusters of closely related issues. Finally, several clusters were combined and two critical uncertainties selected to serve as the axes of a two-by-two scenario matrix.

Horizontal: External Influences: environmental/economic health (negative to positive) Vertical: Social Conditions: ethnic, educational, economic structure (worse to better)

A Tale of Two Valleys Scenario Script: Imagined commencement address by Latino Graduate in 2025"... we have a great challenge and a great opportunity facing us here in the Valley. California is on its way toward becoming the first majority Latino state in the union. We will elect more Latinos to Congress. We will change the face of electoral politics in the United States.

"We must step up to the responsibilities that will be vested in us by the power of our numbers. Or we will remain, in effect, an underclass of under-educated, underemployed peasants. Sure, some of your parents attended college. Yes, we are beginning to see a Latino middle class in California. But you know as well as I that class divisions in California remain closely tied to race and racism, both between Anglos and Latinos, and among middle-class Latinos and other new immigrants.

"These are harsh words. But these are harsh times. You all know about the white and the able fleeing from Fresno and Bakersfield. You all know about the pitched battles between the gangs and the police.

"We cannot allow this rift between the Two Valleys to continue. We must find ways to heal the divide and grow a civil society that joins light and dark, rich and poor, in a way that reduces the distances among us.

Figure 6.5 Planning scenario selection from the Valley Futures Project.

mutual learning. The boundaries of knowledge depend on the kinds of reasons that people offer as each listens and adapts arguments that recommend goals and attachment. As we craft a plan we use cases as precedent and simulations that model plausible outcomes – but outcomes imagined as part of the deliberation.

Practical judgment draws upon emotions as discussed in Chapter 2. Memories, stories, ideas, images – the cognitive products of mental life take shape using an emotional scaffold. Emotions not only motivate by activating our attachment to a choice or option, but they also inform how we conceive objects as worthy of attention and desire. They not only push us toward a cognitive goal, but shape how we select and conceive the goal. The concepts and feelings that together bind representations to intentions include the influence of institutional conventions, social relations, political expectations, and more. The distillation of the relational mix into situations provides the context for the judgment and action used to make, test, revise and adopt plans (Sennett 2008).

The research on plan making still consists of parallel streams of inquiry. Some contours are disciplinary and others methodological. The steepest slopes reflect differences in belief about the theoretical, moral and practical relevance of important relationships shaping urban complexity. I cast this separation as the difference between representation and intention. Insisting that plans combine both, I hope to motivate colleagues to consider taking Donaghy and Hopkin's (2006) message to heart. Consider modifying how you make plans as well as how you study them by seeking coherence rather than consistency. The profession understands the urgency of speaking to practical craft, but usually offers best practices tied to current professional custom, legal convention and political feasibility. The many currents of relevant insight and knowledge generated by academic planning inquiry go untapped. I have tried to show how we might adapt Donaghy and Hopkin's idea of a coherent network to cut tributaries across the diverse channels of academic and professional inquiry. Risking a mixed metaphor we can imagine a confluence of ideas about plan making improving practical judgments about complex urban development. The confluence requires that we learn to use unfamiliar vocabularies to inform how we make practical planning judgments.[12]

The quest of intelligent democratic advice may require much more attention to the legacy of human cognitive and emotional capacities and cultural habits to learn how the short cuts we take in forming judgments may short change efforts to conduct plans that can meet the demands of both social and environmental complexity. The work by Forester (1999) and Innes and Booher (2004) has contributed to our understanding of planning, although they focus less on plan making and more on the varieties of planning conduct. If everyone plans, and our democratic sensibility urges us to listen, how do we practically discern among clever, stupid and wise plans? Not only do we face obstacles in collective decision making (Saeger 2002), but we need demonstrate to fellow plan makers how the intelligent representations we professionals create improve the validity and reliability of plans. I take up how professionals evaluate plans in the next chapter.

Notes

1 Mandelbaum's communitarian sensibility envisions civility, tolerance and prudence animating stakeholder and citizen deliberation fostering liberal public orders. People use these virtues to negotiate and adjust memberships across different social communities without losing grip on an underlying sense of continuity and identity. The community members may speak at cross purposes or disagree, but they continue the conversation because they publicly recognize and respect one another. "For Mandelbaum we adopt many tools to anticipate and manage the complexities of social coordination, but he worries about those analysts and experts who hope to remedy social complexity. It appears an inevitable condition that accompanies a pluralistic society" (Hoch 2006a, pp.128–129).
2 They distinguish explanation and justification as they classify different 'issue' domains: plans, organizations, process and collective choice. The selection treats 'plans' as an issue area we can explain or justify – the act of abstract segmentation treats plans as a kind of knowledge and not a kind of practical judgment. They describe how we can study plans and distinguish this study from other issues confused with plans. But they do not tell us how we combine cognitive insight with desires and hope to craft plans.
3 The concept of habits was discarded by sociologists in the late 1920s as they struggled to legitimize their scientific status in competition with Psychology.
4 Mandelbaum distinguishes thick community solidarity from the more abstract thin contracts of more complex and encompassing organizations. He envisions individuals acting within the bounds of overlapping communities that both reinforce and challenge the larger organizational order. My conception draws upon a more developmental and evolutionary conception of social learning. The explosion of knowledge about our natural history as *homo sapiens* gives reason to explore more carefully the causal and emotional depth of solidarity tied to genetic legacies underlying cultural experience. Peter Marris (1996) helped me appreciate the critical importance of individual development within these revised versions of human evolution.
5 Minsky (1988) contrasts a strictly logical path of inquiry with a common sense path. When we argue logically we strip away tangential references to other forms of knowledge relying solely on a formally consistent sequence. The greater the internal consistency and coherence; the more we believe the argument. But when we argue from common sense we draw upon different sources of knowledge as evidence for claims. The argument lacks consistency and internal coherence and so must draw upon a much wider range of incomplete knowledge to offer convincing support for the claims (pp.140–141).
6 The wicked problems that Rittel and Weber (1973) identified proved daunting because Rittel's list included those features of practical judgment not susceptible to the then popular model of rational optimization.
7 The different theories about coping with social and environmental complexity attend to different aspects of many layers of organizational and institutional order. Any holistic order remains provisional and incomplete.
8 Marvin Minsky uses the model of a 'difference' engine to describe the cognitive infrastructure for the 'satsificing' judgment that Herbert Simon (1982) believed better accounts for how we make decisions. Different biological agents within us activate in response to the difference between an actual and desired situation seeking to diminish the difference. Practical judgments about complex urban relationships rely upon vast layers of such agents whose work remains dimly understood (Minsky 1988, p.78).
9 Donald Schon (1983) wrote eloquently about the conceptual power of metaphor. Niraj Verma (1998) makes the case for similarity in the conduct of planning inquiry.
10 See the work by Marvin Minsky, most recently *The Emotion Machine* (Minsky 2006). Minsky offers a more detailed set of conceptual distinctions to describe how we think than I am doing here.

11 Efforts to insist upon consistency often turn to sources of authority, usually government, to impose sanctions to assure compliance. But enforcing a plan subverts the persuasive underpinnings of the activity. The threat of force may elicit compliance with the purpose represented in the plan, but it may not generate a change of heart among those who comply unwillingly. Plans inform the intentions of actors who use the plans to pursue some purposeful action. Critics of this view insist that compliance takes time and that a change of heart will be forthcoming if not among those forced to change, then those who come later without knowledge of prior practice. Sometimes we need comply with unpopular mandates and subordinate our personal or local plans to the plans of others. But consistency will rarely provide a legitimate rationale for such imposition.
12 Martin Meyerson (1956) wrote an article arguing for a middle range planning that would bridge between specific planning decisions (e.g., zoning) and the more abstract principles of the comprehensive plan. He was right at the time and my work echoes his concern – although the scope of our enterprise now includes much more than it did seventy years ago.

References

Alexander, E. (2001). The planner prince: Interdependence, rationalities and post-communicative practice. *Planning Theory & Practice*, 2(3), 311–324.

Alexander, E. (2005). Institutional transformation and planning: From institutionalization theory to institutional design. *Planning Theory*, 4(3), 209–233.

Berke, P. and French, S. (1994). The influence of state planning mandates on local plan quality. *Journal of Planning Education and Research*, 73(4), 237–250.

Burnham, D. H. and Bennett, E. H. (1909). *Plan of Chicago*. Chicago: The Commercial Club.

Burton, R. (2008). *On Being Certain*. New York: St Martin's Press.

Donaghy, K. P. and Hopkins, L. D. (2006). Coherentist theories of planning are possible and useful. *Planning Theory*, 5(2), 173–202.

Faludi, A. (2000). The performance of spatial planning. *Planning Practice and Research*, 15(4), 299–318.

Fischer, F. (2003). *Reframing Public Policy: Discursive Politics and Deliberative Procedures*. Oxford: Oxford University Press.

Forester, J. (1999). *The Deliberative Practitioner*. Cambridge, MA: MIT Press.

Gronow, A. J. (2011). *From Habits to Social Structures: Pragmatism and Contemporary Social Theory*, Peter Lang. ProQuest Ebook Central, https://ebookcentral-proquest-com.proxy.cc.uic.edu/lib/uic/detail.action?docID=1054750

Hoch, C. (1984). Doing good and being right: The pragmatic connection in planning theory. *Journal of the American Planning Association*, 50(3), 335–345.

Hoch, C. (1994). *What Planners Do*. Chicago: Planners Press.

Hoch, C. (2002). Evaluating plans pragmatically. *Planning Theory*, 1(1), 53–76.

Hoch, C. (2006a). Planning to keep the doors open for moral communities. *Planning Theory*, 5(2), 127–146.

Hoch, C. (2006b). Emotions and planning. *Planning Theory & Practice*, 7(4), 367–382.

Hoch, C. (2007). Making plans: Representation and intention. *Planning Theory*, 6(1), 16–35.

Hopkins, L. (2001). *Urban Development: The Logic of Making Plans*. Washington, D.C.: Island Press.

Hopkins, L. and Zapta, M. A. (2007). *Engaging the Future: Forecasts, Scenarios, Plans and Projects*. Hollis, NH: Puritan Press.

Innes, J. (1995). Planning theory's emerging paradigm: Communicative action and interactive practice. *Journal of Planning Education and Research*, 14(3), 183–190.

Innes, J. (1996). Planning through consensus building: A new view of the comprehensive ideal. *Journal of the American Planning Association*, 62(4), 460–472.

Innes, J. and Booher, D. (2004). Reframing public participation: Strategies for the 21st century. *Journal of Planning Theory and Practice*, 5(4), 419–436.

Kelley, E. D. and Becker, B. (2000). *Community Planning: An Introduction to the Comprehensive Plan*. Washington, D.C.: Island Press.

Lakoff, G. and Johnson, M. (1980). *Metaphors We Live By*. Chicago: University of Chicago Press.

Lakoff, G. (2006). *Whose Freedom? The Battle Over America's Most Important Idea*. New York: Farrar, Straus and Giroux.

Lee, D. B. (1973). Requiem for large-scale models. *Journal of the American Institute of Planners*, 39, 163–178.

Mandelbaum, S. (2000). *Open Moral Communities*. Cambridge: MIT Press.

Manson, S. M. (2007). Challenges in evaluating models of geographic complexity. *Environment and Planning B: Planning and Design*, 34(2), 245–260.

Marris, P. (1996). *The Politics of Uncertainty: Attachment in Private and Public Life*. New York: Routledge.

Meyerson, M. (1956). Building the middle-range planning bridge for comprehensive planning. *Journal of the American Institute of Planners*, 22(2), 58–64.

Minsky, M. (1988). *The Society of Mind*. New York: Simon & Schuster.

Minsky, M. (2006). *The Emotion Machine*. New York: Simon & Schuster.

Pendall, R. (2001). Municipal plans, state mandates, and property rights: Lessons from Ma.inc. *Journal of Planning Education and Research*, 2(2), 154–165.

Rittel, H. and Weber, M. (1973). Dilemmas in a general theory of planning. *Policy Sciences*, 4(2), 155–169.

Saeger, T. (2002). *Democratic Planning and Social Choice Dilemmas: Prelude to Institutional Planning Theory*. Burlington, VT: Ashgate.

Saeger, T. and Ravlum, I. A. (2004). Inter-agency transport planning: Co-ordination and governance structures. *Planning Theory and Practice*, 5(2), 171–195.

San Francisco Planning Department (2018). *San Francisco General Plan; The Market and Octavia Neighborhood Plan*. San Francisco, CA: Department of Planning. Downloaded 08/19/2018http://generalplan.sfplanning.org/Market_Octavia.htm

San Jose Redevelopment Department (2001). *Strategy 2000: San Jose Greater Downtown Strategy for Redevelopment*. San Jose: Field Paoli Consultants for San Jose Redevelopment Department, p. xiii. Downloaded 08/19/2018https://www.sanjoseca.gov/DocumentCenter/View/55573

Schon, D. (1983). *The Reflective Practitioner: How Professionals Think in Action*. New York: Basic Books.

Schon, D. and Rein, M. (1994). *Frame Reflection: Toward the Resolution of Intractable Policy Controversies*. New York: Basic Books.

Sennett, R. (2008). *The Craftsman*. London: Penguin.

Shunneli, D. F., Kaufman, S. and Ozzawa, C. (2008). Mining negotiation theory for planning insights. *Journal of Planning Education and Research*, 27(3), 359–364.

Simon, H. (1982). *Models of Bounded Rationality*, Vols. 1 and 2. Cambridge, MA: MIT Press.

State of California (2017). *General Plan Guidelines*. Sacramento: Governor's Office of Planning & Research, p. 17. Downloaded 09/19/2018 http://opr.ca.gov/planning/general-plan/guidelines.html

Susskind, L. and Cruikshank, J. (1987). *Breaking the Impasse: Consensual Approaches to Resolving Public Disputes*. New York: Basic Books.

Susskind, L. and Ozzawa, C. (1984). Mediated negotiation in the public sector: The planner as mediator. *Journal of Planning Education and Research*, 4(1), 5–15.

Thagard, P. (2001). How to make decisions: Coherence, emotion, and practical inference. In E. Milgram (Ed.), *Varieties of Practical Inference* (pp. 355–371). Cambridge, MA: MIT Press.

Thagard, P. (2007). *Hot Thought*. Cambridge, MA: MIT Press.

Tomasello, M. (2008). *Origins of Human Communication*. Cambridge: MIT Press.

Tomasello, M. (2014). *A Natural History of Human Thinking*. Harvard University Press. ProQuest Ebook Central. https://ebookcentral-proquest-com.proxy.cc.uic.edu/lib/uic/detail.action?docID=3301383

Verma, N. (1998). *Similarities, Connections and Systems*. New York: Lexington.

Webster, C. and Lai, L. (2003). *Property Rights, Planning and Markets*. Cheltenham: Edward Elgar.

7 Evaluating Plans

Introduction

The intuitive assessment that accompanies first impressions about a problem for a place prepares us for action. Unconscious emotional responses to situational details trigger and release memories tied to perceptions, sensations and behaviors learned earlier and bound to social habits. Afraid or angry in the face of unexpected regulatory demand we may automatically comply or fight. Feeling compassion or suspicion for a homeless beggar may prompt giving or withholding. As we engage conscious reflection and deliberation in either case we may suspend these initial responses. The protocol of professional expertise commands that spatial planners rise above these sorts of impulsive sentiments and assume a posture of logical review. Even as I have argued in prior chapters that emotions and feelings shape the judgments professionals make conceiving problems and composing plans; should professionals not embrace objective rationality evaluating the plans they make? Should they not avoid the impulsive and prejudicial impacts of unconscious emotions?

This chapter like earlier ones explores how objective evaluation cannot deliver on the rational promise of certainty. The complexity of places, people and the institutions that fuel their mutual interdependence do not succumb to linear systems logic. The clever rational evaluation approaches that professionals developed to assess spatial plans can do important work assessing plans for familiar breakdowns or routine disruptions. But they do not offer much help adopting different kinds of plan evaluation for complex spatial problems. This chapter compares the conventional use of the rational protocol against a pragmatist approach. The pragmatist trades off the quest for global certainty for the more modest embrace of situational relevance. Pragmatic rationality seeks to test the cognitive value of emotional responses rather than transcend these.

The Blind People and the Elephant

Most of us are familiar with one or another version of the story about the blind people and the elephant. Several blind people each positioned at a different place along the body of an elephant offer conflicting descriptions: snake, pillar, wall, etc. The tale warns us about the importance of context to perspective. Planners usually use it to illustrate how we who study the same cities and policies using concepts drawn from different disciplines may speak past one another. The economist, sociologist and political economist describe the city using different concepts (e.g., market, migration and voting). But the story also warns us about the danger of misplaced inference, taking the part for the whole. It's not that cities don't include markets, migrants and voters, but that we go astray when we take one of these descriptions as inclusive of the whole. It also reminds us that none of us inhabit a position beyond the confines of one of these situations. None of us can see the whole picture unencumbered by the history and meaning of our position.

But what if the blind people had spoken with one another about their observations. At first each might have insisted upon the integrity of their own judgment, emphasizing the veracity of their sensual experience (or superiority of their respective discipline). Some versions of the tale do have each blind person proclaiming to the others the obvious conclusion that the elephant is most evidently a snake or wall. What if the blind people had listened to one another? How might they have come to recognize their differences as less due to commission than omission? The rush to judgment seals each blind person off from each other. The differences in their experience had less to do with their character, reasoning or abilities, than their shared privation – a fixed position along the length of the elephant. Each imagined a part of the elephant as the whole. This imagining was not contemplative or fanciful but tacit and experiential. The attachment to their conclusion was all the greater because of this contact. What must happen for the blind people to recognize not only that they inhabit different positions, but that such differences distort their judgment about the whole elephant?

Rationality and Pragmatism

In this chapter I focus on plan evaluation. Professionals can craft plans, but even as these efforts take shape goals may shift, new data inspire doubts and unexpected events inspire correction. Complexity persists. I compare two approaches. One uses Rational analysis the other pragmatic rationality. I argue that spatial planners should place less emphasis on Rational analysis and adopt a pragmatic approach when evaluating plans. Rational analysis may offer objectivity and precision, but like the judgment of the blind people, it sacrifices context and continuity. A pragmatic outlook embraces context and seeks continuity among diverse viewpoints. It avoids the separation between analysis and action. The Rationalist asks what we need know to assure our analysis is correct and certain. The pragmatist asks what we need we know to cope with the problems we face.

I capitalize Rationalist to refer to those theorists who want their ideas to provide a more important – because more logical and precise foundation for evaluating plans and planning. The pragmatic approach does not search for a conceptual foundation but uses conceptual inquiry as one among many tools (e.g., craft, feelings, intuition, experience, custom and so forth) we possess to cope with the problems we encounter. The pragmatists do not believe theoretical ideas and methods can trump the practical effects of human language, history, culture, evolution and so forth. For instance, the belief that professional planning analysis may be value neutral relies upon Rationalist expectations. In contrast, the belief that professional planning analysis must include the purposes of the relevant audience reflects a pragmatic outlook. The Rationalist wants ideas to illuminate the value of plans like sunshine illuminates the world. The pragmatist evaluates plans holding and pointing a conceptual flashlight (Hoch 1995).

The pragmatists cannot prove that ideas remain inescapably tied to historical and geographic context. They simply re-describe beliefs and claims about the meaning and value of plans in ways that show how they foster or frustrate specific purposes. The pragmatists believe that organizing such inquiry using democratic means will prove more useful than others in coping with complex uncertainties and meeting diverse purposes. This belief does not treat such democratic behavior as inevitable or necessary. The pragmatists do believe democratic inquiry represents the best approach we humans have invented so far to cope with the uncertainties we face. Knowledge does not protect us from contingency and surprise but may prepare us to more clearly and effectively cope with unexpected difficulties.

Critics of pragmatism do not usually disagree with pragmatist belief in deliberative democracy but attack the prominence and centrality of this belief. Forester anticipated such criticisms in his earlier work by focusing on planning and power (Forester 1989). The intellectual sparks fly when pragmatists turn epistemological debates into political debates. Forester faced this criticism in his work. See his article in *Space and Society* and the ensuing criticism and rejoinder (Forester 1983; Forester and Roweis 1983). For a more contemporary example read the debate between myself and Mickey Luria and Marsh Feldman edited by Patsy Healey in the predecessor to the journal *Planning Theory* (Healey 1997b).

The pragmatists abandon the grand separation between theory and practice. The Rationalists insist upon this distinction believing that the power of ideas will trump the uncertainties we face. We need theory to guide practice. The pragmatists, like many current postmodern thinkers, worry that the quest for certainty becomes a power trip as those with little democratic sensibility use Rationality to subject others to purposes that masquerade as necessary and inevitable conditions (Harper & Stein 1996). Pragmatists tie abstraction to context. Sometimes we use the formal and logical properties of a social theory or urban model to abstract from details that obscure a structural order or causal sequence. We go astray when we use this abstraction to substitute for the contingent complexity that always accompanies and shapes the abstracted order. The pragmatists avoid the theory practice dualism because historically powerful people have used the elevation of Rationality to justify modes of inquiry and social control not for reasons the weak find compelling, but for reasons that make the purposes of the powerful appear natural. Adversarial prowess substitutes for the democratic pleasures of diverse modes of inquiry. In his recent book, *The Return to Reason*, Stephen Toulmin offers an historical account for this unfortunate divorce in philosophy. He argues for the sort of reunion pragmatists hoped to enjoin.

> In this respect, Dewey was right to suggest that Pragmatism is not just one theory on a par with all others. Rather, it represents a change of view, which puts *theorizing* on a par with all other activities. From now on, honestly productive craftsmen need not apologize for vulgarity, nor do we need to put logic above rhetoric, ethics above casuistry, metaphysics above sophistry, or the Prophets above the Pharisees. For the time being that game is over; and when Plato declared that Gorgias and the Sophists prostituted their skills by setting up 'knowledge shops' (*phrontisteria*), it was he who was guilty of vulgar libel. Academic jealousies turn out to be as old as the Academy itself (Toulmin 2001, p.172).

This chapter emphasizes what many planning theorists often leave behind in their intellectual ambition to get things right (Hoch 1984, 1992). Rationalists want to construct theories that provide a foundation for future claims about the world. Rationalists imagine theory as a platform or superstructure for our claims about plans and values. American pragmatists Charles Pierce, Oliver Wendell Holmes, William James and John Dewey tried to sidestep this approach over a century ago.

> They all believed that ideas are not 'out there' waiting to be discovered, but are tools like forks and knives and microchips that people devise to cope with the world in which they find themselves. They believed that ideas are produced not by individuals, but by groups of individuals that ideas are social. They believed that ideas do not develop according to some inner logic of their own, but are entirely dependent, like germs, on their human carriers and the environment. And they believed that since ideas are provisional responses to particular and unpredictable circumstances, their survival depends not on their immutability, but on their adaptability (Menand 2001, pp.xi–xii).

Planning Advice and Evaluation

We make judgments all the time about our future. We anticipate, forecast, and predict events and behaviors. Our account of future events informs our judgments. When we make plans we offer advice to ourselves or others.

Planning implies forethought and intention. When we produce plan documents we expect people to read them and use the advice to inform and influence their own judgments about the allocation of public resources, the use of property and so forth. Implicit in such sincere and often urgent effort is the belief that planning will improve the quality of the judgments and that these improvements will produce more effective consequences on the use of resources, property or whatever. If we did not expect plans to make a useful difference, why would we make them?

If we imagine planning as a kind of forethought, then the regular act of monitoring achievement means remembering the earlier intention as a framework for assessment. This framework serves not only as a cognitive reference, but an emotional benchmark as well. AI made this commitment. I don't want to break it. Contrast this with the conception of deferred gratification. This concept treats deferment as a kind of contract. I must go through all the hoops before I receive my reward. Evaluating plans may offer a taste of fulfillment each step of the way. So, for instance, the planner who implements zoning and other development regulations with an eye on the larger plan may express satisfaction with the incremental results. [This does not mean that the same planner is blind to a larger and longer view point that weighs the increments within a larger whole and asks, "Do these implement the plan?"]

Professional planners make plans and use them to justify a variety of regulatory, investment, project and assorted development activities. But rarely do professional planners evaluate plans, or at least not in the same manner as they go about making them. There are many practical reasons for this; lack of time and money for instance. I want to argue, however, that there may be social and conceptual reasons as well. Planners make plans that combine a multiplicity of viewpoints and voices. Most plan making includes analysis, but few planners would expect that analysis alone 'makes' a plan. In contrast, plan evaluation often means analyzing the plan according to select parts, relations and purposes. Practitioners imagine objective analysts conducting rigorous tests of a plan. Some may have witnessed such a study, disappointed that it left out so much, yet excusing the omissions for practical reasons. Furthermore, analysts frequently conduct plan evaluation using only one kind of measure (e.g., economic) or a specific ideological approach (e.g., deep ecology). I am arguing that the pursuit of objectivity and methodological rigor may, like the blind persons and the elephant, offer an unnecessarily limited assessment of the plan.

Evaluating Plans: Comparing Rational and Pragmatic Approaches

"How would you know a good plan if you saw one?" author William Baer (1997) asked in an article published in the *Journal of the American Planning Association*. Baer distinguishes four targets for plan evaluation: plan alternatives, plan outcomes, impact on public good and impacts on professional practice. Baer makes these distinctions, I think, to remind us that the meaning of an evaluation depends crucially on the goals and methods used to conduct it. Baer's classification identifies what I will render as four different viewpoints, or sticking with the metaphor, standpoints – one for each blind person. Just as the blind judges imagine and project parts for the whole, so too do plan evaluators. In this chapter I argue that the blindness comes less from difference in method and more from reliance on a kind of Rationality that often limits and even distorts efforts to comprehend the effectiveness of a plan. I show how these limits work by contrasting a Rational against a pragmatic approach to evaluation for each of the four standpoints Baer identified.

Plan formation: How well does the plan evaluate alternatives?
Plan implementation: How well do after plan outcomes meet plan objectives?
Plan critique: How well does the plan serve the public good?
Plan competence: Does the plan improve professional planning practice?

In each case the first example will describe a Rational evaluation that anticipates precision, correspondence, principles and expertise; the second, a pragmatic evaluation that anticipates relevance, similarity, consensus and stewardship. I am not arguing against rational analysis, but against a Rationality that elevates theory above practical reason. The Rational approach evaluates plans reflecting on conceptual coherence and fit. The pragmatic approach evaluates plans anticipating purpose and consensus. The comparative reviews that follow illustrate the difference in approach for each type of evaluation.

Plan Formation: How Well Does the Plan Evaluate Alternatives?

Formal and Precise

Planning analysts use trip distribution models, soil erosion schemes or cost benefit ratios to evaluate planning judgments. The tools of rational appraisal define what count as measures of quality and merit at the outset of inquiry. Planners possess a vast array of techniques for measuring and calculating changes in value. For instance, in his recent book *Community Impact Evaluation* (1996), Nathaniel Lichfield describes 10 plan evaluation methods that test outputs (e.g., checklist, multi-attribute, linear programming), three that test inputs (threshold analysis) and 12 that do both (e.g., cost benefit analysis, optimization and community impact analysis). Virtually all of these provide means for measuring and calculating value using increments of utility. Lichfield briefly reviews the many disagreements among evaluation analysts and admits that applying different methods yields different evaluations of the same place and project. But after admitting that context matters in the use of methods he spends the bulk of the text discussing improvements to method rather than explore relationship to context (Lichfield 1996, pp.33–45).

Lichfield makes the argument that economizing represents the primal value for members of modern society. We may have many layers to our lives, but all must build upon economic prosperity. Hence, for Lichfield scarcity shapes all other values by its insistent necessity. The efficacy of the varieties of economically oriented cost benefit methods flows from this view of our social relationships (p.47ff). This enables him to reduce the vast assortment of human attachments, activities, beliefs and so forth to a relatively modest set of monetary measures that he can use in his impact analysis. The complexity returns later, but in the form of residual externalities.

Such sweeping abstraction simplifies as it offers access to a diverse assessment of relationships that we cannot comprehend relying solely on our own common sense. The method lifts us out of our conventional mind set offering a detached calculus for comparing and weighing the impacts of alternative decisions. The chunky tradeoffs among environmental, social, physical and economic issues once translated into an instrumental framework of calculation provide a legible and efficient source of feedback for analysts and decision makers. But when taken too far or relied upon too exclusively, such analysis generates exaggerated claims. This happens when analysts seek to escape the practical contingencies of social and political life through careful deployment of method alone. The problem results not from the pursuit of clarity and precision, but the elevation of strict methodological guides as boundaries for meaningful discourse about what counts as good advice. The brilliant instrumentalist, like the drunk, searches for lost keys only where the light shines (Kaplan 1964).

Relevant and Plausible

In their edited book, *Evaluation of the Built Environment for Sustainability*, editors Brandon, Lombardi and Bentivegna (1997) classify and compare 40 papers delivered at an international conference. Several authors conducted multi-attribute plan evaluations. This approach does not use a uniform measure of value to enhance the powers of calculating difference (e.g., cost benefit analysis), but seeks to identify and measure different preferences people express comparing specific policy choices. These preferences (usually ordinal measures of social, physical, environmental and other valued conditions) are combined into relatively legible and graphically accessible preference scores for different planning alternatives. For instance, Peter Nijkamp and L. Arusto compared three planning alternatives: current commercial development, adjustment to preserve historic features and a sustainability alternative with tough environmental controls on parking and rehabilitation B all for the historical downtown of Bassano del Grappa, Italy (Nijkamp & Arusto 1997). The simultaneous assessment of multiple attributes helped policy makers understand how development decisions might produce multiple related impacts. For instance, attributing economic value varied with choice of impact on property values, commercial revenue, or employment.

This approach provides an accounting scheme to help decision makers in complex and contentious policy arenas compare the relative merits of different combinations of likely outcomes. Most importantly, the method provides a tool for improved deliberation in a collective decision making context rather than a substitute for such deliberation.

Plan Implementation: How Closely Do After Plan Outcomes Meet Plan Objectives?

Did people follow the plan and did the actions they take yield the expected outcomes? Many classic case study accounts of comprehensive planning offer a rather dismal account of the planning enterprise. Consider the works by Meyerson and Banfield (1955), Alan Altshuler (1965) and Peter Hall (1982); all highlight the failure of various planning schemes. Not only did people not follow plans, but worse, the plans when followed did not produce the anticipated results. Recent research, more focused and less sweeping in its claims, offers more hopeful assessments.

Methods Guide Purpose

Emily Talen (1996) uses spatial statistics to test claims about the geographic relationship between park access and the characteristics of city residents in Pueblo, Colorado. Talen compares park access in 1996 with planned park access in 1966. Interestingly, Talen does not test whether or not the parks proposed in 1966 got built. She admits that overlaying current parks and planned parks showed little fit. The district did not follow the 1966 plan. She focuses on outcomes instead.

Talen measures whether or not park facility access improved after the plan. She uses spatial statistics to compare the pattern of accessibility among residents in relation to the entire system of park facilities before the plan (1966) and long after (1990). High access residential areas score above the mean, low ones below it. Talen uses four different models of spatial distribution to assess accessibility from the center of each census tract to each park.

In the end Talen admits that the choice of spatial model defines the kinds of pattern one finds in the data. The use of abstract statistical measures, however, also shifts the evaluation criteria away from the deliberations of park planners, officials and users. If the park facility plans proposed in 1966 were not followed by public officials (which Talen admits), should we use the proposed planning facility locations as a planning norm? In effect, if we know after the fact that the plan was not followed, what does it mean to evaluate the plan? Talen's use of GIS shifts attention to outcomes and criteria bound tightly to method, but only loosely tied to purpose and plan.

Purposes Guide Method

Michael Stegman and Michael Luger conducted an evaluation study of a home ownership subsidy program for the Town of Chapel Hill (Stegman & Luger 1993). Local planners and officials had designed a program using public money to subsidize the purchase of homes by moderate income households that would, without the subsidy, remain renters. The program pursued two goals. First, assist moderate income renters to enter the home owner market. Second, build equity over time so that when and if the owners sold their subsidized home they would acquire enough equity to pay back the original subsidy and still make a down payment on a new home. Stegman and Luger believed these goals were not complementary, but mutually exclusive. They believed that the town had to choose to invest the subsidy for individual household equity accumulation or recapture the subsidy at time of sale for use by other moderate income renters, not both. Stegman and Luger used spread sheet analysis to compare the financial outcomes for each approach over time. The analysis showed that the effort to serve both goals simultaneously fell short of achieving either. Households did not escape the need for subsidy and the Town only recaptured a portion of their original capital. The study reframed the town officials' belief that they could serve both ends and gave them reason to choose between the two. Once offered plausible evidence about the likely consequences of their policies, the local council reconsidered its original commitments and chose the wealth enhancing program forgoing efforts to recoup the program funds.

Plan Critique: How Well Does the Plan Serve the Public Good?

Baer places planning critics in this category: analysts whose vocabulary is alien to the participants doing the planning. This includes political economists of both the ideological right and left, as well as those postmodern thinkers challenging the very prospect of planning at all. The critics from both left and right despite their many disagreements leave room for planning, but postmodern critics hope to junk the entire enterprise. I will tackle the most challenging.

Postmodern Critique

James Scott (1998) argues in his book *Seeing Like a State* that four elements combine to turn the modern state into a nasty imperialistic and autocratic surveillance system. First the state imposes administrative order on nature and society. The state classifies diverse people and landscapes into abstract categories that increase the ease with which the state can manipulate people, the land and their possessions. Second, the ideology of high modernism promotes a blind faith in the power of scientific and technical progress. The pursuit of this rational order inspires confidence in the efficacy of physical and aesthetic designs; build new towns and grand housing blocks that implement state organized utopian improvement schemes. Powerful state officials have often embraced high modernist optimism, putting the ideals to use as conduits serving their interests in expanding and extending the reach of the state and their authority as officials. The third element includes an authoritarian state regime that combines the surveillance system and high modernist designs into an especially coercive system of subjection. Such regimes prosper in societies fragmented by social upheaval: war, revolution, depression or civil disruption. Finally, successful state growth requires a weak and divided civil society. If people can organize themselves to resist the imposition of the surveillance state, then the despotic state can be kept at bay.

> In sum, the legibility of a society provides the capacity for large scale engineering, high-modernist ideology provides the desire, the authoritarian state provides the determination to act on that desire, and an incapacitated civil society provides the leveled social terrain on which to build (p.5).

The four elements may be clustered into two domains: rationality and authority. Standardization and high modernism together produce the rationality post moderns love to hate, while despotic officials and civic passivity foster the authoritarian state long associated with the red menace of the now dismembered USSR during the cold war years. Scott's case against rationality cuts more deeply and critically than his treatment of the elements related to authority. First, the rational lends itself to such critique because homogenization takes the same shape across all the diverse landscapes of the world. Cultural, social and individual differences lose value. The variety of authoritarian regimes make a grand critical argument less compelling. Second, Scott wants to warn us, as did, I believe, Foucault, about the loss of the diverse individual particularities that makes freedom worthwhile (Foucault 1975). Scott may admit the necessity of a paradoxical state reigning in his anarchistic impulses. But when it comes to the rational elements of legibility and high modernism he makes a more heroic and romantic critique. The rational organization of the concepts used to make plans and conduct planning evaluations imposes an order that subjects more than it liberates. Planning paves over differences generating homogeneous spaces that can be more easily managed and controlled. Whether narrow cost benefit analysis or robust multi-attribute analysis, rationality packs a powerful repressive wallop.

This grand critical narrative awakens us to the dangers of a rational government in modern times. Ironically, Scott's strong rejection of the tools of rationality, government regulation and their application in planning schemes for the improvement of human settlement leaves little room for meaningful public planning. Scott does qualify his argument. He admits we need not apply it across the board. But the rhetorical structure he adopts does not show how such planning would work without subjecting, leveling or excluding multiple voices. He holds to an underlying ideal about practice that offers very little practical meaning.

Critical Participation

Leonie Sandercock provides an ambitious postmodern critique of city planning. The rational methods that inform government planning in the name of a greater public interest fail. The powerful and prosperous receive benefits the weak and poor can only imagine. But unlike Scott, who ties the power of knowledge to the power of the state, Sandercock explores fissures in the relationship between knowledge and authority. She studies seven examples of insurgent practices that she contends offer hopeful examples of local democratic resistance and innovative social mobilization directed at community improvement (Sandercock 1998).

Against the long standing planning ideal of a unified public interest, Sandercock proposes a civic ideal of a multiple or heterogeneous public. Practically, this means giving democratic voice to the many different groups and interests in a society, relying on an overarching set of shared principles. Planning should be regarded not simply as an instrument of the state, but as a tool for social mobilization and the practical articulation of new civic ideals. Instead of expanding the rational ties of the global marketplace, planning rationality should emphasize forms of reasoning tied to local experience, face to face dialog, hands on experimentation and active engagement. She insists that nonverbal forms of learning as well as contemplative knowing be included as well. The good plans, the insurgent, democratic plans, inspire dialog, conduct active hands on learning with those individuals and groups who will most likely live with the consequences. Sandercock is no less critical than Scott, but she focuses that criticism on purposes tied to current practice.

Plan Competence: Does the Plan Draw Upon and Contribute to Better Planning Practice?

The conventions that a professional brings to the plan making task will include the mandates, regulations, procedures and tools of his craft. These are described and catalogued in Planning Advisory Service reports prepared by the American Planning Association, planning legislation, the conventions of professional practice and a variety of manuals, guides and reference texts. Each planner, however, adopts the knowledge and criteria within their own particular practice. As planners make judgments about the elements of the plan they do more than just follow instructions and guidelines. They select and compare the meaning and value of different planning elements as they compose the plan. The final written form may resemble the framework imposed by mandate or other requirements, but this resemblance does not necessarily mirror the preceding thought and activity used to make the plan. I use the word craft here to suggest that the quality of plan making includes activities that cannot currently be identified and isolated with sufficient precision to enable routine independent performance. Plan making, unlike some computerized regulatory planning tasks, cannot be easily rationalized into specialized chunks done by nonprofessional clerks. As I described in Chapter 6, as planners write, draw and calculate they compose a narrative, make arguments and envision relationships that speak to an audience. These audiences include the sponsors associated with a plan mandate, but also include a diverse assortment of potential critics, colleagues, citizens, officials, and most important, oneself. The plan maker anticipates the expectations and judgment of these audiences. This distinction provides a much richer conception of plan assessment than Baer considers. As professionals make plans they make judgments about the adequacy, merit, fit, feasibility and rationality of the document in relation to a variety of audiences.

Planning Incompetence

Social psychologist Dietrich Dorner uses computer simulation games to test planning competence. Assigned planning roles, participants make choices among a list of possible choices and then use calculated computer feedback to assess the impacts their choices have on the modeled relationships. For instance, one simulation requires participants to plan and manage resources for a rural community of herds-people in a third world setting. Another has participants enact the role of mayor influencing a variety of policy and program choices for a mid sized city. The simulations test for competent planning judgment in the face of controlled complexity.

Dorner studied not only outcomes, but how participants conduct their inquiry. Ineffective participants make few decisions, focus on a single goal and set effects, fail to make and test hypotheses, fail to follow up on insights and issue commands while avoiding responsibility. They act in a narrow Rational fashion. In the words of planning analyst Donald Schon (1983), the participants improperly frame problems. They mistakenly elevate their familiar, rational expertise at the expense of a more complex open learning (Dorner 1996, p.34). The emotional and political demands of planning practice often encourage planning practitioners to adopt familiar rationales that promise more than they can deliver (e.g., zoning) (Baum 1983, 1987; Hoch 1988).

Planning Competence

Dorner lays out a pragmatic version of the rational model as the appropriate way to cope with complex uncertainty. However, he uses the model not as an ideal type, but a practical guide for assessing the quality of judgments made in complex situations. Effective participants tend to make frequent decisions, seek out causal and systemic links, offer and test hypotheses, follow up on hunches and take responsibility for errors. They use pragmatic inquiry for comprehending a complex, changing and obscure situation. Dorner, a social psychologist, provides evidence for a pragmatic versus rational planning.

Planning researchers have long studied what planners do (Watson 2002; Dalton 1989). Recent research on planning practice, whether autobiographical accounts (Jacobs 1978; Krumholz & Forester, 1989), case studies (Baum 1998; Grant 1994; Gunderson & Light 2000; Healey 1997a; Majoor 2015; Throgmorton 1996) and interviews (Forester 2009; Baum 1983, 1987; Krumholz & Clavel 1994; Hoch 1994; McClendon 1988) evaluate planners, favoring those who demonstrate political savvy, moral sensitivity and active learning. The meaning of good practice comes to us in the details of practical conduct carried out in a specific context. Ironically, the good planners are not necessarily those whose efforts mobilize great power or who achieve stunning success. Good planners in these accounts foster useful planning deliberations that challenge misleading, unjust or otherwise destructive preconceptions. The good planners find ways to make judgments using practical democratic intelligence sensitive to future consequences.

A Pragmatic Sensibility

We often evaluate plans like blind men studying an elephant because we elevate the rationality that abstracts from the complex contexts and multiple purposes that accompany plans to serve as the proper framework for judgment. A pragmatic approach helps us find ways to compensate for the limits of our rational blindness and fixed position. Pragmatism does not provide a miraculous cure, but modest practical steps for recognizing and assimilating differences. Many years ago, Donald Schon made the case for reflection in action in his book *The Reflective Practitioner* (Schon 1983). He reminded us that judgment uses knowledge in action. We learn *to do* things in a different way than we learn *about how* the same things work or *why doing* those things matter. Professional planners use knowledge all the time to resolve problems enough to satisfy officials, superiors and citizens. But when the planners encounter problems that do not lend themselves to their tacit knowledge, they may pause and think about their current knowledge. Schon does not expect planners to use rational analysis at such moments (whether market or class analysis), but a kind of pragmatic inquiry that generates new metaphors to bind together the confusing and troubling aspects of inquiry.

He describes the case of engineers at MIT trying to design a synthetic brush that would lay paint as effectively as a horsehair brush. During their evaluation efforts, one of the engineers stopped thinking about the structural properties of the materials and considered how painters used brushes. Instead of analyzing the effectiveness of the brush as a conduit he imagined its usefulness as a pump. Painters pump a brush to control the flow of paint. Once equipped with this metaphor the engineers reframed the problem and set off a new round of more successful tests.

We use the concept of evaluation in different ways to help us negotiate the complex ambiguities and uncertainties people face making judgments about plans. The pragmatic attention to the consequences of use uncovers and invents an intricate web of meanings. The pragmatic insight provides a vocabulary that turns attention away from the pursuit of a rational order outside practice. James Throgmorton (1996) uses the metaphor of a web to describe the relationships among advocates, analysts and clients in the use of argument. We do not make meaning unilaterally, but through a network of interconnected filaments that bind us to one another. In one sense this metaphor reflects the inescapable inter-connectivity of language. We strive to invent new metaphors that push the margins of conventional comprehension (e.g., sustainability or deep ecology).

Turning Rationality into rationality

A pragmatic rendering of Baer's four types of evaluation would soften the edges emphasizing continuity and similarity rather than detachment and difference. When we evaluate plans our judgments do differ as we select alternatives, compare consequences, conduct critiques or assess competence. But these ideas flow less from the logic of rational method and more from fitting purposes to context, helping blind persons learn to speak to one another. A pragmatic viewpoint encourages us to refine our practical reasoning critically and contextually, but without the confinement of rational precision, fit, principle and expertise. So how do we judge a good plan pragmatically? Consider what a pragmatic approach brings to each type of plan evaluation.

Plausibility versus Precision: Does the plan include alternatives that show potential consequences vividly and plausibly for the relevant stakeholders?
Similarity versus Correspondence: Do relevant stakeholders use the plan, resist the plan, grudgingly submit or perhaps ignore it altogether? Do people take the plan to heart and remake their lives in terms of its purposes?
Consensus versus Principle: Did the plan propose or otherwise inspire consensus building measures that relevant stakeholders used to improve deliberations about plan policies, options or outcomes?
Stewardship versus Expertise: Do the plan makers make their intentions known in ways that anticipate and include shared responsibility for plan consequences?

Selecting Alternatives: Plausibility versus Precision

What do planners do when they cook up new planning alternatives? How do they make good plan alternatives? How do planners compose plausible alternatives from among a vast array of possibilities? Consider how popular TV detectives conduct their investigations. They do not move from general principles to the particular, but construct and compare plausible accounts of how each suspect might have committed the murder. Hilda Blanco (1994) argues that planners use a similar kind of thinking when they plan. Planners usually face problems with geographically unique and historically contingent properties that defy the limits of rational analytic inquiry. Planners do not analyze so much as imagine how general goals apply to more specific, practical policies and projects. They do not compose plans deductively or inductively, but (and here Blanco uses ideas from pragmatic philosopher, Charles Pierce) abductively. Planners offer plausible interpretations of what goals mean in specific situations.[1]

The wicked problems (Ritel and Webber 1973) so common to planning and so difficult to handle with induction or deduction can be abducted. Planners propose plans that offer new institutional relationships or a new way of life. They design plausible yet ideal arrangements that readers or viewers can use to re-describe and re-imagine the current activities that accompany the problem. The pragmatic deployment of abduction renders rational what analysis casts aside. The tools of technical and instrumental rationalists work well where certainty and agreement are great. Planning offers a vocabulary for tackling messy and disagreeable situations. It trades off certainty for relevance. Offering people plausible alternatives to settled but problematic ways of life will not prove anything about causality or structure. We can analyze plans and planning but should beware relying on analysis alone to plan or evaluate plans. The criteria we use to judge the effectiveness of a plan should attend to the diversity of meanings associated with the consequences of the plan. A pragmatic approach anticipates these meanings from the moment planning gets underway.

Consider what this means for planners as they discuss the merits of different plan alternatives. All the varieties of human communication and comprehension: storytelling, reasoning by analogy, debate, persuasive argumentation, drawing, and so on now count as legitimate tools for rational inquiry. The authority and legitimacy of a pragmatic evaluation of plan alternatives depends less on the deployment of a rigorous and narrow analysis and more on the use of a forgiving and robust narrative. Practitioners frequently recognize the wisdom of such evaluations, but then deny the validity and rationality of their judgments because the activities that make their practical inquiry meaningful do not fit the vocabulary of Rational analysis. The arguments they construct, the stories they tell and the drawings they make appear soft compared to the hard precision of scientific analysis. But considered from a pragmatic viewpoint, these efforts appear quite reasonable. Furthermore, the demands of relevance and contextual fit impose demanding evaluation criteria. They are hard to do well. They just do not require the use of detached objective analysis.

Evaluating Consequences: Similarity not Correspondence

When we judge how well a plan is followed, we anticipate correspondence between blueprint and product. We use models to identify relationships and assign criteria to test the fit. For instance, we use ideas about utility and markets to describe the relative costs and benefits of a proposed project. Typically, we calibrate the model to assess how well it predicts relevant consequences of current relationships using historic data. Then we apply the model to expected or planned future relationships measuring the likely relationships. We analyze trends. Daily weather forecasts offer a widespread example of this type of evaluation. The forecasters use meteorological data from previous days to estimate future behavior. Short run forecasts prove much more reliable than long term because the complex relationships that compose weather violate short run trends. Interestingly, the reliability of forecasts tends to be scale dependent. The more geographically and temporally inclusive the outlook, the more reliable the forecast. Ironically, the value of such grand forecasting diminishes for those who hope to put the forecast to practical use. We want to know what the weather will be like in our own community next week to prepare for our planned trip. But the model cannot answer this problem. These models work best where the uncertainty associated with the modeled relationships remains relatively stable and scale invariant. These conditions are not common for urban planning problems that involve, like the weather, increasing uncertainty as the frame shifts from the regional to the local.[2]

Models represent a prosaic, specialized variety of metaphor. Planners use more robust and less precise metaphors to bind purpose and practice. They leave behind the clarity of the blueprint. Instead of seeking correspondence they pursue coherence. The mechanical, ecological or cybernetic metaphors inform images, descriptions and narratives that illustrate how multiple seemingly antagonistic goals and desires might cohere together. Looking back, after the fact, we model relationships that make what happened an obvious and perhaps inevitable fit. Looking forward the same logical reasoning proves frustratingly dogmatic. We use metaphor to reach towards our future.

Metaphor – evocative similarity – fuses an unfamiliar but useful juxtaposition into a new habit of practical judgment. Robust metaphors are scale invariant. We use them to describe collective and individual action at both large and small scales. Sustainablity has now become a central concept in planning parlance. For years resource management and environmental assessment co-existed as parallel enterprises accommodating one another from afar. Each tradition described the same set of development relationships in overlapping yet distinct terms. The experience of continuous effort common to many human endeavors is mapped onto the relationship between the natural and the human. Such a mapping would have proven much less popular without the practical groundwork laid by environmental reformers, movement activists, planning innovators and so forth. How the shift to sustainability occurred requires careful study and analysis. My point is that the sustainability concept currently bonds human development and environmental protection together in a new and useful manner. How useful? Well, planners can use the concept to discuss site specific water retention, as well as region wide flood management issues. The concept leads us to identify and assess at each scale the interdependencies whose damage or repair might increase or decrease the symbiotic relationship between human and natural environments.

Serving the Public Good: Consensus versus Principle

Planners seldom work solely on their own – lone scientist in a lab or solitary artist in studio. Planners work with others in a variety of organizational settings. Planning judgments with meaningful authority must speak to a diverse assortment of institutional and organizational members: elected representatives, agency officials, neighborhood residents, community activists, business lobbyists, developers, and so forth. A pragmatic approach not only includes these purposes and interests when selecting and comparing options but anticipates a wider democratic consensus. Planners rarely bring matters to a close like researchers announcing the results of an experiment or politicians taking a vote. But planners can foster activities that encourage decisive deliberations among the diverse assortment of antagonists and allies. A pragmatic outlook supports public deliberations about a plan, not as civic window dressing for professional expertise, but a crucial source of practical comprehension useful for building consensus (Fox and Miller 1995).

Planners too often adopt legislative or court room mentalities, imagining all forms of democratic activity as a form of adversarial voting or adjudication. Planners present truthful analysis and principled testimony to public representatives divided into factions. Given the close alliance that has developed between government and planning in the last fifty years, this hardly seems surprising. But the emphasis on these arenas of judgment exaggerate the effectiveness of objective analysis as a source of truth in adversarial contests that often shape how the public evaluates plans. Advocacy planners were the first to point out the limits of this approach – that many public goods requires planners to choose among them – urging planners to take the side of the weak (Davidoff 1965; Krumholz & Clavel 1994). A professionalism that links the authority of expertise with one or another principle prepares planners to take sides when they evaluate plans. Rationality becomes a weapon of objectivity in a polarized political debate. A pragmatic planning tries to avoid adversarial contests by fostering consensus building. Emphasizing negotiation and deliberation may not resolve a dispute, but it can inform, invent and even inspire democratic agreements that prevent and pre-empt adversarial blow outs. When planner consider how well their plans build consensus, they adopt a pragmatic outlook (Innes 1995; Healey 1997a; King & Stivers 1998).

Evaluating Authorship: Stewardship versus Expertise

Good problem solvers in complex situations, Dietrich Dorner found, tend to form positive, specific goals clearly and explicitly laid out, identifying contradictory or troubling overlaps. The bad problem solvers adopt negative goals that are vague and general, unclearly identified while relying on implicit assumptions. But rarely did any participant accomplish this all the time in different experimental simulations. Dorner measures differences in how well participants score in the simulations. No one was perfect.

Dorner explores the fuzzy relationship between general and specific goals; what planners often describe as the difference between goals and objectives. Achieving multiple goals requires that people neither form too deep an attachment to a specific decision nor avoid taking any action for fear it will violate a larger goal. Dorner (1996) proposes the awkward phrase, 'efficiency diversity'.

> A situation is characterized by efficiency diversity if it offers *many different possibilities* ('diversities') for actions that have a high *probability of success* ('efficiency'). In chess, examples of such situations are control over the center of the board, more men, and strategic placement of pawns (p.53).

This conception of strategic rationality resembles Andreas Faludi's consequentialist approach (Dorner 1996), but without the rationalism. Niraj Verma's (1998) scholarship, following the pragmatist William James, argues that the emphasis on rational analysis detaches planners from purposes and sentiments. Verma, not only reminds planners to tie conceptual distinctions to consequences rather than formal logical relations; but he also argues that feelings, belief s and commitment shape our expectations. Judging the meaning of consequences for the purposes at hand requires attention to the continuity and connections among different experiences. Good evaluation requires that we take relevant feelings and beliefs into account because they mark the attachments that bind purpose and experience (Marris 1996).

Conclusion

The pragmatic approach reviews the plausibility of plan alternatives, the similarity binding plan and product, the breadth and depth of any agreement the plan informs and the responsibility the plan inspires among those able to follow it. These prudent pragmatic judgments provide theoretical coherence for the practical common sense that wise planners acquire on the job. Instead of promoting an exaggerated distance between the judgments of experts and practitioners, it invites a critical engagement. The pragmatist does not fault the practical side of practitioner judgment, but the tendency among practitioners to stress a combination of occupational (e.g., transportation versus housing, long term versus short term) and disciplinary (e.g., economics, geography) attachments that unnecessarily reinforce premature conceptual, political and moral convictions.

The pragmatic approach does pose risks. First is the threat of a cynical pragmatism. The cynic shapes purpose to fit context or ends to fit means turning evaluation into a 'snow job' or a damning critique. This common practice undermines the legitimacy of a pragmatic approach making it all the more important to reclaim the proper meaning and practice. Second, the pragmatic outlook can serve as justification for a conservative incrementalism where relevance means conformity and similarity translates into sameness. The practical safeguards against either risk do not come so much from improvements in method, as close attention to shared consequences. In a democratic society people can and do monitor plans in just this fashion. Pragmatism provides a vocabulary that can improve the quality of such evaluations, even as cynics and conservatives obscure the view (Harmon 1995).

Adopting a pragmatic planning outlook will not restore vision to the blind persons standing round the elephant. There are real practical and institutional differences among the diverse standpoints taken when evaluating plans. Fearful owners, powerful developers, prejudiced neighbors, selfish petitioners and the host of people who inhabit, influence and direct the organization of settlements comprehend and judge plans differently. Instead of trying to tame the contingency and uncertainty of the planning enterprise through a privileged Rational method and Professional expertise, we should try to comprehend and organize the different viewpoints and the ambiguity among them by adopting a pragmatic outlook. The pragmatic approach recognizes the inescapable plurality of these differences and then proposes a vocabulary that the blind persons can use to speak to one another as they review together the merits of a plan. It turns methodological competition or disciplinary debate into shared deliberations that use multiple methods and purposes. Theory does not replace the political and moral values with conceptual trump but invites the use of such values within a democratic arena focused on shared consequences more than shared assumptions.

Notes

1 This interpretation of the planning process is precisely what Dewey had in mind in his theory of value. The planning process operationalizes values. It gives meaning to vague and abstract preferences by identifying the conditions under which such preferences can be actualized, and the consequences they are likely to entail. Such a process enables us to make informed judgments about conflicting values and, in itself, provides us with the means to actualize them. Planners, through their plans, essentially engage in the kind of value construction and analysis that Dewey believed would flow from the application of the method of social intelligence. Planning can thus accumulate knowledge on social values through its practice (Blanco 1994, p.162).
2 One of the promising features of GIS is the ability to easily shift the visual representation of geographic relationships at different scales. The traditional land use plan at 1:24,000 exhibits choropleth blobs that at 1:50 become building footprints, lot lines and landscape details familiar to local inhabitants. The increasing ease of scale shifting with computer aided imagery erases technical barriers to assessing the effects of planning policies across scales. This increases the accessibility of the information to a much wider audience of viewers who may grasp the detailed local maps more readily than the more abstract images for an entire region. However, the detailed maps do not so much answer questions as provide an enriched context for interpretation. The arrangement and selection of layers of information introduces the visual equivalent to the multi-attribute analysis using demographic and economic values.

References

Altshuler, A. (1965). *The City Planning Process*. Ithaca, NY: Cornell University Press.
Baer, W. (1997). General plan evaluation criteria: An approach to making better plans. *Journal of the American Planning Association*, 63(3), 329–344.
Baum, H. (1983). *Planners and Public Expectations*. Cambridge, MA: Schekman.
Baum, H. (1987). *The Invisible Bureaucracy: The Unconscious in Organizational Problem-solving*. New York: Oxford University Press.
Baum, H. (1998). *The Organization of Hope: Communities Planning Themselves*. Albany, NY: State University of New York Press.
Blanco, H. (1994). *How to Think About Social Problems: American Pragmatism and the Idea of Planning*. New York: Greenwood.
Brandon, P. S., Lombardi, P. S. and Bentivegna, V. (Eds.). (1997). *Evaluation of the Built Environment for Sustainability*. London: Chapman & Hall.
Dalton, L. (1989). Emerging knowledge about planning practice. *Journal of Planning Education and Research*, 9(1), 29–44.
Davidoff, P. (1965). Advocacy and pluralism in planning. *Journal of the American Institute of Planners*, 31, 331–338.
Dorner, D. (1996). *The Logic of Failure: Recognizing and Avoiding Error in Complex Situations*. Reading, MA: Addison-Wesley.
Forester, J. (1983). The Geography of Planning Practice. *Environment and Planning D: Society and Space*, 1, 163–180.
Forester, J. (1989). *Planning in the Face of Power*. Berkeley: University of California Press.
Forester, J. (2009). *Dealing with Differences: Dramas of Mediating Public Disputes*. New York: Oxford University Press.
Forester, J. and Roweis, S. (1983) On planning practice: Materialism and politics. *Environment and Planning D: Society and Space*, 1, 481–491.
Foucault, M. (1975). *Discipline and Punish: The Birth of the Prison*. New York: Random House.
Fox, C. J. and Miller, H. T. (1995). *Postmodern Public Administration: Toward Discourse*. Thousand Oaks, CA: Sage Publications.
Grant, J. (1994) *The Drama of Democracy*. Toronto: University of Toronto Press.
Gunderson, L. H. and Light, S. S. (2000). Adaptive management and adaptive governance in the Everglades ecosystem. *Policy Sciences*, 39, 323–334.
Hall, P. (1982) *Great Planning Disasters*. Berkeley: University of California Press.
Harmon, M. M. (1995). *Responsibility as Paradox: A Critique of Rational Discourse on Government*. Thousand Oaks, CA: Sage Publications.
Harper, T. and Stein, S. (1996). Postmodernist planning theory: The incommensurability premise. In S. J. Mandelbaum, L. Mazza, and R. W. Burchell (Eds.), *Explorations in Planning Theory* (pp. 414–429). New Brunswick, NJ: Center for Urban Policy Research.
Healey, P. (1997a). *Collaborative Planning: Shaping Places in Fragmented Societies*. London: Macmillan.
Healey, P. (1997b). Ed. Planning theory, political economy and the interpretive turn: The debate continues! *Planning Theory*, 17(Summer), 10–87.
Hoch, C. (1984). Doing good and being right: The pragmatic connection in planning theory. *Journal of the American Planning Association*, 50(3), 335–345.
Hoch, C. (1988). Conflict at large: A national survey of planners and political conflict. *Journal of Planning Education and Research*, 7(4), 25–34.

Hoch, C. (1992). The paradox of power in planning practice. *Journal of Planning Education and Research*, 11(3), 206–215.

Hoch, C. (1994). *What Planners Do*. Chicago: Planners Press.

Hoch, C. (1995). Teaching ethics and planning theory. In S. Hendler (Ed.), *Planning Ethics: A Reader in Planning Theory, Practice and Education* (pp. 281–300). New Jersey: Rutgers, Center for Urban Policy and Research.

Innes, J. (1995). Planning theory's emerging paradigm: Communicative action and interactive practice. *Journal of Planning Education and Research*, 14(3), 183–190.

Jacobs, A. (1978). *Making City Planning Work*. Chicago: American Society of Planning Officials.

Kaplan, A. (1964). *The Conduct of Inquiry: Methodology for Behavioral Science*. New York: Harper & Row.

King, C. S. and Stivers, C. (Eds.). (1998). *Government Is Us: Public Administration in an Anti-Government Era*. Thousand Oaks, CA: Sage Publications.

Krumholz, N. and Clavel, P. (1994). *Reinventing Cities: Equity Planners Tell Their Stories*. Philadelphia: Temple University Press.

Krumholz, N. and Forester, J. (1989). *Making Equity Planning Work*. Philadelphia: Temple University.

Lichfield, N. (1996). *Community Impact Evaluation*. London: UCL Press.

Majoor, S. J. H. (2015). Resilient practices: A paradox-oriented approach for large-scale development projects. *Town Planning Review*, 86(3), 257–277.

Marris, P. (1996). *The Politics of Uncertainty, Attachment in Private and Public Life*. New York: Routledge.

McClendon, B. and Quay, R. (1988). *Mastering Change: Winning Strategies for Effective City Planning*. Chicago: American Planning Association.

Menand, L. (2001). *The Metaphysical Club: A Story of Ideas in America*. New York: Farrar, Straus and Giroux.

Meyerson, M. and Banfield, E. (1955). *Politics, Planning and the Public Interest*. New York: Free Press.

Nijkamp, P. and Artuso, L. (1997). Methodology and application of sustainable environmental concepts for the built environment. In P. S. Brandon, P. S. Lombardi and V. Bentivegna (Eds.), *Evaluation of the Built Environment for Sustainability* (pp. 435–450). London: Chapman & Hall.

Rittel, H. W. J. and Webber, M. M. (1973). Dilemmas in a general theory of planning. *Policy Sceinces*, 4(3), 155–169.

Sandercock, L. (1998). *Towards Cosmopolis: Planning for Multicultural Cities*. New York: John Wiley.

Schon, D. (1983). *The Reflective Practitioner: How Professionals Think in Action*. New York: Basic Books.

Scott, J. C. (1998). *Seeing Like a State: How Certain Schemes to Improve the Human Condition Have Failed*. Princeton, NJ: Yale University Press.

Stegman, M. A. and Luger, M. I. (1993). Issues in the design of locally sponsored home ownership programs. *Journal of the American Planning Association*, 59(4), 417–434.

Talen, E. (1996). After the plans: Methods to evaluate the implementation success of plans. *Journal of Planning Education and Research*, 16(2), 79–92.

Throgmorton, J. A. (1996). *Planning as Persuasive Storytelling; The Rhetorical Construction of Chicago's Electric Future*. Chicago: University of Chicago Press.

Toulmin, S. (2001). *Return to Reason*. Cambridge, MA: Harvard University Press.

Verma, N. (1998) *Similarities, Connections and Systems*. New York: Lexington.
Watson, V. (2002). Do we learn from planning practice? The evolution of the practice movement in planning theory. *Journal of Planning Education & Research*, 22(2), 178–187.

8 How Planning Theory Informs Planning Practice

Introduction

The complexity of places will not submit to a single conceptual viewpoint. Pragmatism searches for ways to integrate and adapt different ideas to specific situations as problems emerge. But how might this work? In this chapter I apply ideas from different theoretical viewpoints to compare two comprehensive plans for nearby suburban municipalities on the edge of the Chicago Metropolitan Region. After a brief review of Chicago suburban development, I describe how professional planners working for the municipalities of Frankfort and Orland Park craft comprehensive land use plans for each suburb. This sets up the case.

I do not compare the plans against a single standard but show how different theoretical ideas inform judgments of planning craft and what this means for interpreting plan quality. The analysis in this chapter provides an example of how a pragmatist does theory using ideas from different planning theorists. Searching for distinct yet complementary insight across theories focuses attention on different meanings for familiar plan making activity. The comparison does not diminish the theoretical differences, even as it can improve the range and depth of the judgments that practitioners might learn to take as they compose plans for places with others.

I conclude that both plans work as advice for their respective municipal audiences; but that one plan offers better quality advice because it draws upon a wider range of theoretical ideas that improve the practical scope of its message. Both plans fail to meet the normative expectations set by political economy or scientific rationality. Taken pragmatically, theoretical ideas can work like prosthetic attachments enhancing the cognitive craft for plan making rather than as justifications for moral perfection or scientific certainty.

Suburban Development and Spatial Planning in Chicago

Urban development happens in waves of investment. The cycles of boom and bust imprint their legacy on the physical form of metropolitan regions. Most of Chicago's suburban places developed as clusters of rapidly constructed subdivisions that reflected the physical styles and spatial arrangements promoted by private developers, popular with home buyers and compliant with county zoning and subdivision regulations. Successive waves of investment flow outward. Greenfield developers promote and advertise images of place that emulate attractive low density suburban living tied to ownership of a single family dwelling within a niche landscape: pastoral, recreational, rural and the like. Each subdivision developer promotes and advertises the character for an arrangement of parcels for a small slice of a vast expanse.

In many of these newer suburban municipalities the developer shapes the urban fabric. Since the 1950s, physically, the average dwelling size has increased, and so has the system of roads as traffic to these places increased. Developers often work at the neighborhood or sometimes even municipal scale. The subdivided residential areas became their own neighborhoods, insulated from commercial districts. The shift from the traditional grid pattern to curvilinear residential streets shifted the overall suburban development. The cyclical flow of finance lead to periods of rapid build-out followed by consolidation. Spatially, the bulk of new single family development happened on peripheral sites. The physical character of neighborhoods and municipalities followed the private plans of home builders offering dwellings targeted to home owning households within different income segments.

Although occasionally land developers work at a large neighborhood and even municipal scale; most operate at an intermediate scale (Buzzelli 2001). Land development follows the boom and bust cycles of the larger economy sensitive to federal policy offering tax subsidies for home ownership. The many competing developers carve up chunks of suburban land following the aesthetic and spatial conventions. The resulting spatial geography of relatively rapid suburban development does not follow the social contours set by households living together over generations in the same place. Shared expectations include an attachment to increasing amounts of space inside the home and the surrounding yard and a strong conviction that neighboring dwellings need be the same size or larger.

Eran Ben-Joseph (2003) surveyed and studied how subdivision regulations affect the design of residential developments in rapidly growing regions. He did a nationwide survey of jurisdictions experiencing rapid growth.

> Most developers indicated that they want to build higher density single family areas and more multifamily units and would create more varied site and structural plans if they had the opportunity. In the majority of cases, developers applied for more dense development, yet an overwhelming majority (72 percent) had to design a lower density

development because of existing regulations. These observations have remained consistent in the last 25 years.

Population increase has always fueled metropolitan urbanization. But in the United States the spatial impact on suburban expansion increased in recent decades due to increases in the number of households and the increasing size of dwelling units built in suburban green field areas. Research tracking land conversion using satellite evidence found that for midwestern regions including Chicago that the rate of urban land absorption between 1980 and 2000 exceeded population growth rates by a factor of four (Pijanowki & Robinson 2011). The rapid expansion on the periphery was accompanied by the decline and in some cases hollowing out of neighborhoods, commercial centers and industrial locations in the central city and aging first ring suburban municipalities. These first ring suburbs include the suburbs incorporated before 1970. In Chicago these include municipalities formed almost a century earlier as well as those formed to capture the waves of post WWII sprawl. The older suburbs possess a kind of urban character that distinguishes them from the *cul-de-sac* laden subdivisions arranged in homogeneous clusters of increasingly larger homes (Lee & Greenleigh 2005). But age and location do not allow for simple classification. Some inner suburban municipalities have attracted ethnic immigrants with a range of occupation and income, while neighboring suburbs fill up with low income African American households subjected to long standing segregation. In Chicago the black African American outmigration has concentrated in the southern and some western suburban places.

During the boom years of the early 2000s many older prosperous municipalities experienced demand for housing conversion. The early wave of post war housing built small 1200 square foot dwellings on large lots; lots that a generation later could accommodate dwellings two or even three times as large. These infill developments began to proliferate as land values skyrocketed in high demand suburban locales. Lanyi Charles (2013) studied tear down activity across the entire scope of inner suburbs for the Chicago region. She found that tear down redevelopment started in prosperous predominantly white areas and later spread to less prosperous but still middle-class areas with ample lot sizes. The doctrine of home ownership and the preference for single family dwellings with increasing amounts of space continues to drive metropolitan decentralization.

Case Selection and Method

The plans selected for this comparison were part of a much larger collection of 69 comprehensive plans prepared for suburban municipalities for the Chicago region between 2009 and 2013. I and my research assistant Jacqueline Henrikson read these plans and classified them as part of a larger study about plan content and quality. Two three-hour interviews were conducted with two planners for each municipality. The planners consented to the interview and use of their names. The illustrations come from the comprehensive plan documents.

Orland Park and Frankfort were small rural towns in the late 19th century that eventually became suburbs as the Chicago region expanded. Both remain deeply wedded to the development doctrine of sustained growth refining and expanding the availability of single family dwellings with access to high quality physical infrastructure and schools. Suburban planners making comprehensive plans for a local municipality composed of polyglot subdivisions search for community character a spatial identity that can bind together the diverse and fragmented subdivisions built by individual developers. The household life cycle fuels cohorts that travel through the housing stock. In prosperous places young married couples move in with child rearing at the center of attention, mid-life households upgrade to a larger home pursuing new life style choices or empty nesters cluster in retirement settlements. Social bonds flow less from residential proximity or neighboring, and more from family life cycle experience using nearby school facilities, recreational facilities, parks and commercial places. Trying to anticipate and accommodate the local flow of household members with the expectation of a stable community takes shape in comprehensive plans as a quest for character. [Ironically, the language of identify does not seem to vary much regardless of the physical characteristics and socioeconomic standing of a suburban place. The aging inner ring suburban municipality with small homes and modest income households tells the same story about itself.]

The Orland Park Case

In the 2012 Comprehensive Plan for Orland Park the planners seek to balance urban and suburban community benefits. They describe the future offering a mix of "big-city opportunities" but "with a lot more green space and a lot less stress" (Orlando Park Planning Department 2013, p.17). The planners embrace the city-in-the-country ideal. Most plans for green field communities make the same claim. Each suburban municipality hopes to carve out a unique spatial identity along the outward trajectory of residential and commercial development. The Orland Park planners meet the challenge use storytelling to frame the plan. The introduction introduces the married Smith couple as they move to Orland Park from Chicago's Northside with young daughter in tow. Their journey ends in a place that similar future newcomers will also enjoy – a cosmopolitan child friendly place with low intensity high quality green scape. The planning districts are mapped in Figure 8.1 (Orland Park Department of Planning 2013).

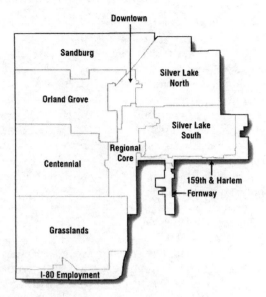

Figure 8.1 Orland Park planning districts.

The Plan Situation

The senior staff planner offered a succinct set up. I paraphrase from a longer interview:

> *The practical impetus for the plan emerged in 2000 when the Regional Transit Authority (RTA) conducted a Transit Oriented Development Study of the 143rd Street train station. The planners working on the study raised questions about plan for improvements asking what would generate a sense of place. The public actively participated and showed interest in this idea of doing more than just making functional improvements. The popularity and interest made it onto the radar of the mayor and some of the other elected officials.*
>
> *Nearly a decade after the TOD plan in 2009 we conducted a Strength Weakness Opportunities and Threat (SWOT) analysis with the elected officials laying out the case for taking a longer view of the future of the Village. We did not face an indifferent or hostile audience of elected officials. Mayor Dan McLaughlin on the board since 1983 described how at a meeting with Orland Park youth in the 1990s he asked them about downtown Orland Park. They told him about the mall. He was shocked. The auto friendly mall did not say anything meaningful about Orland Park as a community. McLaughlin realized it would take a conscious effort to draw attention to these places and that plans could provide the stimulus for physical improvements.*

Land Use Plans

We studied a lot of other comprehensive plan but wanted to make sure that plans for future development and redevelopment would contributed to an Orland Park identity. We and local developers had already started shifting away from a regulatory compliance approach to a plan review focus. Our expertise and interest in urban design meant that visual form and appearance of subdivisions or infill projects set principles for future spatial location and arrangement. We paid attention to the regional planning efforts by the Chicago Metropolitan Agency for Planning (CMAP) integrating regional issues into the plan. The combined conventional land use planning ideas with form-based code ideas introduced by 'New Urbanism'. These made sense for our own work.

We copied a modified version of the page layout from the award winning 2011 Champaign Illinois Comprehensive Plan. We liked that their plan offered simple and easy to read developer friendly maps. The maps include notations tied to parcel and infrastructure problems and potentials. We had hoped to include detailed subarea plans to show building footprints and layout ideas for future subdivisions but had to pull back as time ran out.

Instead of describing passive land use categories the plan focuses attention on potential variations in the spatial form and intensity of physical development within each. The planners hope to foster a mix of uses that leverage the environmental and spatial features of existing neighborhoods. Publicly sensitive infrastructure improvements and the spatial integration of uses can provide a unified character for each district. Explicit plan principles offer guidance for how to do this. For instance, urging developers to avoid uniform density blocks and to produce graduated densities that taper from spatial activity nodes outward toward peripheral areas.

For instance, the Centennial Planning District description includes residential, green field open space and employment. The current homes were built in the two decades between 1990 and 2010. The text details some of the policy recommendations for the future: creating pedestrian and bike friendly streets, annexation of unincorporated islands of land while encouraging infill development that incorporates the intensity of surrounding use and environmental amenity into development plans. The maps provide detailed locational representations of the policy ideas offering explicit direction about the spatial meaning of each policy in relation to other parallel policies. The map images combine detailed information about developer plans, capital improvements, land use, transport mode split, incorporated status and prior public agreements. Unlike conventional land use maps that offer static snap shots of future land use polygons, these district maps enable the user to review and compare how different land policy proposals interact with prior plan decisions and some developer expectations. The maps do not offer fixed illustrations of a uniform

138 Part III

singular plan for each place, but rather capture the complex interaction among a variety of expectations in play among developers, municipal policies, elected officials and others with a stake in the future of the land for each planning district. The maps visually translate abstract planning policies of the municipality into a more complex array of the many expectations and issues shaping future development for each place (see Figure 8.2).

Instead of evoking a simplistic and nostalgic conception of character for a mythic place, the plan offers up practical and useful development ideas closely aligned with each place. The text arrayed across the surface integrates the plans of stakeholders with the underlying land use proposal and existing infrastructure.

> *We wanted to ensure that each map could stand as a legally defensible policy document. But we also wanted a map that elected officials, developers and planning commissioners would use to guide their judgments about what to approve. As staff planners we had learned that developers face a serious information gap as they conceive what they want to build on a site while trying to imagine fitting their idea into the local subdivision and zoning code requirements. We had each experienced trying to do this sort of translation in meetings with developers experiencing joint frustration trying to show what different adjustments and tradeoffs would mean for the proposed project. The maps we created for the comp plan included the kind of information that would reduce the ambiguity and difficulty of this sort of exchange. We reviewed every potential development site within each district map at our weekly meetings. We sent these out to other municipal departments for feedback. How did*

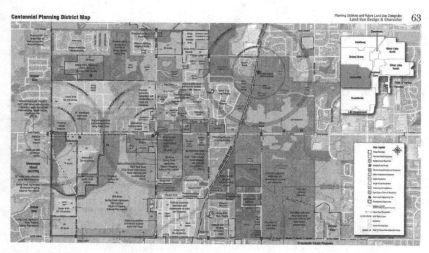

Figure 8.2 Layered Orland Park land use map detailing many plans in play.

infrastructure proposals square with public works expectations? How did land use plans fit with land use policy expectations? No staff pushed back or complained. We presented the maps as provisional drafts open for comment. As we worked on the plan and shared drafts the public works and engineering colleagues really came to like the approach. They found the visual display of the combined information useful for their own work.

Translating goals

We worked hard to integrate policy, principle and objectives into the plan. The map provided a visual display of these judgments in ways that we thought developers, officials and residents could all use to comprehend future development options. We can compare how we assessed a large development area.

The original 1990s subdivision included density and open space requirements consistent with the comp plan at the time. But today (2010) the land remains vacant. The question was how do we plan for future development using new principles? The locational principle for residential subdivision favors variation. Instead of a uniform spread of density across the subdivided site, the subdivision design locates more intense physical use along exterior boundaries (e.g., arterial roadways) tapering off toward the center of the site. Apartments butt up against the edge (R4) and then an interior seam of lower density multifamily dwellings gives way to low density R2 dwellings.

The plan includes concentric pedestrian travel circles that urge the viewer to consider the difference commercial nodes that populated the street grid as walking and not just driving destinations (Figure 8.3) (Orland Park Planning Department 2013, p.63). The circles translate a pedestrian policy into a familiar geographic display for travel behavior. The maps include a mix of site specific public work project proposals, proposed subdivisions, road extensions and current land marks and neighborhoods. The maps offer a tentative tableau for future infrastructure and land use improvements that enables the viewer to see each in relation to the others. The near term changes include more detail, while the more speculative distant proposals offer provisional indicators.

Frankfort Case

In 2004 the Village approved an update of the 1996 comp plan. The Policy Framework provided a 'bridge' between current land use decisions and ideal future land use. The authors hoped these policies would ensure Frankfort coordinated public investments to support short term and long-range development and so maximize opportunities to meet Village's goals. This growth focused efficiency update came in response to the booming real estate activity along the southern border of the community; the portion of unincorporated county land undergoing rapid urbanization.

140 Part III

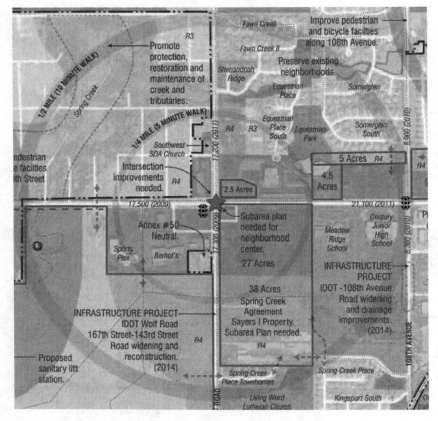

Figure 8.3 Zoomed in portion of Figure 8.2 land use map showing plans in play.

Just six years later the Village undertook another update focusing on the same area (Figure 8.4) (Frankfort Planning Department 2010). Despite the real estate recession that emerged in 2006 and had yet to peak, Village officials responded to the Will County board approval of subdivisions totaling more than 1,600 parcels in Green Garden Township adjoining its southern boundary. The Village had annexed subdivisions on its southern boundary in 2004 and 2006 but wanted to take a forward thinking strategic approach.

The Plan Situation

Two staff planners set the stage for the comp plan update. I paraphrase interview responses into a short narrative:

> *There was a lot of development happening in adjacent Green Garden Township under county authority. Will County adopted a land resources*

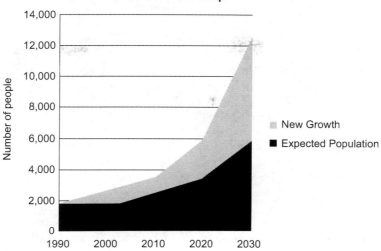

Figure 8.4 Frankfort projected population growth from migration.

management plan (these included a series of plans for land use policy starting in 2002 and culminating in a 2011 plan for a proposed airport in nearby Peotone). The area included large lot residential parcels using groundwater wells and septic systems. Scattered parcels cut everything up. Population was increasing. Residents liked that they had access to urban services while enjoying the 'country life'. The local township leadership did not recognize the emerging infrastructure demands for roads, sewer and water.

In 2010 as staff we realized that new development was not flowing from Frankfort south. The haphazard subdivision growth could potentially cut off growth opportunities for Frankfort and constrain future village expansion. This worry set in motion the impetus to make land use plans for this area assessing the prospects for continued growth and village involvement.

Zach and I got in the car and spent an entire day driving around and taking photographs and tried to understand area at a greater level of detail. Traveled every single section road up and down. Documented existing uses. We photographed them and we then created a GIS map that documented and displayed the current land uses. Coming up with categories was interesting. We identified enough kinds to capture the variety of use and so understand what was happening as we viewed the map images. We did not want to be too specific creating a million categories that made visual pattern analysis impossible.

The Big Picture

The two staff studied the plans of other institutional actors likely to build large scale regional commercial and transport facilities in Will County in the coming decades. Additionally, they paid attention to the plans of municipalities to the south proposing their own ambitious growth plans. Even as the development surge diminished the Village officials welcomed reconsideration of the comp plan to respond to the plans of other actors shaping their strategic interests.

Staff prepared estimates of local population growth for a three percent annual rate that matched suburban growth overall, but if one or more of the large regional developments happened in the next two decades they offered an eight percent estimate for residential demand in the Green Garden Township. The goals statement for the update anticipates capturing and managing any growth that happens providing room for commercial and industrial firms while complementing the low-density estate scale residential development in place. Conservation of flood sensitive water shed areas complements the mix of equestrian and residential farming uses. The Village wants to assure that the quality of future more conventional subdivisions meets their standards rather than the less restrictive Will county requirements.

Land Use Plan

> Sleepy Frankfort is part of a greater whole. We know that the town includes subsets of civic activists: long-timers with ties to the old town as a place to protect, others who see Frankfort as an exurb to protect and conventional suburbanites who see the place as a bedroom community serving the region. Showing the county map locating intermodal freight centers and major transport improvements helped them all grasp the possible impacts of these drivers. Local resident demand for more services, shopping, employment will increase in the future. The fragmented subdivision activity to the south is not a fluke, but a response to the increasing demand.

Figure 8.5 from the updated 2010 plan illustrates the location of potential large scale economic and transportation facility development that will attract new residents. The planners prepared narratives that outlined the strategic focus of these facility plans and their potential impact on the Frankfort study area.

The Frankfort addition to the comp plan laid out a provisional locational sketch for future development. The generalized use zones rely on idealized functionally homogeneous projections. Unlike the county wide map detailing the intentions of other strategic actors making plans nearby, the map in Figure 8.6 shows imagined results solely in terms of Village interests (Orland Park Planning Department 2013). The future residential and commercial uses channel expected growth into contiguous subdivision development tied to Frankfort.

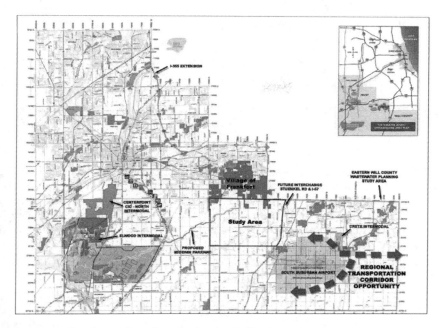

Figure 8.5 Sketching other plans in play for Will County in 2010.

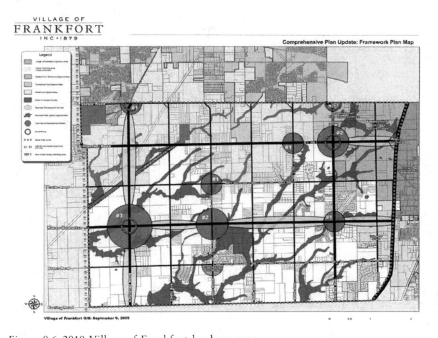

Figure 8.6 2010 Village of Frankfort land use map.

Using Three Different Planning Theories to Compare the Cases

Many institutions shape the complex spatial uncertainties that accompany suburban development. Professional planners make public plans for a local government using practices and protocols culled from the planning movement and discipline. But a vast array of plans (private citizens, developers, investors and others) compose the encompassing field of planning. Unlike professions like law and medicine the authority for conceiving and enacting decisions for city plans does not possess institutional presence and stature like the system of courts or a health care system of hospitals and clinics. This is not a failure of the planning discipline, but a product of the focus on spatial interaction tied to specific places across the globe; as well as the ubiquity of plan making among people and the vast variety of institutions and organizations they create. The field of spatial planning includes so much that efforts to encompass all the various actors and their interaction becomes abstract and superficial. The professionals for Orland Park and Frankfort did not make superficial plans. They each adopted a different approach for framing and selecting future land planning issues. How would different planning theories analyze these differences and interpret their meaning and relevance?

Answering this question, I compare how each planning theorist conceives how plans can and should work. The analysis focuses on three practical aspects of professional plan making: representing, interpreting and judging? These reflect the pragmatist approach: Grasping the situation includes setting problems and opportunities. Anticipating and conceiving spatial interaction through active imaginative consideration of potential future consequences prepares people for the unexpected. Adaptation and not optimization frames imaginative anticipation. Collaboration taps the experience and knowledge of relevant actors with a stake in the future for a place. They are not sequential, but iterative and synthetic. How did the professional spatial planners?

Represent: that is select, describe and assess the salience of causes for local suburban spatial change?
Interpret: Identify and compose goals, objectives, solutions, options and strategies as options for the plan?
Judge: Imagine and evaluate future effects for the municipality and its environs?

See Table 8.1 For a comparison of planning theory analyst approaches.

Emily Talen

Represent: Emily Talen urges professional spatial planners to pay attention to land use rules and how they pre-empt the purposeful wisdom of an urbanist sensibility sensitive to the demands of place. She looks to the

Table 8.1 Comparison of planning theory analyst approach.

	Talen	Beauregard	Hopkins, Knapp, and Kaza
Representing Causes	Rules and norms guide spatial arrangement and use of space using antiurban modernist functionalism; study and embrace complexity for a place instead	The role of things as agents shaping spatial interaction effects; the material actants animate constraints and opportunities across scale for relevant place	Identify complex spatial interactions of interdependence, irreversibility, indivisibility and uncertainty among people and the world for specific place.
Interpreting Purpose	Use urbanism principles to mediate and judge spatial complexity for places: diversity, connectivity, equity, publicity	Identify and mediate spatial relationships creating sites using principles to construct baroque enunciations that inform publics animating a place	Focus on identifying and improving decisions about land development showing how to include future interaction effects that embrace complexity
Judging Future Effects	Focus on physical spatial relationships searching for historical continuity, contextual meaning and aesthetic coherence	Besides framing options for spatial improvements for a place, articulate the meaning of these changes for relevant agents (human and non) inspiring publics to alter old habits achieving more democratic and just consequences	Instead of striving for a single vision for many agents; help improve how agents signal future intentions improving coordination to improve the effects of their collective decisions

historical practices of urbanism to discover spatial planning that offers prescriptive recommendations for place-based improvements tied to explicit conceptions of spatial form and order. She recoils against the antiurbanism of modernist rationality that imposed functional compromises on urban landscapes that sacrifice traditional beauty and form to placeless planning processes. Rational planning and even the communicative turn that challenged it distracts from the important mission of place-based planning committed to guiding development of beautiful settlements. Analyzing the spatial complexity of urban places requires assessing the legacy of development tied to existing rules and conventions. The uniformity and segregation of suburban places was the product of zoning and subdivision rules untethered from a proper understanding of urban complexity and diversity (Talen 2012).

Interpret: Talen (2005) casts plan making as part of a tradition of urbanism. She identifies four traditions that each fit within different levels of urban intensity (urban to rural transect) and urban order (prescribed or emergent). Regionalism (low intensity emergent) fits low intensity urban settlements within the ecological limits of an enveloping countryside. Think Geddes and MacKaye. Incremental urbanism (high intensity emergent) embraces mutually responsive interaction among individuals and local groups using urban places as resources for urbane enjoyment. Jane Jacobs takes center stage. Plan making (high intensity prescribed) that justifies targeted infill redevelopment and urban renewal fulfilling publicly sanctioned civic purpose. Burnham and followers go here. Planned communities celebrate new development on peripheral undeveloped land (low intensity prescribed). Howard, Unwin and Parker in the UK and Stein and Wright in the US play prominent roles. Talen elaborates the historical development of each tradition hoping to revive interest in judgments about the physical structure and form of urban settlements at the core of urban planning theory. Good spatial planning draws on these traditions to assess spatial situations and compose plans.

Talen expects professional planners to conceive the principles for good place plans based on the experience of city building distilled into traditions that include ideas and conventions. The urbanism principles include diversity, connectivity, mix, equity and public space. Diversity is most important. She contrasts these with uniformity, separation, homogeneity, efficiency and privatism of anti-urbanism. Good planning practice seeks to put the principles of urbanism to use guiding the spatial order for places. For instance, Talen embraces a physical (not determinist) version of comprehensiveness as she conceives plans for urban development. The geographic transect (promoted in New Urbanist 'Smart Codes') links general and long term goals of a comprehensive plan with local decisions about specific short term development projects. Instead of regulating current land use zones that rarely anticipate future land plans using a 'transect' integrates plan making as part of project approval. "The plans that make up the Smart Code are specific guiding principles of good urban form that are used to provide a framework for the various transect zones" (Talen 2002, p.303). The transect describes the geographic interdependence of urban development project effects both for a specific site and along a reference axis from a fixed center point in a settlement to the far edge of its periphery.

Judge: Talen understands that plans anticipate specific outcomes even as these may take a long time to emerge or may change with use. She studies how rules influence the practice of planning and the effects that follow over time. The zoning and subdivision rules that now foster racial exclusion and social inequality across the metropolitan regions were once envisioned as tools to reduce the spatially unfair burdens of slum living. The form-based codes on the New Urbanism she celebrates still require interpretation and deliberation that use planning principles about pattern, form and use to offset the perverse effects of rigid zoning and subdivision regulations.

Embedding planning principles in the design and use of rules can in her view improve the prospects for improved places. Judgments about good places require familiarity with exemplars and precedents, but also competent practice using principles and rules to guide plans for streets, neighborhoods and other places along the transect.

Bob Beauregard

Representation: Beauregard (2016) compares two state sponsored spatial planning conceptions of urban complexity: Romantic and Baroque. A romantic account casts regional economic inequality among booming and shrinking cities as functional parts of a global economy with losers and winners located within a nested hierarchy. The parts make sense in relation to the whole. The state manages from above. The baroque account describes the parts as nodes within networks of interdependent relationships. The global view does not exist independent of these relations, but articulates their interaction paying attention to the contextual details tied to different local nodes. The qualities of a place, the local government policies and other local actions shape what happens and so the possibility for change. The conditions within a place do not define the location of that part but animate the growth or shrinkage of that locale in relation to all the other places. Beauregard wants spatial planners to shift from the romantic to baroque outlook to grasp the promise of complexity.

Interpretation: Beauregard distinguishes two strains of spatial planning: those meeting the social needs of people and those improving the spatial order for places. He frames this as a theoretical dilemma. He critiques the over reliance on a rational approach to plans that impose a too simple order on a complex place. Beauregard focuses on the moral responsibility that democratic planning requires including the kinds of tools deployed, the relevant actors and the principles used to conceive future concerns and proposals for a place. He uses Bruno Latour's critical focus on the practical technological and material things to remind professional planners that grasping the complex interactions shaping a place requires a sensitivity not only to the interplay of people and their institutions, but the interdependent ebb and flow of relationships among things. Street signs and speed bumps act just as much as policemen.

Beauregard uses three concepts to analyze how spatial plans work: site, context and setting. Site refers to the provisional spatial conception professionals provide in a plan. Professionals represent the site using principles that combine causal and normative beliefs to select and focus attention. Imagine a map detailing land use. Context describes the geographic location in terms of the many existing historical and ecological conditions that people inhabit and use; and that possesses meaning for them and others with ties to the place. Think of a video capturing pedestrian and vehicle traffic at an intersection. The physical, environmental, social and symbolic features that compose a place exceed the bounds of any purposeful site carved out by professional planners. The material features of the place actively shape how people live and the expectations civic publics take for granted. Imagine the layers of attachment people use and remember for the places each inhabits.

Beauregard maps Latour's critical assessment of context onto the planning analysis of place. Planning analysts use place to refer to a more inclusive backdrop of material conditions that inadvertently introduce a kind of stability and order not subject to inquiry (obduracy). Instead of presuming context as a background, treat these seemingly inanimate features as part of the action. If the plan hopes to reduce fragmented land development then it must show how indifference to spatial interdependence shapes current practice. Narrow residential streets to slow traffic and bump out curbs at corners to signal intersection crossings.

Beauregard wants to awaken professionals to the practical norms each urban dweller relies upon grasping and navigating the material and social features of a setting. The setting includes the material tools, location and embodied tradition of the office, consultancy, and other stuff used to make plans. The practical authority of these judgments relies upon the relationships with elected officials, other government workers, supervisors, petitioners, activists and so forth; all mediated by how professionals deploy their tools in the environs of the meeting rooms and other places. Animating the dynamic ensemble of relations can help professionals grasp a wider and deeper scope of understanding of overlooked complexity. The principles guiding judgments about cause and effect should include attention not only to the ideas about spatial continuity, but for what this might mean across the layers of relationships that need to change to bind together the location and form of future subdivisions.

For instance, as people recognize the legacy of fossil fuel dependence and its consequences for global warming they reinterpret the past. The interstate highway system that once was the pathway to progress now appears as a narrow transport conduit for gas guzzlers. But the inertia of the prior commitments, what Latour describes as an assemblage, resists easy change. Those working to promote the 'reality' of climate change must work hard to overcome these commitments. For Beauregard spatial planners seek to make climate change 'obdurate' – the 'new normal' for energy policy guiding urban development.

Judgment: Professional planning ideas and efforts do not substitute for organizing and political choice; but the plan advice offers alternative conceptions of the future that include interactions among competing ideas including practical tradeoffs and compromise described in terms of specific physical and environmental changes. Beauregard warns against embracing unifying schemes or one-sided proposals that masquerade as the public good. He recognizes that the meaning of future consequences requires that the relevant agents be included in the deliberations before (or as) decisions are made. The spatial planners can and should organize such involvement, but not as advocates for one or another agent or interest. They can and should make recommendations for an option if publicly and critically informed deliberation about the imagined effects offer evidence of beneficial consequences. The complexity of each situation precludes certainty. Taking responsibility for such practical judgment requires courage along with political sensitivity and strategy.

Beauregard embraces liberal democracy of the pragmatist sort. He recognizes that professional planners rarely pursue elective office or organize communities; but they can and should make plans that identify and describe problems that publics can 'gather round' (p.187). Beauregard calls this the politics of enunciation. This means telling people how a complicated set of government institutions and practices can shape their concerns and offer useful solutions while showing how local governments are constrained as well. How can such activist public planning work? Beauregard imagines a strong federal welfare state demonstrating how its powers may trump cavalier capital mobility and local suburban municipal inequality.

Hopkins and Knapp

Hopkins and Knapp want professional planners to focus on plans as tools for shaping intentions about specific development related options. He envisions plan making as ubiquitous, provisional and advisory. Professional planners should enter any planning situation or setting for a place identifying the other actors who care about the future for the place and include their plans. Hopkins (2001) study of plan making tells professionals what to look for and more recently how to collect and offer information to those involved to improve the quality of decisions for future land development.

Representation: Hopkins urges professional spatial planners to focus on decision situations that emerge as opportunities for plan making. Causes flow from the nexus of decisions and actions shaping land development. Instead of following the familiar protocol for comprehensive plans, consider making plans according to their relevance and meaning for complex development decisions that pose serious consequences for the actors tied to the future place. He proposes the following:

Identify important development related decisions
Describe the specific situations tied to these decisions
Identify opportunities to influence such decisions with advice
Set the scope to include the mix of interactions functionally relevant for the situation
Identify and assess future consequences for interactions considering four I's
Include relevant actors fostering attention and response to their plans for the situation.

Interpretation: Plans may take shape as an agenda, vision, policy, design or strategy. Select one or more depending on the kind of decision situation. If making and using a list of actions to set priorities, allocate resources, or more describes the situation; then set an agenda. If articulating and expressing beliefs about future expectations describes the situation; then focus on shaping a vision. If concerns about making and following a set of rules consistently describes the situation; then focus on shaping policy. If detailing the logical order for the development of a place describes the situation; then focus on improving the design. If concerns about the interaction among the interests and intentions of many actors describes the situation; then focus on strategy making. In this last instance Hopkins offers some prescriptions for selecting among 'decision' situations facing relevant agents based on interdependence, irreversibility, indivisibility and uncertainty generated by interactions with the environment (context), other agents and among different beliefs/values.

Judgment: Spatial planners compose alternative options within each form comparing different actions and imagined effects for resolving the situation. These may occur within a deliberative setting, but as the scope increases so do the number of agents pursuing different plans for a place. The publicly organized planning meetings by professional staff include only a small portion of the many land development discussions and decisions that organize investment, construction and more.

Hopkins and Knapp (2018) propose that spatial planners make a public plan of ordered expectations for a municipality, county or public agency; but also collect and prepare information about the provisional schemes of other development actors. Make this information available so that all actors can better comprehend and judge how to collaborate and compete. Agents involved in complex development for a place may compete or contest with others over the purchase and disposition of land and property. In these settings where political competition and contest can preclude deliberation, the actors may make it known that they have made plans and so taken steps to act. Some actors might use knowledge of their respective plans to find common ground for coordinating their actions to favorably influence political competition in their favor. Hopkins urges professionals to help articulate information about these plans helping agents signal their intentions and then learn from these how to modify and pursue their plans. This can encourage a more robust and democratic contest for political attention and decision.

This approach reduces the gap between plan and implementation (Kaza, Hopkins, & Knapp 2016). Hopkins wants to move beyond a too rigid 'plan then act' distinction adopted by scholars who envision plans as conduits for doctrine, policy or action. The plan may work like a blueprint or design with implementation describing how closely the constructed place conforms to plan proposals. The degree of correspondence measures the degree of implementation. Treating plans as provisional signals captures the active quality of plans as tools for directing attention and effort to specific ends susceptible to review and alteration. Help agents navigate the currents of strategic uncertainty.

Interpretive Findings

How can we use ideas from each planning analyst to understand the plans and the planner accounts of how they made their respective plans? I apply the ideas of each theorist using the relationships among conceptions of planning offered in Chapter 3. Movement refers to professional and government conceptions of urban plans. Discipline includes the scientific, artistic and academic conceptions of urban plans. Field encompasses the vast diversity of plans people use that shape urban places (see Chapter 3). This approach enables the user to use each theory putting their different interpretations to practical use making sense of plan making.

Movement to Discipline

Talen's approach would embrace the new urbanist focus of the Orland Park planners over the regulatory land planning by the Frankfort staff. The Orland Park planners enjoy local leadership that has expressed a commitment to place building rather than rule following land development. Interestingly the developers are on board as well. Even though Talen and Knapp (2003) found little evidence of new urbanist or smart growth implementation in Illinois this case testifies to the diffusion of a place focused approach. The OP planners integrate the principles of physical diversity, connectivity, mix tied to purposeful civic places; even as they sidestep the principle of equity. The Frankfort planners embrace the conventional focus on land management tied to functional norms embedded in zoning and subdivision codes. They hope to improve the efficiency and efficacy of greenfield transformation. The gradual intermingling of small scale subdivision combined with increased land speculation by regional developers offered an interesting adaptation that posed a classification challenge. The update did not provide an opportunity to introduce new principles, but an opportunity to assess the threat of subpar subdivisions not properly aligned with future roadway and sewer system expansion. Theirs was a clever defensive approach assuring that Frankfort land regulation would eventually order new development to the south just as before. Suburban plans serving an anti-urban development system.

Movement to Field

Beauregard would insist planners for both places carved out sites for purposeful action within complex places along Chicago's suburban fringe. The Frankfort planners may not champion new urbanist principles, but they do take steps to alert Village officials in 'sleepy' Frankfurt to awaken to the threats of land development that challenges both the officials' sense of place and municipal authority. The county level map not only helped the staff recognize the wider scope of causal agents (e.g., interstate extensions, multimodal freight centers, airports), including institutional actors and the physical objects that they cast as magnets activating demand for future residential dwellings. The Frankfort staff narrative showed how the tools of the trade (GIS digital computation and display, first hand field observations and meeting with residents about expectations about future land use change) shaped their conception of the planning situation.

Beauregard would recognize the care taken by the Orland Park planners as they framed and articulated the future land plan. The Frankfort staff had handed off most of the plan making work to consultants, but the Orland Park staff composed and produced the plan including elected officials and Village staff not only to build legitimacy, but to improve quality and efficacy in ways that bound intention and action more closely together. The complexity of the visual land maps used to project and display future plans for each municipal district spoke to a diverse assortment of potential users. The brief notes about future intention tied to different features of each site showed how the imagined interaction effects might arise (good and bad) in relation to specific proposals for different types of infrastructure improvements and land use changes. The Baroque enunciation of multiple overlapping possibilities reduced graphic simplicity while inviting reconsideration of current conditions.

Beauregard would note how the Orland Park planners took important steps to build publics for the comp plan; not only the Village board, but municipal staff, other planners, civic activists and local developers. They did not claim superior technical expertise or moral principle but put their methods to use in practical ways that altered their daily routine to carve out times for deliberation among different relevant agents whose life and work might be touched by the plan. Most of these meetings remained close to home involving familiar folks. The shift from rule following to place making integrated the interests and expectations of others into the fabric of the plan. Beauregard would, however, remind us of the limits in play. Equity and diversity remained stunted by the undercurrent of conventional residential income and racial segregation across the region.

Field to Discipline

Lew Hopkins and Knapp would focus on how the planners adopted a scope that included the plans of other relevant actors shaping future land development in and around Orland Park. What started out as an agenda building policy focused comp plan became over time a plan organized to embrace rather than tame the complexity of place making on the metro edge. The staff planners did not project an image of a future land use configuration and then imagine developers fitting into a singular framework. They used new urbanist and conventional land management principles to mediate the future goals. Recognizing the salience of other intentions in play they prepared plans that detailed what these (and related) plan intentions might mean for future land use changes within different parts of the Village.

Hopkins would commend the map notations used in this plan as the staff adopted their approach after a 2011 Champaign Urbana plan prepared by Bruce Knight (then current president of the American Planning Association); who learned some of his planning craft from Hopkins who taught planning at the University of Illinois.

The Frankfort planners literally conducted field research, but their functional classification effort buried the very kinds of detail about future intentions for specific places that Hopkins urges us to study and use. The map they created to make a visual argument about the potential development impact of regional scale improvements was the right idea, but they did not go far enough. What were the plans in play for the agents involved and how did their intended actions intersect and interact? Instead of addressing the strategic complexity the map implied, the Frankfort planners treated the image as a picture illustrating cumulative effects. Their commitment to the comp plan protocol constrained their vision to municipalities competing for jurisdictional control over future county land development.

These brief interpretive accounts of planning theorists offer an illustration of how we can use different theories to offer distinct coherent and complementary understanding of the same comprehensive plan making cases. Why do accounts of planning cases usually rely on a single theory? The pragmatist traces that attachment to prior learning. Students and new professionals learn to adopt that theory as a kind of justifying doctrine guiding research and practice. The same pragmatist sensibility invites us to reconsider that attachment and adopt a more inclusive approach. Theories offer competing conceptions that may offer important insights when used to grasp and inform judgments for urban planning. Planning theories provide tools for inquiry rather than justification for belief.

Conclusion

Plans mostly offer a mix of good and bad advice. Partly this results from the complexity of the causes and purposes. The pragmatist focus on situations anticipates this ambiguity and contingency. Plans for all three theorists conceive plans as dynamic tools rather than blueprints or foundations setting conclusive proposals for future development. Plans offer provisional ongoing reconsideration of troublesome spatial situations susceptible to purposeful intervention.

The comprehensive plan becomes less a convergent culmination or completion of community goals; and more a periodic holistic reconsideration of current spatial challenges and opportunities using different ideas and views about the future. The plan for a single uniform public should be recast as a complex combination of many proposals for the future coordinated through creative provisional experimentation. Good advice fits the functional demands of the spatial situation even as it includes and expands the views of different ideas and people.

I reviewed three very different contemporary planning theories to show how very different views may offer complementary ways to conceive and evaluate the plan making activity of professional planners. We can use these ideas because they do not align with one another along the same dimensions of judgment. Embracing different ideas for planning requires making moral and political commitments as well. Practical social virtues guide how people (including professionals) conceive, judge and act upon their plans in public even as professional principles of spatial planning shape how professional planners compose and offer advice. The craft of combining these moral sentiments shapes the meaning and relevance of the advice for specific actors facing a problem situation. Recognizing complexity means acknowledging moral ambiguity and the provisional quality of choices and decisions even as the professional offers recommendations for action. The good plan avoids didactic lessons or platitudes as it describes consequences in enough detail to allow users to consider the imagined effects of tradeoffs among competing moral and technical effects. The good plan also embodies democratic scientific inquiry improving judgments about collective efforts to remedy problems that include competing values, beliefs and viewpoints. Plans cannot set the good but inform those struggling to do good as they imagine options for action in the future. The next chapter considers how these efforts anticipate conceptions of community that challenge the provincial attachments and views that constrain what spatial planners can do.

References

Beauregard, B. (2016). *Planning Matter: Acting with Things*. Chicago: University of Chicago Press.

Ben-Joseph, E. (2003). *Subdivision Regulations: Practices and Attitudes A Survey of Public Officials and Developers in the Nation's Fastest Growing Single Family Housing Markets*, working paper. Cambridge, MA: Lincoln Land Institute.

Buzzelli, M. (2001). Firm size structure in North American housebuilding: Persistent deconcentration, 1945–1998. *Environment and Planning A*, 33(3), 533–550.

Frankfort Planning Department (2010). *Village of Frankfort 2010 Land Use Plan Update*. Frankfort, IL: Village of Frankfort.

Hopkins, L. (2001). *Urban Development: The Logic of Making Plans*. Washington, D.C.: Island Press.

Hopkins, L. and Knapp, G. (2018). Autonomous planning: Using plans as signals. *Planning Theory*, 17(2), 274–295.

Kaza, N., Hopkins, L. and Knapp, G. (2016). Vain foresight: Against the idea of implementation in planning. Paper presented at the ACSP Conference, Portland, Oregon, October.

Lanyi, C. S. (2013). Understanding the determinants of single family residential redevelopment in the inner-ring suburbs of Chicago. *Urban Studies*, 50(8), 1505–1522.

Lee, S. and Greenleigh, N. (2005). The role of inner ring suburbs in metropolitan smart growth strategies. *Journal of Planning Literature*, 19(3), 331–346. DOI: doi:10.1177/0885412204271878

Orland Park Planning Department (2013). *Village of Orland Park Comprehensive Plan*. Orland Park: Village of Orland Park.

Pijanowski, B. C. and Robinson, K. D. (2011). Rates and patterns of land use change in the Upper Great Lakes States, USA: A framework for spatial temporal analysis. *Landscape and Urban Planning*, 102, 102–116.

Talen, E. (2005). *New Urbanism and American Planning: The Conflict of Cultures*. New York: Routledge.

Talen, E. (2012). *City Rules: How Regulations Affect Urban Form*. Washington, D.C.: Island Press.

Talen, E. and Ellis, C. (2002). Beyond relativism: Reclaiming the search for good city form. *Journal of Planning Education and Research*, 22, 36–49.

Talen, E. and Knapp, G. (2003). Legalizing smart growth: An empirical study of land use regulation in Illinois. *Journal of Planning Education and Research*, 22, 345–359.

Part IV

9 Planning Spatial Community in a Complex Society

Between Solidarity and Contract

Spatial planning is a moral enterprise. As professional planners offer advice about what we should do now to prepare for the future, they make moral claims. According to Seymour Mandelbaum (2000) we often justify these claims either by appeal to universal principles or communal norms. He exhibits little confidence in either the invention or discovery of transcendent guidance and adopts a communitarian outlook that insists we rely on familiar concepts of community to frame our moral deliberation.

Mandelbaum describes three kinds of community: deep, thin and open; each tied respectively to a different social relationship: solidarity, contract and respect. We draw upon each conception of community as we conduct our lives in urbanized liberal democracies. We join religious communities and marry, buy homes and pay taxes, and we negotiate among competing claims that different communities make upon us. He warns us not to extend the expectations of solidarity and contract too far into the public arena of contested collective choice. We should rely instead upon a respect for a kind of deliberation that enjoins and engages competing claims for public attention and collective choice. We should adopt the conception of open moral communities.

The political meaning varies with different theoretical ideas about community scope and inclusion. Rosenblum (1987) distinguishes three sorts of communitarian approaches: direct, latent and pluralist. Benjamin Barber's (1984) work is direct; Alan Wolfe (1979) latent and Michael Walzer (1983, 1995) pluralistic. Mandelbaum shares this pluralist communitarian sensibility that envisions civility, tolerance and prudence animating stakeholder and citizen deliberation fostering liberal public orders. People use these virtues to negotiate and adjust memberships across different social communities without losing grip on an underlying sense of continuity and identity. The community members may speak at cross purposes or disagree. They continue the conversation because they publicly recognize and respect one another.

How do people come to recognize and respect strangers? I believe that the infrastructure for civility requires planning and civic virtue. For Mandelbaum participating in public deliberation requires that neighbors actively shift viewpoints and positions, and that they do this traversing different communities in a liberal society. I will argue that we need not expect so much. It is enough if people making plans for others conduct deliberations to meet expectations for public accountability that include relevant common needs and goods. Publicity offers credible assurance even as it falls short of the kind of deliberation that professional planners often seek to promote.

The Challenge to Plan Deliberation

Public deliberation in the service of a liberal democracy faces three sorts of challenge: cultural differences, social inequality and social complexity. Members of a community who resist any effort to consider the value of other cultures will not enter public deliberation prepared to consider other views. Those people who endure the burdens of poverty, racial subordination and other forms of repression cannot deliberate with those who subject them or benefit from their subjection. People must pass a certain threshold of cultural tolerance and social justice before deliberation will be legitimate and effective. But it is the third criteria of social complexity that has the greatest relevance for planning deliberation. The consequences that ensue from an unexpected natural or social disaster may fall unevenly on minorities and economic subordinates; but the effects can damage the majority and the wealthy as well. The history of urban settlements has always included inequality, but in the face of social and natural adversity and uncertainty solidarity has emerged. The fitful unions established across segmented factions can generate opportunities for military, infrastructure and environmental plans to take shape.

For Mandelbaum (1979) we adopt many tools to anticipate and manage the complexities of social coordination, but he worries about those analysts and experts who hope to remedy social complexity. Complexity accompanies a pluralistic society. He criticizes efforts to tame complexity using systematic rational inquiry. I take his warning, but remind us that we rely upon a vast network of institutional and infrastructure systems that use the powers of instrumental rationality to make urban living predictable for most inhabitants. The experts who design and manage these systems may pursue their specialized ends without attending to the consequences for others, but they may also recognize the interdependence and invent ways to anticipate and coordinate this interaction. I make the case that all of us can and do make plans as we navigate social complexity; a capacity that may inform more ambitious spatial planning efforts for the kinds of community Mandelbaum wants to keep open.

I describe and analyze two brief illustrations of public planning deliberations to illustrate these differences and draw out the implications for how we recognize the democratic quality of planning deliberations and how these insights might lead us to improve plans. We can, I think, take Mandelbaum's critical insight that we enliven and improve the quality of public deliberation using a robust pluralism. However, binding that pluralism together will take more than respectful reciprocity and civic virtue, it requires that we do plans and planning to help guide collective decisions in an increasingly complex and interdependent world. Planning and plan making play an important role coordinating these complex relationships. My argument is less a critique of the eloquent liberalism Mandelbaum describes and illustrates in his book, then an effort to show that using a few pragmatic distinctions and criticisms can make planning an important if more prosaic tool for coping with complexity. The demands of planning practice and the consequences of practical judgment test the limits of an irony that remains too aloof.

Deliberation

In *Open Moral Communities* Seymour Mandelbaum weds moral ideals to the ongoing context of human social life in communities. His viewpoint is inescapably interpretive. Communities should not be confused with places (e.g., a neighborhood or suburb), groups (e.g., women, elderly) and institutions (e.g., City Hall or the Corporation). Although communities assign meanings to places and artifacts (e.g., graffiti, logos, façade style), places do not act. When we say that Chicago works or the flag stands for our honor these actions live only in our rhetoric and not in the objects or their relations. Groups formed by shared characteristics, risk, interest or opportunity (e.g., Hispanics, the homeless, pedestrians and homeowners) do not create community. Community members use shared norms to guide judgment and behavior and the ensuing meaning of membership. The homeless Hoboes a century ago created a community that the current homeless would neither recognize nor enter.

Institutions organize some of the same social territory as communities but emphasize structural order. Communities include the social relations and actions that people use to interpret, comply and shape the underlying order. Members select and modify the rules as they proceed. Mandelbaum adopts a communitarian version of institutions exploring how we invent and adapt institutions to meet community needs or cope with community problems. Community membership invests meaning in the places, groups and institutions. Members receive rights and assume obligations that exclude those unwilling or unable to comply.

Pluralism

We belong to many communities and in our liberal society these multiple memberships may overlap, cohere and conflict without an underlying or overarching community order. The pluralistic variety and complexity requires that each of us reconcile the differences among them. Mandelbaum adopts a prudent voice as he describes the fragmented field of communities. He remains deeply suspicious of new and improved social contracts that promise to sidestep or trump the complex entanglements and interdependencies that sustain a contested and negotiated order across the complex field of interdependencies. Mandelbaum comprehends community by studying the acquisition of habits of action and thought shaped within a particular network of memberships acquired over time. Offering designs for new communities within this outlook should generate rich and detailed accounts of what people do rather than spare analytic reviews of correspondence between covenant and compliance. He admits that this approach appears conservative as the weight of precedent, history, context and complexity tames hopes for sweeping change.

The Tyranny of a Common Good

Throughout his book Mandelbaum shows how efforts to use concepts: theory, story, time, tools, cities and plans to simplify the complexity of a pluralistic world paradoxically betray the hope for coherence and consistency (the complexity persists). Each concept imposes public order and discipline that diminish our freedom and capacity for moral stature. The effort to imagine, design and plan for a singular and complete order leads to paradoxical failure. We cannot and should not use clever ideas to tame complexity.

We adapt to the increasing division of labor and social interdependence of modern life by altering community boundaries in hopes of taming this complexity. Mandelbaum argues that our efforts to produce inclusive and coherent institutional orders to tame the externalities and inequalities among diverse communities impose too abstract a standard at too grand a scale. Adopting an inclusive, uniform and universal standard of desert strips people of their standing as moral actors by abstracting from the specific features of community membership that make moral commitments meaningful. The deserving needy become passive recipients instead of moral actors. We turn communities of actors into groups filled with needy clienteles.

The Cosmopolitan Pluralist

For Mandelbaum the combination of pluralism and openness together takes shape as we shift allegiance between inherited belief and contractual agreement. We learn to release our hold on some elements of communal solidarity and to embrace those elements cherished by members of another community. Mandelbaum as a cosmopolitan believes that meeting with strangers awakens us to important differences that prove useful and fulfilling. But as communities vie with one another for survival, prosperity and ascendancy they risk damaging the network of respect members use to keep the pathways that link them unobstructed. What keeps doors open? How do we learn to respect one another across our differences and maintain it?

Mandelbaum identifies two complementary sensibilities that nurture open communities: a belief in the efficacy of overlapping similarities and a willingness to use public interpretation to navigate the passageways among them. He rejects the idea of adopting an 'original position' (Rawls) to remove injustice or 'ideal speech communication' (Habermas) to remedy distortions in communication. Both appeal to a kind of perfectionism that does not want to submit to the inescapable mix of underlying community relations.[1] An open communitarianism attends to "the conditions that create, sustain, and recreate limited communions; to the work of attracting and transforming resources, socializing new recruits, disciplining members, and relating to outsiders" (Mandelbaum 2000, p.53).

Mandelbaum's rhetorical strategy anticipates an openness many critics may find hard to accept. First, some argue that irony represents a burden, wound or violation. They resent the proliferation of communities, not so much the multiplicity, but the egalitarian sensibility that tolerates plurality and the ensuing moral relativism. Such critics loathe the kind of ironic citizen Mandelbaum takes for granted. These critics may include deep communitarians embracing exclusive doctrinal norms (e.g., religious fundamentalists), but also shallow contractarians emphasizing strong individualism (e.g., the Wise Use movement). These believers prefer synecdoche to irony; doctrines over deals; consensus without compromise.

Second, other critics believe that hope for democratic deliberation among diverse communities remains segmented and stratified by an underlying terrain of social inequality, cultural exclusion, and social complexity. For these critics Mandelbaum presumes what need be more vigorously challenged and reformed. We cannot meaningfully play the role of ironic communitarian shifting among communities because too many doors remain shut and the topography of access woefully uneven. I want to focus on the second group of critics, placing myself among them.

Revising the Deliberative Ideal: James Bohman

Political theorist James Bohman (1996) shares many of the same ideas about deliberation as Mandelbaum, but with a less poetic and more pragmatic orientation. He argues that public deliberation is a form of interpersonal public dialog – the give and take of reasons in social contexts. The dialogue begins with problematic situations where coordination breaks down and succeeds when actors are able to cooperate again. Success does not require consensus for an alternative, but agreement to continue cooperating. So as people publicly cooperate in dialogue exchanging reasons with equal standing and effective voice they find comparisons among alternatives convincing even if the outcome differs from the one they desire. Bohman (1996) distinguishes between public discourse where arguments may prove convincing and public dialogue where participants learn about the effects that make reasons convincing (p.34)

Bohman identifies the conditions necessary for such dialog to succeed: non-tyranny, equality and publicity. Non-tyranny speaks to the central democratic ideal that citizens decide their shared fate and so rely upon some method to prevent or resist the concentration of power. Political equality requires that all citizens be included and that the influence of non-political inequalities (e.g., wealth or status) be excluded. When people use control over distribution of one good to control distribution of another they generate political subordination. Buying votes or harassing subordinates at work are examples of tyranny that generate political inequality (Walzer 1983). Publicity refers to the kind of social space where deliberation occurs and to the kinds of reasons citizens propose. Publicity ensures that all the speakers can participate effectively in the social space of debate. Deliberation has weak publicity if participants know the rationale (e.g., Do we know what's on the agenda for tonight's meeting?), and strong publicity if participants can use the rationale to shape the dialog (Do we know what's at stake at tonight's meeting?). The first two conditions usually take center stage in the analysis of deliberation, but I will focus on publicity because it invites the use of planning.

Publicity

"Publicity works on three levels: it creates the social space for deliberation, it governs processes of deliberation and the reasons produced in them, and it provides a standard by which to judge agreements" (Bohman 1996, p.37). The social spaces range from the jury room to legislative chamber and with respect to planning from stakeholder meeting to public hearing. In each case the space makes room for dialog. The reasons need be comprehensible and potentially acceptable to the participants. Appeals to reasons tied exclusively to a particular community, for instance, a religious community or advocacy group, fail the publicity test.

For Mandelbaum and Bohman it is enough for deliberations to keep the conversation going; consensus may be accomplished, but only on special occasions. Both believe deliberation involves more than argument. Both acknowledge the important role of public deliberation in taming the uncertainty generated by the social complexity of modern societies. Both emphasize that deliberations make it possible to critically consider, compare, reconcile or reject differences.

Mandelbaum distinguishes between thin and thick conceptions of membership. As we engage in public deliberations we do not speak to everyone as members of a group, but as members of specific communities tied together by mutual respect. Public openness mobilizes this respect enabling participants to listen to the reasons offered for different alternatives reaching a joint understanding without imposition of an external frame of reference or viewpoint. We learn to adapt and try out new reasons within a framework of mutual respect at once both familiar and strange.

For Bohman, as we make and offer public reasons we direct them to an unrestricted and hence inclusive or singular audience taking pains to make them comprehensible and testable. This makes the deliberation publicly convincing because reasons are not tied to a specific faction, community or interest. For Bohman, the dialog can lift us out of our pre-conceptions and commitments not because the ideas echo or resemble familiar attachments, but because the reasons speak to a public. Public deliberation is more than the mutual interpretation of diverse reasons among participants. Participants deliberate to solve problems or resolve conflicts. Public deliberation does not edify, but repairs social cooperation

Bohman's conception of publicity is less restrictive than Mandelbaum's concept of public interpretation. Both emphasize the exchange of reasons, but for Bohman the meaning of publicity flows not from mutual respect – recognizing the value of others – but from accountability to the public. Bohman envisions deliberation as a dialogue that depends on "the accountability of intelligible action to others and the reflexive ability of actors to continue cooperation by extending accountability to all actors and to new situations" (Bohman 1996, p.54). When deliberating about a planning policy at a public hearing we need not offer reasons that respect the interests of each participant, but reasons that an indefinite public of citizens find comprehensible and convincing.

Social Complexity and Spatial Planning

Bohman argues that deliberation in the context of complex modern societies face important institutional constraints. Deliberation that addresses a large and inclusive public relies upon a coherent and consistent set of coordinated institutional relationships (Bohman 1996, p.66). Successful deliberation relies upon an infrastructure that affords coherence and consistency over time and space. This echoes the distinctions that Bratman (1987) uses in his analysis of small 'p' planning introduced in Chapter 1. Spatial planning contributes to the formation of this infrastructure by coordinating these relationships temporally and spatially. Planning provides the framework for judging alternatives by relying on collaboration informed and shaped by the institutional linkage of professional intelligence and social reciprocity.

As citizens of post-industrial society we take for granted the engineered systems that enable us to avoid uncertainty and so make our own way of life more predictable. The morning and evening commute, shopping at the supermarket, uninterrupted cell phone service, standard fast food fare and so forth form layers of systematic routine. The vast array of utilities, appliances, conveyances and procedures that make the common pursuit of individual purposes among millions a matter of routine goes largely unexamined until something goes seriously awry.

> The virtue of rationally designed laws, scientific principles, airline networks, telephone systems, and motel chains is that they will work as they are expected to when one calls on them ... The conditions of

freedom in modern society thus depend not only on the rational consistency of law, but on that of a variety of organized, coordinated performances. Whatever the number of competing firms, the 'standard practices' – of the medical system, the housing system, the agricultural system, the educational system – are not discretionary goods and services, produced by the market in response to the varying nuances of consumer demand. They are, rather, structured processes, products of an evolutionary collective process of rational analysis. The justification for such rational enterprises is not so much that they reflect individual will, but more that they represent a sustained effort to reduce the degree of arbitrariness in the provision of an important service (Anderson 1990, pp.104–105).

The problem with social complexity is that it exceeds public accountability. These bureaucratic institutions need be modified to include public deliberation. The work by John Forester (1989, 1999) has focused on this problem offering ways to introduce deliberation into a diverse assortment of institutional settings – especially those doing planning. But Forester adopts a liberalism less tied to aesthetic ideals of autonomy and self-perfection and more attuned to ideals of freedom and justice.

Mandelbaum treats complexity in liberal societies as an expression of plural communities. As we negotiate the boundaries of overlapping communities we support or withdraw from institutions and adjust to the complex demands of inter-organizational fields. We do rely on a complex division of labor and specialized expertise – but these liberal social orders escape efforts to plan them. Plans and planning are simply specialized parts and so unable to coordinate the encompassing field.

Planning, Coordination and Social Complexity

The ubiquity of planning among individuals, organizations and groups generates uncertainty even as each actor carves out a domain of familiar predictable relationships. As each comprehends the meanings that others use to manage their relations they learn to coordinate behavior and successfully adapt to expectations and actions within the family, firm, school and other hands-on domain. How we do this involves both cognitive and emotional learning. Thinking uses concepts to order the relationships while emotional attachments fuel and flavor the repertoire of feelings we rely upon to select, compare and inform our actions. We learn to plan as part of our development from child to adult; and render a complex social and physical world susceptible to coordinated action.

The social complexity of modern urban living involves us in interactive systems where our tacit planning skill proves less useful. The practical fit between plan and intention that made coordinating a meeting easy proves elusive in the face of competing goals, institutional segmentation, overlapping communities, technological variations, specialized knowledge and more.

Trying to tame this complexity using systemic knowledge abstracts the contextual and relational details needed to fit plan and intention. Rational plans that envision forms of order that simplify relationships within a more general and abstract hierarchy do not work. Mandelbaum provides a compelling critique of such plans. He does an excellent job analyzing the rhetorical problems inherent in writing comprehensive rational plans for socially unequal and politically complex cities and regions. The authors for the wrote to an ideal audience portraying a simple and unified conception of a complex region.

Reading Plans Critically

Mandelbaum reads the *Plan for Philadelphia* in three complementary ways: offering arguments about policy, design opportunities and as stories. Policy claims fit inputs and outputs together as elements of the city system. Mandelbaum analyzes some unsubstantiated and vague policy claims to show how a critical rewrite can clarify the claims and offer choices to new audiences previously ignored. Reading for design opportunities Mandelbaum finds incoherence as descriptions of Center City alternate between purposeful actor and passive object. His analysis uncovers multiple audiences with conflicting relationships. Finally, he recasts the plan into stories, elaborating alternative plots for policy claims; and creating characters, relationships and actions that turn ambiguous design opportunities into competing narratives.

Mandelbaum punctures the rhetoric of certainty highlighting the ambiguity that accompanies the effort to make comprehensive plans for big city. This analytical insight encourages a skeptical readership but does not tell what professionals might do as they make spatial plans for complex places. He does warn the professional to find ways to take responsibility even as spatial plans take shape as composite artifacts. Mandelbaum reminds us that as spatial plans are made, the relevant actors (professionals, politicians and many other participants) craft a set of policies, designs and processes that anticipate future decisions about a specific set of inescapable interdependencies and uncertainties. The spatial plan provides the scaffolding for a tentative agreement about future activities within a limited context (e.g., center city, the corridor, a product cycle) speaking to different audiences. The plan and the publics whose future it considers remain a work in progress.

The plan cannot work like a deal or contract offering a firm *quid pro quo* for the future. It must remain ambiguous and incomplete: ambiguous because as people use the plan to guide decisions, the ensuing consequences generate unexpected interdependencies and uncertainties that require adjustment; and incomplete because the plan remains open to future changes in goals and methods. These qualities pose a serious problem for the professional authors. The author cannot write the plan as a narrative without excluding many of those affected, and as Mandelbaum's critique makes evident, seeking to write like God will encourage no serious readership at all – at least among those who read with irony. It may be better to think of a plan as a kind of reference document that combines elements of dictionary, a tour guide, a chart and a map that all direct attention to a set of ongoing relationships that those using the plan can recognize and use to coordinate future collective action in time and space. This book offers arguments and examples for doing this. How do we discriminate plans that offer good advice from those that do not?

Telling Good Plan Deliberation from Bad

I compare two brief illustrations of planning deliberation about plans to illustrate how the distinctions Bohman uses provide a useful frame of reference for comparing the quality of deliberation and so assess opportunities for improving plan deliberation.

The Chicago Housing Authority Case

In November of 1999 the Chicago Housing Authority (CHA) held its last public meeting on the HOPEVI Plan for Transformation in an auditorium at the Chicago Merchandise Mart. Over 300 public housing residents attended, most delivered by CHA supplied buses. Hundreds of copies of the draft redevelopment plan were stacked at tables outside each entrance to the hall. The meeting included presentations by the city appointed executive director, Phillip Jackson, and the then newly appointed chief of staff for the mayor, Julia Stash. Both Jackson and Stash had a history of community and public accomplishment. Neither comes to their position through the ranks of the aging patronage machine.

Staff roamed the hall with microphones and clip boards. After the speeches ended and comments began individual tenants voiced particular grievances about their dwellings and buildings, raised doubts about the prospects for future security and voiced concerns about their future role implementing the plan. In each case Jackson and Stash respond with diligent respect. Staff people record the comments on their clip boards. In some cases Jackson sent staff scurrying to the site of a complainant to offer immediate attention and assistance. Some in the audience roll their eyes, others cluck their tongues and a few offer up hefty sighs of painful resignation – all signaling skepticism and disbelief.

The plan was largely set. Residents did not oppose improving their living environments. The older and more experienced ones had witnessed similar, if less dramatic, reforms before. Results had rarely squared with the proposal. The history of failure and legacy of abuse was not reviewed. The new leadership and staff played out the roles of sales managers making their proposed product line attractive to a skeptical target audience. The audience kept pushing for improvements and assurances at the margin, but offered only grudging acceptance. Discussion among staff and residents was formal and directed mainly to the two leaders standing at the front. The gulf of social and economic inequality separating managers and clients kept the exchange lopsided.

The Oak Park Case

A local resident completed a study documenting increasing racial concentration of students within some of the eight elementary schools for the Oak Park District 97 Elementary and Middle School District. The results made their way into the local newspaper and a political issue was born. Activists, officials, citizens, teachers and others began calling the District, the Village and the newspaper voicing concerns about the prospects of racial re-segregation in a suburban municipality with thirty years doing racial integration. District and Village officials together sponsor a special all day Saturday meeting to discuss the issue of racial change in the schools.

Three speakers open the day-long meeting. They do not defend current practices but raise questions about current policy. The questions do not attack current administrators but focus attention on different views about the problem of residential racial segregation in schools and housing. The problem has multiple dimensions that reflect different views about race, integration and the consequences of intervention strategies. The speakers represent these differences in their persons, views and reasoning. Empirical evidence of emerging segregation in several elementary schools provokes a flurry of heated exchanges as people offer different interpretations. After a morning of presentations with questions, answers and debates, the afternoon consists of break out groups. People engage in discussions about their views and attend to the views of others. The comments are recorded and eventually sent out to the participants who registered.

The results of the meeting are taken up at a meeting of the village council three months later. The council forms a joint Housing Education and Community Investment task force, carefully including members from the active constituencies. The officials ask the task force to make plans for actively reducing the threat of re-segregation while involving the efforts of the different parties. The issues raised in the earlier meeting are not lost, but organized into an ongoing action agenda. The committee includes members from the District, Village, Board of Realtors, civic associations, housing integration agencies, educational groups and individual citizens.

Comparing Cases

Despite the sincerity of the new CHA leadership and the genuine effort to invite participation, the meeting did not share access to the plan itself. Given a voice without authority the participants had difficulty taking the plan to heart. Most had not read the document that possessed the rhetorical features

Mandelbaum critiqued in his analysis of the *Plan for Center City* Philadelphia. It appeared more a threat than a promise. Conversation consisted mainly of strategic negotiations at the margins: concessions, adjustments and tradeoffs residents hoped to secure for their building before relocation officials showed up on the doorstep. The large public setting was not part of an ongoing dialog, but a crescendo marking a policy shift initiated by HUD and carried forth by a local reform administration. The public deliberations did not meet the test of publicity. The plans for mixed income residential settlements introduced lease agreements, price strategies and building schemes that changed a way of life replacing it with uncertain commitments. The residents had little understanding of what these proposals meant for them and what they could do to shape the options.

In contrast, the Oak Park citizens enjoyed public standing at the very outset. What participants said mattered enough to shape the local agenda. The exchange of ideas stimulated more involvement which resulted in a meeting where diverse ideas and arguments competed for attention and consent. The discussion resulted in formation of a task force that included people holding different viewpoints, but sharing a willingness to collaborate on an action plan to remedy racial concentration in the elementary schools. They agreed to continue cooperating even as they suspended final consent.

In the CHA case the efficacy of publicity was undermined by the incredulity of the claims the leadership made and the inability of the participants to hold the speakers accountable. In the Oak Park case the participants listened to their differences in a setting that enhanced the credibility of public officials while spreading responsibility practically among those people willing and able to take action. The politics of interest and advocacy took place among various parties but did not capture the planning activity nor lead into dead end conflicts. The different parties agreed to keep talking and planning together.

The Oak Park deliberations started out describing the facts of social inequality and cultural differences within the school and the community, providing a vocabulary for discussing planning ideas that sought remedies to school quality while anticipating and addressing the distortions of long-standing inequities and racial differences. The plans designed to remedy the complexities of demolishing and building new housing did little to reduce uncertainty among the CHA residents. The antagonism and mistrust between officials and residents inflamed cultural misunderstanding, while the optimistic promotion of income mixing inspired greater feelings of vulnerability and subordination.

The CHA plan did not inform deliberation but became another symbol of continued subordination. The proposals for helping remedy the complex problems besetting Chicago public housing were neither received nor comprehended by the residents. The Oak Park planning agenda provided a scaffold for the dialog that participants conducted. It did not detail outcomes, but raised questions and issues that participants used to create the relevant problem domains and avenues for directing future attention and inquiry. The Oak Park planning during the meeting distills a large array of issues and concerns into a set of related problems susceptible to independent coordinated action. The two examples illustrate even in this schematic version how planning can detract from or contribute to public deliberation.[2]

Conclusion

Citizens possessing strength of character and civic virtue can sustain shifts in public involvement during deliberation. They draw upon multiple layers of trust formed in diverse community memberships and then use these to cultivate a richer sense of self that can find a home in different places. This cosmopolitan character does not rely upon the skepticism of the calculating rationalist, but the aesthetic sensibility of poetic fulfillment. Mandelbaum critiques the Plan for Center City Philadelphia for projecting a mythic image that obscured the plurality of voices, viewpoints and interests. He deploys a critical detachment that makes practical collaboration for plan making seem too risky or foolish. Writing for an audience of scholars critical irony provides a shared recognition of differences. As scholars we adopt critical irony for our own enlightenment and edification. But the same irony proves much less useful finding common ground among diverse communities using their own idioms. As we write to a wider audience about the conduct of public deliberation critical irony may not leverage understanding, but stimulate mistrust, defensive withdrawal and resistance to cool detachment

Taking a pragmatic approach offers a division of cognitive labor that reduces the distance between planning expertise (large 'P' Planning) and common sense (small 'p' planning). This requires not only a belief that citizens possess the capacity to deliberate but requires a vigorous review of the institutional and contextual relationships that foster barriers to such an integration. As Bohman (1999, p.590) points out, the pragmatic attraction to deliberative forms of democracy does not simply mean plunking down face to face town hall meetings in every setting and locale. The social and institutional complexity of modern life require not only open debate among citizens, but

> socially organized deliberation on how best to achieve effective consensual ends. The latter requirement meant that democracy should not only employ the free and open deliberation of citizens, but also the best available methods of inquiry. Those methods are the methods of science, broadly understood as all cooperative and critical inquiry (Bohman 1999, pp.590–591).

Social Complexity, Communities and Communication

Difficulties emerge as political deliberation about plans and planning takes form in segmented domains of knowledge that frustrate and discourage public deliberation. This requires the creation of deliberative situations and institutions in which those affected by public decisions can assess the credibility of the specialists and influence the terms of their ongoing collaboration. No one can be competent in all domains of specialized knowledge. In effect, the intricate division of labor and social organization means that people must rely on others not only to cooperate, but for what they contribute to social intelligence. "Such dependence on others is a consequence of seeing intelligence as a genuinely social property, not merely as the extension of individual capacities and powers" (Bohman 1999, p.594).

We cannot rely upon trust and respect to make interdependent access to expertise feasible among members of a community. Bohman argues that trust cannot be the basis for such feasibility without sacrificing freedom from the tyranny of expertise. He argues that deliberation in the face of complexity, inequality and difference, relies upon public communication open to challenge. Publicity and not shared trust provides the practical basis for practical democratic deliberation. Publicity for Bohman (1996) means speaking to citizens who enjoy equal standing. The reasons offered in the dialog "must be communicated in such a way that any other citizen might be able to understand them, accept them, and freely respond to them in his or her own terms" (p.26).

For Mandelbaum prudent planning guides deliberations rather than a too egalitarian conception of justice. This prudence acknowledges and negotiates among, for instance, the complex division of authority organizing local governance. Prudence respects the complex overlapping memberships and commitments of different local governments and communities. This works but asks too much to outlook and character. Only the most articulate and cosmopolitan speaker can use irony as a tool for detachment without losing touch with her communities and becoming estranged. These cosmopolitans remain a relatively small community.

Finding Common Ground

When Mandelbaum critiques Rawls and Habermas as perfectionists, he rejects their quest for justice tied to universal rationality as imposing too great a loss in human freedom. They sacrifice the complex attachments to overlapping and antagonistic communities that make our freedom interesting and meaningful. He imagines us trading social meaning for abstract assurance. But these theorists point out social resources that we can access to resist and improve illiberal and repressive actions, policies and arguments. We can critique the trap of universal certainty without rejecting the possibility of filaments of rationality informing how we make sense of our obligations to one another no matter the communities that we claim or that claim us.[3] Our plans can still offer useful advice even as differences and conflict continue.

The two brief planning stories I constructed from my observations illustrate important differences in planning deliberations that attend to cultural differences, social inequalities and social complexity and those that do not.

As scholars and analysts, we use these distinctions to judge the moral superiority of the Oak Park to the CHA deliberations. But to make sense of the comparison we need also draw upon a belief in the legitimacy and efficacy of deliberation for both cases.

The public housing residents expressed cynicism precisely because they expected that their interests and voices would be part of the planning deliberation. The public order that sustains the hopes of the CHA residents even in the face of continued disregard relies upon a combination of thin and thick forms of solidarity The combination forms a union based on shared hope. The door symbolically portrayed in the public meeting remains shut, but they peer through the window and imagine what it would mean to travel through to the other side. This imaginative image rests upon expectations that include the absence of prejudice and cultural disregard. On the thick side, the plan describes goals and projects where such injustice is banished. The residents anticipate the plausibility of a new way of life deliberations where they enjoy the same public standing as anyone else. The CHA deliberations meet Bohman's publicity standard even as they fail to produce the kind of mutual learning and consensus that work by such planning theorists as Innes, Forester, and others describe. As scholars we recognize the irony in the CHA account, but it was not the irony that the residents can see. They expect the plan to make a difference.

The Oak Park residents used deliberation to help reduce and remedy the cultural and social divisions that undermined how the district managed school membership. They adopted participatory deliberation that emphasized interests rather than positions, ensured equal standing among participants, anticipated political distortion, fostered joint learning as part of the planning activity. The joint planning helped ensure thick layers of publicity.

Planning deliberation with this pragmatic emphasis seeks to identify and formulate planning alternatives for all those touched by the consequences. This expansive demand does not require a unitary summation or reconciliation of different schemes, but sufficient elaboration of each to enable people to recognize the meaning of the consequences and make comparisons about the relative merits of each. In the concluding chapter of his book on planning deliberation John Forester (1999) identifies three kinds of practical judgment as resources for doing this work: technical, political and social. As we combine efforts to assess the scope of the problem, set parameters, identify measures we find that we must ask questions about values, interests, preferences, attending to the many differences that emerge speaking with others whose characteristics, history and location set each apart and yet bring them together in public deliberation. The planning craft seeks to combine and coordinate these judgments in ways that draw upon the thin bonds that tie us together to frame the relevant assortment of values and meanings used to select and compare options. Wisely, I think, Forester does not tell a story that people should follow to plan well but uses the stories of many people doing planning to tell us how well we might plan. The irony in this inquiry loses its capacity to leverage critical detachment and instead fosters critical engagement. The next chapter focuses on how professional planners adopting a pragmatist approach can engage in morally sensitive and politically meaningful judgments as they craft spatial plans.

Notes

1 Mandelbaum is referring here to a reading of John Rawls and Jurgen Habermas respectively that treats each as more Kantian than pragmatic in their viewpoints.
2 We can subject these examples to the critical scrutiny of an ironic critique, and I made them easy prey. But the point here is to consider that when we try to bridge divides among participants that irony may not serve us very well and planning may.
3 I think Stan Stien and Thomas Harper offer useful examples of how a pragmatic adoption of Rawls insight as 'wide reflective equilibrium' can avoid any of what Philosophers would term a transcendental or Kanntian legacy. The work by John Forester has done the same for the ideas of Habermas. For a very thorough critical revision of Habermas using pragmatic ideas, see the book by Heath (2003).

References

Anderson, C. (1990). *Pragmatic Liberalism*. Chicago: University of Chicago Press.
Barber, B. (1984). *Strong Democracy*. Berkeley: University of California Press.
Bohman, J. (1996). *Public Deliberation: Pluralism, Complexity and Democracy*. Cambridge, MA: MIT Press.
Bohman, J. (1999). Democracy as inquiry, inquiry as democratic: pragmatism, social science and the cognitive division of labor. *American Journal of Political Science*, 43(2), 590–607.
Bratman, M. (1987). *Intention, Plans, and Practical Reason*. Cambridge, MA: Harvard University Press.
Forester, J. (1989). *Planning in the Face of Power*. Berkeley: University of California Press.
Forester, J. (1999). *The Deliberative Practitioner*. Cambridge, MA: MIT Press.
Heath, J. (2003). *Communicative Action and Rational Choice*. Cambridge, MA: MIT Press.
Mandelbaum, S. (1979). A complete general theory of planning is impossible. *Policy Sciences*, 1(1), 59–71.
Mandelbaum, S. (2000). *Open Moral Communities*. Cambridge, MA: MIT Press.
Rosenblum, N. (1987). *Another Liberalism: Romanticism and the Reconstruction of Liberal Thought*. Cambridge, MA: Harvard University Press.
Walzer, M. (1983). *Spheres of Justice: A Defense of Pluralism and Equality*. New York: Basic Books.
Walzer, M. (1995). *Thick and Thin: Moral Argument at Home and Abroad*. Notre Dame, IN: University of Notre Dame.

10 Ethical Planning Judgment

Introduction

Normative arguments about urban planning frequently follow paths philosophers make distinguishing judgments based on rules, consequences or virtue. In this chapter I consider how each approach considers compromise as an ethical problem. Adopting a pragmatist approach, I argue that rather than a moral problem, compromise offers an important moral resource for integrating different moral sensibilities and values making plans for complex practical problems. The ethical significance of compromise includes the integration of rules, goals and conduct in plans that anticipate and cope with complex environmental and social change. Compromise for planning does not abstract moral norms as guides independent of historical context and practical possibility. The shifting compromises fit within a developmental approach; testing the record for better outcomes tied to innovations in democratic conduct responsive to context over time. On this account compromise is not inherently bad even if it may yield bad outcomes. Pragmatic thought embraces enough give and take to explore the emergence of an uneven and incomplete common good sustained despite mutual antagonism. This robust conception of compromise can reconcile a diverse range of social differences and disparate moral claims. Good compromises typically include a mix of competing norms, goals, interests and desires that yield improvements judged better than prior or current practice. Good judgments about common goods from this pragmatist view distill the public interest even as many stakeholders remain dissatisfied. Some 'rotten' compromises will fail to do good because they increase suffering, foster exploitation, encourage domination or justify subjection that destroys reciprocity. These compromises fail the pragmatist test for goodness even as their proponents may produce convincing plans.

In many cases, the idea of compromise also denotes a kind of moral failure. For instance, the practitioner who glosses over the facts, selectively distracts a client raising a valid critique, or occasionally lies to meet client expectations violates a threshold of social trust. Compromising the truth to persuade clients that a plan correctly responds to a problem is on this account wrong (Wachs 1985). Additionally, the practitioner who adjusts forecast assumptions to make a future infrastructure project appear more efficient and fiscally feasible compromises the efficacy of moral assessment (Fyvberg 2005). Cases where professionals compromise ethical principles to achieve political and personal advantages deserve moral censure (Barrett 2001). The pragmatist treats the singular and legible violation of rules, distortion of truth or character flaw as matters for routine correction and sanction. The tough ethical issues emerge as multiple goals and goods compete for attention in complex situations that compose the places people inhabit.

Pragmatism rejects the quest for moral perfection whether tied to moral integrity, optimal utility or heroic virtue. These normative orientations reflect philosophical theories that offer doctrine and method as foundations for action. Pragmatism considers ethical norms within the context of a developmental conception of human evolution and history. The modern promise of self-development both as a resource and product of purposeful inquiry and practical experimentation (Unger 2007) adopts different meanings in disparate circumstances. One size does not fit all. Instead of relying upon moral ideals to guide conduct planning, I believe professional practitioners can and should focus upon constructing forms of compromise that improve the provision and allocation of complex goods for places. Ideals set a moral horizon, but do not offer useful signposts for making an ethical journey. The efficacy and meaning of better planning, as seen from this perspective, depends on how well those sharing the consequences of the plan comprehend, consent and benefit from inescapable practical tradeoffs made conceiving the paths to take.[1] Ethical compromise reconciles goals as situational tradeoffs informing intention at the threshold of action (Sheppard 2003).

I recast the strong distinctions between public, common and private goods as differences in degree, not kind. Ethical relevance for planning practice depends on how practitioners conceive relevance, context and use in specific spatial situations. Instead of exhorting practitioners to be just or accomplish the optimal good, we would do better exploring how different plan makers conceive and reconcile many ethical beliefs and ideals as they make and persuade others to follow their spatial plans. Professionals can and should learn the laws, rules, customs and methods that describe the range of norms and principles relevant for the discipline. But meaningful practical ethical judgment requires paying attention to what plan makers do in the context of a complex situation where moral, social and political differences shape the problems that emerge. We can learn from detailed narrative accounts of plan making and implementation in complex settings.

Compromise and Moral Judgment

Philosophers have distilled philosophical approaches to moral thought into three types of moral judgment: rules, consequences and conduct (MacIntyre 1990). MacIntyre contends that these arguments about the ethics of cultural identity, legal obligation and justice focus on transcendent universal norms. The books written about planning ethics acknowledge these intellectual contours (Wachs 1985, Hendler 1995; Thomas 1994), even as they recognize that practitioners make practical judgments that fall short of ideals. Practical compromise appears a moral failure.

The pragmatic approach combines an Aristotelian attention to virtue with a developmental naturalism. Aristotle recognized that sound ethical judgment integrates competing virtues to address the ambiguity, conflict and relevance of practical demands in a specific situation (Schwartz & Sharpe 2005). The conduct of practical wisdom contrasts with utilitarian practical intelligence. Intelligence fits ends to means while wisdom reconciles differences in purpose and method. Much social science evaluation uses clever methods to assess the impact of social norms or individual preferences for global or aggregate measures of satisfaction or happiness (Abbott 2000). However, these studies abstract from crucial temporal and contextual relationships crucial for planning. The talk of modernist moral failure usually includes the foolish deployment of a clever utilitarian analysis like net benefit analysis for some huge engineering project (Hall 1982; Flyvbjerg 2005). The pragmatist does not reject using a utilitarian calculus but limits the use for familiar predictable social problems.

The pragmatic approach embraces practical reason that combines the cognitive and emotional powers of memory, imagination and feeling to compose plans sensitive to conduct and consequence; virtue and purposeful good. This approach does not offer rational generalizations about what to do as rules or principles. Pragmatic rationality treats plan making as part of the very architecture of judgment. The imaginative creation of alternatives for action that plausibly and meaningfully address consequences for others integrate evaluation and analysis. The critical assessment of consequential interaction effects for select combinations of goals and methods among stakeholders makes ensuing compromise more intelligent and ethical (Fesmire 2003).

Pragmatist planning weaves compromise into the very fabric of any practical proposal composing, judging and selecting a joint project or action. The meaning of a 'good' plan emerges from the practical efforts among those involved to include the many intentions and interests at play. Instead of imposing rational conventions, norms and purposes from outside or above, the pragmatist studies how prior conventions and practices unperturbed by the disruptive challenge at hand (e.g., drought, flooding) might be leveraged to construct alternative solutions. The judgment of moral salience flows less from norm fitting or legal compliance and more from involvement with those involved conceiving how combinations of purpose, interest and practice might resolve the situation so those involve gain security and responsibility. The merits of these proposed efforts combine sensitivity to damaging or complementary consequences for persons and places with prudential consideration of how actors use precedent, causality, context and circumstance to compose plans for action (Bartels et al. 2015; Ansell 2011).

Instead of handing off moral standards to an external judge or transcendent ego, the pragmatists turn to the practical historical efforts of civilization celebrating efforts to expand the breadth and diversity of membership in communities that support individual development. Here, it is important to note that the invention and adaptation of inclusive social practices and attendant cultural norms has emerged unevenly across different places while the variety, scope, quality and form of democratic deliberation as a resource for these places remains a work in progress (Knight & Johnson 2011). Individual freedom and flourishing routinely struggle with the powerful constraints of traditional cultural prejudice, capitalist economic excess, nation state political hegemony and technological instrumentalism – as all these play crucial roles shaping prospects for democratic governance. The pragmatist viewpoint casts the prospect for moral improvement within the complex interaction of these constraints imagining actions that people can do widening the path to freedom.[2] This makes the practice of critical reform an inherently practical effort that take shape as historical compromises. But it also elevates the status of plan making from a blueprint means focused activity to a resource for imagining what improvements might be done, evaluating their consequences and reconsidering the possibilities for meaningful choice and purposeful action together with others in different situations (Unger 2007). The plans foster and improve political compromises that advance joint projects and policies that fall between what each party expects and what they can currently accept.

Planning for the Public Interest and Public Good

The idea of a public good, which often animates planning work in important ways, provides an expansive conception of moral responsibility even as the legacies of a rationalist philosophical focus, reflected in the debates between deontological (duty) and utilitarian (consequences) conceptions, continue to influence the discourse around public goods. But how should planners anticipate and cope with the moral differences that emerge among different planning actors and communities about public goods? How and to what extent might communities identify and support the interests of those outside their own community, even if their interests clash?

Communities tend to include others in their conception of a wider public good depending on the levels of shared interdependence (roadway), vulnerability (flood plain) and solidarity (citizenship). Pragmatists assess the relevance and value of moral goods along a continuum from private to public with the middle ground tied to common goods – goods like highways, aquifers, air basins, fisheries and parks. Conceiving interests as exclusively public or private tends to exaggerate adversarial differences in the possession and use of many urban goods and amenities.

But geographic and social distance typically reduces our sense of moral responsibility. Adam Smith posed this question well as he noted that we would attend to the pain of a minor cut on our finger much more than the great loss suffered by thousands of strangers facing famine or disaster who live abroad (Smith 2000). The instrumental calculus of the misery demonstrates the need and the analysis of social responsibility affirms their dessert. As we engage in deliberate reflection, the rational evidence outweighs the merits of attending to our own needs; and yet we persist (Haidt 2001). On the one hand, we lack the resources and means to remedy the greater need of these strangers. Unable to offer meaningful assistance we attend to what we can control. On the other hand, the vast cumulative need does not appear morally meaningful. The fate of these people does not connect with our own sense of moral responsibility (Kamm 2007).

If theorists frame moral obligations in terms of laws or social norms, they may find rational grounds for placing moral priority on the needs of strangers suffering from disasters. Theorists may claim that everyone regardless of their social identity and membership possesses certain universal rights (Schwartz 1994). The pragmatic approach frames these rights as goals rather than obligations because pragmatists do not believe in any larger encompassing authority at work authorizing the rights. The pragmatist tradition recognizes that we humans share the same species, but not any inherent moral value. These values follow the historical creation of institutions, norms and practices that seek to remedy the problems of childrearing, hunger and exploitation. We do not start from scratch but build on millions of years of adaptive trial and error (Wright 1994).

Instead of conceiving the public interest as aggregate instrumental benefits, which might ensue from a policy or as a form of legal or moral right inspiring and directing policy compliance, the pragmatist focuses on the meaning of consequences or rules for practical judgments about what to do in specific situations. For spatial planners these situations often emerge as breakdowns in conventional habit require attention to the conflict over the use and disposition of common goods. The pragmatist frames these situations attending to the context of social relationships that shape the contours for moral judgment. The sources of suspicion and trust flow from these relations (Graham et al. 2013; Holden & Scerri 2014).

There exist plenty of nasty social conventions, institutional practices, cultural habits, technological systems, economic inequalities and political conflicts that undermine social learning and environmentally adaptive change. Conceiving and promoting practical possibilities for political change that tame complexity of many interests, remedy social inequalities and embrace diversity of cultural identity will rarely achieve the full complement of goals as envisioned. The complexity of competing values frames every practical judgment people learn to make while imagining and comparing their impact before taking action. The pragmatist outlook casts this effort in functionally adaptive terms that dovetail with the concept of capability introduced by Amartya Sen (1999). But how can individuals and communities use these insights for making plans that both tackle social complexity and foster common good? That is the focus of next section.

Human Interdependencies, Social Complexity and Common Goods

Order in complex societies requires both tolerance and respect. But there is a hierarchy of sorts. I may tolerate others without respecting them. We recognize liberal societies because members create and sustain institutions that provide scaffolding for tolerance. Strong liberal rationales describe these institutions as rights and justify them by drawing strong ties to human nature. I agree with Mandelbaum (2000) and Walzer (1982) that trying to make democracy appear inevitable because an expression of some deeper and more enduring qualities of human nature leads us astray. Pragmatists embrace tolerance and nurture respect because these qualities of institutional governance sustain differences among the various communities within a nation, region, metropolis or neighborhood. I prefer a future oriented pragmatic outlook that has us aspiring to democratic ideals within various practical settings. We imagine small scale democracies and try them out in different settings learning from what succeeds in fulfilling our expected hopes and what does not.

Walzer captures with Mandelbaum the crucial insight that negotiating the plurality of competing claims to membership and the distribution of goods within and between communities cannot be determined by some external standard without distorting or subjecting these claims to some higher authority. Mandelbaum warns us about the tyranny of imposing a too abstract reason and Walzer warns us about the tyranny of using the organization of one good to control the distribution of another (e.g., wealth controlling political authority). But neither tells us how we might interpret, anticipate and negotiate shared goods among communities. Mandelbaum argues that we adopt what he terms 'sensibilities': pluralistic tolerance that respects the boundaries of diverse communities and a commitment to a mode of public interpretation based on reading in public. Walzer envisions a political community based on mutual respect for difference.

But respect seems more a building block for a republican rather than democratic order. We need only tolerate rather than respect others to make democratic coordination feasible. Respect acknowledges the community of belief held by others because that community acts in ways familiar to our own. Tolerance only requires that we agree to coexist with others regardless of familiarity. Lest tolerance seem too timid a threshold, contrast it with indifference and the range of antagonistic relationships that can undermine democratic collaboration. Conducting planning in a pluralist society requires both in order to avoid tyranny of expertise and social hegemony.

The array of institutions that compose the modern world impose conventions and rules that people absorb becoming members. We inherit memberships. These interconnected and overlapping memberships pose a moral challenge as we each awaken to the challenge of voluntarily forming an individual identity. On a larger scale, the overlapping complexity of markets, political parties, religions, firms, unions, movements and communities generate a dense field of interdependencies that produce unexpected consequences. Each person may choose to resist, contest and modify these institutional rules to carve out greater personal autonomy. The normative contours of private, public and common sector good shape deliberation about the social meaning of this pursuit (Mandelbaum 2000).

The contrast between public and private good tends to dominate moral debate. In this chapter I focus on a kind of good that falls in between – the common good. Common goods are especially relevant for settlement oriented spatial plans that create and tap resources susceptible to depletion. The literature on the commons imagines rational individuals each taking what they can, generating a social dilemma as this behavior depletes the common good. The work by Elinor Ostrom (1990) on what she calls *common pool resources* considers how people govern the common good and avoid exhaustion while working together. She studied how users design and adopt a collaborative institution of rules and practices. They communicate with each other relying on social trust. Trust provides a threshold of assurance for members to voluntarily moderate resource use before cooperation unfolds.

In doing so, and rather crucially, the users create a plan for future cooperation that promises adequate and reliable yields for each individual while sustaining the common resource each tap. Informed both by trust and a plan (even if tacit and spontaneous), such collaborations work as each coordinate use fairly and competently. The combination of knowledge and solidarity tied together in a plan for the future provides a remedy for the tragedy generated by the competitive exploitation of a shared resource. Collaboration emerges as a strategic resource giving purpose to the underlying relationship of give and take (Fung 2007; Unger 2007; Goldstein & Butler 2009).

Spatial plans for common goods respond to the relevant forms of complexity described by Lew Hopkins (2001): interdependence, uncertainty, indivisibility and irreversibility. The plan for any common good tied to place includes practical judgments about the relevant meaning, usefulness and feasibility of a coordination practice. Each practice combines moral, political and technical features that may help appraise and classify current common good use or appraise and compare imagined future scenarios (Schwartz & Sharpe 2005).

Each of us makes plans that help facilitate an understanding of the world of relationships individuals and communities inhabit. Using the process diligently, each of us can learn to comprehend the meanings that others use and so coordinate our mutual behavior to successfully adapt to respective expectations and actions. How people learn to do this involves both cognitive and emotional responses. Thinking uses concepts to order the relationships while emotional attachments fuel and flavor the repertoire of feelings people rely upon to select, compare and inform actions. Individuals learn to plan for daily and longer-term activities as part of development from child to adult; and each use plans to render a complex social and spatial world susceptible to coordinated action (Marris 1996; Haidt 2001).

The provision of complex common goods among cooperating individuals and communities require social, economic and political coordination as those cooperating usually take steps to monitor and manage use. Knowing how to choose the proper kind of practice to fit the common good problem requires practical wisdom and prudence. Additionally, external ecological, market, government, and demographic or technological changes can disrupt sustained cooperative use of a limited shared good. The moral quality of the plans and their legacy on this account will rarely reach the threshold of moral perfection (just, efficient or beautiful) but offer up compromises among those using the common good and other external changes (Kamm 2007; Deyle & Slotterback 2009). Professional knowledge for planning blends scientific and political understanding offering feasible options along collaboratively sustained continua of possibility.

Thus, compromise plays a key role in planning practice because professional practitioners who sincerely plan for common goods face the challenges of complexity and the threat of external constraints. However, compromise often generates ambivalence because those who do it combine a good act (cooperating on one goal) and a bad act (subverting another goal). Avishai Margalit (2010) embraces compromise as a crucial dimension of political democracy:

> On the whole political compromises are a good thing. Political compromises for the sake of peace are a very good thing. Shabby, shady, and shoddy compromises are bad but not sufficiently bad to be always avoided at all costs, especially not when they are concluded for the sake of peace. Only rotten compromises are bad enough to be avoided at all costs (p.16).

But there are those compromises that fail to meet the basic thresholds of moral decency. These include rotten compromises that embrace evil and foster corruption. These often include plans that encourage lending, borrowing and exploitation practices that displace externalities onto the vulnerable. Less reprehensible but still morally destructive are those compromises that ensue from misplaced confidence in a single dimension of practical improvement insensitive to complex interaction effects. These plans impose an instrumental focus on efficient infrastructure development or egalitarian distribution scheme that ignores the interaction effects of complex common goods. In contrast, some compromises deploy a common good strategy attentive to fit with local complexity conditions and sensitive to the consequences of the plan for current and future residents. The public interest activates the plan ideals even as the details of the options for the future require tradeoffs among the interests and purposes of stakeholders and places (Innes & Booher 2010; Holden & Scerri 2014).

An Ethical Planning Example

So what features of plan making help us meet and cross ethical thresholds creating compromises that together bring the horizon closer to current reality? What moral force does plan making offer to help fuel improved ethical judgments across the complex relationships that accompany any large planning effort? Consider the following story,

Norah Beck and the Historic Pullman Plan

Fire destroyed the historic Pullman clocktower factory building on Chicago's south side in 1999. The structure was part of a model company town constructed by rail car manufacturer George Pullman in the 1880s. A Chicago Landmarks Commission Task Force was created to study and recommend a plan. Chaired by former Governor Jim Thompson, a long-time supporter of Pullman's development, the Task Force immediately began demanding tens of millions of dollars from the government to rehabilitate the property. Norah Jones tells the story of her planning mentor during an early professional internship in the City of Chicago.

> Recognizing the ineffective nature of their actions, my boss (who was, in effect, the only staff person working with the Task Force), established a time line to guide Task Force procedures. He divided the upcoming year into two major parts, separated by an Interim Report that would set out the goals of the Task Force. He invited members of the Task Force to voice their feelings about the site and invited community members to speak at those occasions as well. Satisfied that enough documented political opposition to demolishing the site had been recorded, my boss turned Task Force attention to gathering information from similar cases elsewhere. Because of the enormous financial and labor commitment needed to repair the buildings in Pullman, he needed to demonstrate that rehabilitation could be done and could prove successful. Next, he collected initial estimates from consultants for the scope of work needed to repair the buildings. Hiring consultants interested in the project and in preservation projects generally insured positive feedback in the reports. Selecting a broader range of consultants to provide a full range of alternatives would have included demolition, truly the most economically feasible option. The consultants issued reports demonstrating existing market support for Pullman's rehabilitation including options for feasible funding. None recommended demolition.

The interim report offered up stories about the future redevelopment of the Pullman factory that appealed to many different interests.

The report offered five major 'stories' associated with the Pullman site: 1) The best example of a planned town in America, 2) The opening up of the American West, 3) American industrialization, 4) Labor history and the Great Migration of blacks to the North through employment as a Pullman Porter, and 5) Work, social, and cultural history of Pullman employees, many of whom were immigrants. Appealing to such a wide range of interests, the report garnered support from a variety of government and community groups. Technical information in the report was abstract, providing only that information necessary to show the bell tower and factory buildings could be rebuilt.

Guiding the Task Force involved clever maneuvers to foster communication.

Economic realities and social stigmas associated with the south side of Chicago rendered most conventional development impossible. My boss decided to look more closely at alternative developments for the site. The National Park Service was identified as a potential financer/operator of the site. NPS designation would insure continued funding ... but the consultants were not used to working with such a large government bureaucracy and were unsure of its utility. My boss arranged a meeting between NPS officials and the consultants. Through this conversation, the consultants gained a better understanding of the designation, and the federal officials were able to provide suggestions for improving the application for designation ... including alternative designations that allowed for more creativity and partnerships with for-profit operators. My boss showed the consultants options shaped by feasible potentials, not barriers.

The Task Force staff recommended this blended strategy contrasting it favorably against either a for profit or non-profit option.

Because of the many focus group meetings held throughout the year, as well as staff's responsiveness to appointee questions, the Task Force felt as if it had done the work and offered the best possible recommendation. My boss and I had done most of the work sifting through available information and deciding what and how to present options for Task Force review.

It took many years, but the redevelopment was eventually done. The Pullman Site received national park designation in 2015.

This practitioner story offers a useful example of a pragmatist ethos in action. The rational duty focused moralist would find much to critique. The professional planner did not embrace objective detachment nor adopt the conventions of market assessment. The place possessed unique historical significance complicated by the economic and social decay of surrounding neighborhoods. Anticipating the racial prejudice and cultural indifference of opponents, the planner collected negative testimony that focused overwhelmingly on project infeasibility. He adopted this frame and focused on imagining future alternatives for redevelopment that would prove feasible. This deflected the political impact of opponents. None cared enough to respond and challenge this move at the time.

Instead of developing arguments among the different interests and viewpoints of the Task Force members the planner used their participation to craft options that included these differences as part of future development options. The inclusion of diverse purposes and views did not diminish the moral quality of the plan but enabled the different participants to recognize and acknowledge the legitimacy and relevance of the recommended plan that finally took shape.

The planner in Nora's story did not pursue the best or most optimal plan. The planner responded cleverly and sensitively to a complex situation. He worked on the site related economic and construction issues with bidding consultants. Feasibility was not just a question of assessing moral and political risk, but working out the practical costs of financing, construction and operation. The brief story does not drill down into those details, but the planner bridged both domains using plan making as scaffolding. Pragmatists do not separate fact from value; but explore how their relationships influence future consequences. The final plan embodies a mongrel combination of integrated values and interests tied together as a provisional conception of a common good for the future – the Pullman redevelopment plan.

Conclusion

In the context of liberal societies, provisional plans may fail to achieve ambitious goals and yet still offer incremental improvements and practical hope for the improved allocation (more efficient, just and sustainable) of a complex common good. The deployment of practices that rely upon increased trust and reciprocity improves the prospects for more deliberate and legitimate plans. Plans do not justify the judgments people make, but help people conceive and compare the meaning of future imagined effects. Justification flows from the prudential assessment of these consequences among those holding competing purposes and interests; as well as those witnessing these efforts (Hoch 2002; Holden & Scerri 2014).

Consider the continuum between moral horizons and ethical thresholds. The professional associations for planning create detailed codes about thresholds for conduct and vague musings about the moral horizon (AICP Code; RTP Code). The leadership expects most members to be morally decent but recognize that only a few will be heroic. This distinction proves challenging however for planning practice. As professionals offer advice about what options to consider anticipating and preparing for the future they look to the horizon. This practical imaginative work often requires crossing many moral and political thresholds tied to cultural and social customs and beliefs that rarely converge but require active sustained political effort to come together. The practical potential for change takes place in the middle range between threshold and horizon (Graham et al. 2013; Verma 2009).

The politics of planning, in this sense, does not require that planners engage directly in the political work done by community organizers, elected officials, administrative executive officers, political activists, lobbyists and common good users. However, it does require that planners attend to the practical nexus of social and political differences attending to different moral claims shaping the plans as well as the moral practices shaping the conduct of plan making. This means that planners will make compromises. When seen using the practical continuity of the continuum, splitting the difference, scratching backs, rolling logs and the other euphemisms describing political deal making represent both moral accomplishments as well as moral failures (Guttman & Thompson 2010). Idealistic or cynical plans that fall at the extremes may justify the dreams of those who make them, but they tend to abstract from practical problems rooted in social and spatial complexities that accompany human settlements everywhere. Plans that offer compromise attend to these details offering practical advice with mixed moral results. A pragmatist outlook evaluates the merits of such advice within the context of the evolving historical situation but does so searching for incremental progress toward a more inclusive good based on democratic deliberation.

Notes

1 The social welfare principle informed by utilitarian moral ideas envision a calculus that can aggregate the diversity of purpose and interest that center in common goods like roadway placement, groundwater use or congestion relief. But complex interactions among spatial, political and social differences can often make such rational abstraction perverse. Collaboration and coordination may be settled though a market pricing system, but planners often face challenges where purposeful deliberate coordination need be done.
2 Sen (1999) uses the notion of capability to describe the necessity of going beyond conventional development goals and measures of success (like basic utilities, economic goods and social services) and take into account overall improvement to human potential. Development, in Sen's scheme, is therefore about developing the capabilities of people by increasing the options available to them.

References

Abbott, A. (2000). *Time Matters: On Theory and Method*. Chicago: University of Chicago Press.
Ansell, C. (2011). *Pragmatist Democracy: Evolutionary Learning as Public Philosophy*. New York: Oxford University Press.
Barrett, C. D. (2001). *Everyday Ethics for Planners*. Chicago: APA.
Bartels, D. M., Bauman, C. W., Cushman, F. A., Pizarro, D. A. and McGraw, A. P. (2015). Moral judgment and decision making. In G. Keren and G. Wu (Eds.), *The*

Wiley Blackwell Handbook of Judgment and Decision Making. Chichester, UK: John Wiley.
Deyle, R. and Slotterback, C. S. (2009). Group learning in participatory planning processes: An exploratory quasi experimental analysis of local mitigation planning in Florida. *Journal of Planning Education and Research*, 29(1), 23–38.
Fesmire, S. (2003). *John Dewey and Moral Imagination: Pragmatism in Ethics.* Bloomington, IN: Indiana University Press.
Flyvbjerg, B. (2005). Design by deception: The politics of megaproject approval. *Harvard Design Magazine*, 22, 50–59.
Fung, A. (2007). Democratic theory and political science: A pragmatic method of constructive engagement. *American Political Science Review*, 101(3), 443–458.
Goldstein, B. E. and Butler, W. (2009). The network imaginary: Coherence and creativity within a multiscalar collaborative effort to reform U.S. fire management. *Journal of Environmental Planning and Management*, 52(8), 1013–1033.
Graham, J., Haidt, J., Koleva, S., Motyl, M., Iyer, R., Wojcik, S. and Ditto, P. H. (2013). Moral foundations theory: The pragmatic validity of moral pluralism. *Advances in Experimental Social Psychology*, 47, 55–130.
Guttman, A. and Thompson, D. (2010). The mindsets of political compromise. *Reflections*, 8(4), 1125–1143.
Haidt, J. (2001). The emotional dog and its rational tail: A social intuitionist approach to moral judgment. *Psychological Review*, 108, 814–834.
Hall, P. (1982). *Great Planning Disasters.* Berkeley: University of California Press.
Hendler, S. (1995). *Planning Ethics: A Reader in Planning Theory, Practice and Education.* New Brunswick, NJ: Center for Urban Policy Research.
Hoch, C. J. (2002). Evaluating plans pragmatically. *Planning Theory*, 1(1), 53–75.
Holden, M. and Scerri, A. (2014). Justification, compromise and test: Developing a pragmatic sociology of critique to understand the outcomes of urban redevelopment. *Planning Theory*, 14(4), 360–383.
Hopkins, L. (2001). *Urban Development: The Logic of Making Plans.* Washington, D.C.: Island Press.
Innes, J. E. and Booher, D. E. (2010) *Planning with Complexity: An Introduction to Rationality for Public Policy.* New York: Routledge.
Kamm, F. M. (2007). *Intricate Ethics: Rights, Responsibilities, and Permissible Harm.* Oxford, UK: Oxford University Press.
Knight, J. and Johnson, J. (2011). *The Priority of Democracy: Political Consequences of Pragmatism.* Princeton, NJ: Princeton University Press.
MacIntyre, A. (1990). *Three Rival Versions of Moral Enquiry.* London: Duckworth.
Mandelbaum, S. (2000). *Open Moral Communities.* Cambridge, MA: MIT Press.
Margalit, A. (2010). *On Compromise and Rotten Compromises.* Princeton, NJ: Princeton University Press.
Marris, P. (1996). *The Politics of Uncertainty.* London: Routledge.
Ostrom, E. (1990). *Governing the Commons.* Cambridge: Cambridge University Press.
Schwartz, S. H. (1994). Are there universal aspects in the structure and contents of human values? *Journal of Social Issues*, 50(4), 19–45.
Schwartz, B. and Sharpe, K. (2005). Practical wisdom: Aristotle meets positive psychology. *Journal of Happiness Studies*, 7, 377–395.
Sen, A. (1999). *Development as Freedom.* New York: Random House.
Sheppard, J. W. (2003). The nectar is in the journey: Pragmatism, progress, and the promise of incrementalism. *Philosophy & Geography*, 6(2), 167–187.

Smith, A. (b. 1723–d. 1790). (2000). *The Wealth of Nations*. Introduction by R. Reich; edited, with notes, marginal summary, and enlarged index by E. Cannan. New York: Modern Library.
Thomas, H. (1994). *Values and Planning*. Aldershot: Ashgate.
Unger, R. M. (2007). *The Self Awakened: Pragmatism Unbound*. Cambridge, MA: Harvard University Press.
Verma, N. (2009). Pragmatic ethics and sustainable development. In F. Lo Piccolo and H. Thomas (Eds.), *Ethics and Planning Research* (pp. 40–53).Burlington, VT: Ashgate.
Wachs, M. (Ed.). (1985). *Ethics in Planning*. New Brunswick, NJ: Center for Urban Policy Research.
Walzer, M. (1982). *Spheres of Justice: A Defense of Pluralism and Equality*. New York: Basic Books.
Wright, R. (1994). *The Moral Animal: The New Science of Evolutionary Psychology*. New York: Random House.

Index

Abbot, A. 45, 177, 186
accountability 160, 165–6
adaptation 14n8, 51–52, 62, 78, 88, 144, 151, 178
adversarial 113, 126, 178
advice; compose 77, 105; craft 27; good 3, 30, 71, 116, 153, 168; imaginative 66, 148; institutional 73, 78; practical 28, 40, 94, 113, 186; professional 1, 79, 99, 154, 159, 185; provisional 4, 52; public 9, 114; quality 9, 72; relevant 63, 78, 86; useful 54, 72, 132, 172
affordable housing 15n10, 39, 55, 58–60, 75, 89
African American 134
agenda viii, 20, 31, 51, 72, 73, 88, 150, 152, 164, 169, 170
Albrechts, L. 69, 78–79
Alexander, E. R. 42, 46, 49, 55, 63n3, 64, 96, 107
Allmendinger, P. 75, 79
Allport, D.A. 19, 36
Altshuler, A. 117, 129
ambiguity 1, 11, 87, 89, 103, 128, 138, 153–154, 167, 177
American Institute of Certified Planners (AICP) 39
American Planning Association (APA) 39, 40, 41, 53, 64, 81, 97, 107, 108, 114, 120, 129, 130, 153
Anderson, C. 166, 174
Ansell, C. 177, 186
anticipate 115; consequences 11, 27, 40, 49, 62, 71, 113, 121, 124, 135, 142, 154; complexity 4, 13, 85, 88–90, 100, 102, 106n1, 153, 160, 175; consensus 126; future 1, 3, 9, 11, 18, 72, 78, 90, 95, 146, 167; goals 20, 67, 121, 180; institutional relationships 50, 58, 68, 160, 180; other plans 2, 54, 96, 123; problems 10, 173; uncertainty 1, 70, 95
appraise 30, 93, 94, 95, 96, 181
Archibugi, F. 42, 45, 46,
Ariely, D. 54, 64
Aristotle 177, 187
Artuso, L. 130
Assche, K. V. 73, 79
assemblage 148
Association of European Schools of Planning (AESOP) 47
attachment; civic 33n5; disciplinary 48, 56; emotion 9, 18, 25, 26, 30, 32, 70, 91, 127, 154, 166, 181; expertise 57, 94; habit 77, 132, 153, 165; meaning 56, 105, 111, 116, 127, 172; place 65, 133, 148
authority 74, 124, 126, 169; planning 30; decisions 50, 93, 144; expertise 126, 179–80; government 51, 57, 107n11, 119–20, 148, 151; political 54; legal 61

Baer, W. 114–18, 121–3, 129
Bagozzi, R. P. 31, 34
Bailey, F. G. 28, 32, 33n, 34
Banfield, E. 117, 130
Barber, B. 159, 174
Barrett, C. D. 176, 188
Bartels, D. M. 177, 186
Batty, M. 48, 64
Baum, H. 7, 27, 34, 71, 75, 77, 79, 121, 122, 129
Bauman, C. W. 186
Bauman, Z. 69, 79
Beatley, T. 41, 46,
Beauregard, B. 145, 147–9, 151–2, 154
Becker, B. 89, 108
Ben-Joseph, E. 133, 154

Bennett, E. H. 6, 100, 107
Berke, P. 99, 107
Beunen, R. 73, 79
bias 15n11, 17, 18, 20, 21, 22, 34, 70, 75
Blanco, H. 12, 15, 123, 124, 128n1, 129
Bohman, J. 163–8, 171–174
Boninger, D. S. 20, 34
Booher, D. E. 54–8, 61, 64, 74, 78, 80, 96, 105, 108, 182, 187
Brandon, P. S. 116, 129–30
Bratman, M. 10, 13, 15n11, 15, 165, 174,
Bruner, J. 69, 80
Burgess, P. 19, 35
Burnmham, D. H. vi, 99–100, 107, 146
Burton, R. 91, 107
Butler, W. 181–187
Buzzelli, M. 133, 154

calculation 51, 90–3, 116
Campbell, H. 44, 46
capital improvements 99, 137
coordination; adaptive 52, 145; market 61, 62; plans and 11, 13, 92, 100; social 55, 56, 60, 85, 106n1, 160, 163, 180–2, 186n1
Champaign, Illinois 137
Channon, S. 34
Chicago 34, 35, 58–9, 78, 81, 99, 107–8, 130, 132–5, 137, 154, 61, 168, 170–4, 183–4, 186
Chicago Housing Authority (CHA) 168
choice; collective 63n4, 87, 89, 106n2, 135, 148, 159; compare 19, 54–55, 69, 116–7; guide 11, 14n2, 21– 3, 49, 75–7, 91–94, 121, 154, 167, 178; justify 3, 72; trust 30, 67, 105
Churchill, S. 26, 34
Clark, A. 11, 15
Clavel, P. 122, 126, 130
client 2, 9, 27, 43–5, 51, 55, 69, 71–2, 74, 77–9, 92, 96–7, 99, 100–2, 123, 162, 169, 175
Coates, L. 34
cognitive psychology of planning 19, 33, 34, 35, 36
cognitive science 15, 34, 91, 95
coherence 12, 13, 43, 48–9, 55–6, 62–3, 89–93, 99, 105, 106n5, 109, 115, 125, 127, 145, 162, 165–7, 187
Cole, R. 27, 34
collaboration 2, 57, 61–3, 96, 144, 165, 171–2, 180–1, 186
collective action 64, 77, 103, 168
collective effort 40, 41, 154

commercial development 116, 135
common good 50–1, 56–8, 60–1, 162, 175, 178, 179, 180–2
communicate, communicative 42, 46, 56–8, 66, 107–8, 130, 145, 174, 181
communication 20, 33, 55, 80, 85, 89, 109, 124, 163, 171–2, 184
communitarian 87, 106n1, 159–61, 163
community 26–9, 40, 43, 46, 66, 73, 77, 87, 92, 102, 106n4, 108, 115, 120–1, 126, 130, 135–6, 139, 142, 153–4, 159–73, 178, 180, 183–6
compassion 17, 18, 26, 31, 110
comprehensive plan 4, 15n, 26, 42, 51, 55–6, 89, 107n, 108, 117, 132–5, 137, 146, 149, 153–5, 167
compromise 3, 66, 68, 96, 145, 148, 163, 175–8, 182–3, 186–7
conflict 2–4, 10, 35, 45, 47, 51, 55, 66–7, 73–4, 81, 86, 89, 95, 98, 11, 128n, 129, 155, 161, 165, 167, 170, 172, 177, 179
consequences; anticipating 49–57, 148–9; evaluating 14–5, 17, 20, 25, 62–3, 120, 118–28, 175–82, 185, 187; imagined 2, 3, 10–12, 29–32, 67–9, 114, 144–5; plans and 71, 73, 86, 88, 90, 154, 160–1, 167, 169, 173; scenarios and 76–7
consistency 12, 13, 56, 59, 60, 62, 63, 89, 91, 97, 98, 99, 105, 106n5, 107n11, 162, 165, 166
consultants 99, 102, 108, 152, 183–185
contextual meaning 56, 89, 145
contract 29, 87, 106n, 114, 159, 162–163, 167
Cooper, M. 34, 73, 80
cooperate 12, 14n4, 56, 67, 163, 165, 170–2, 180–2
correspondence 20, 80, 91, 115, 123–5, 150, 162
cosmopolitan 75, 135, 162, 171–2
counterfactual thinking 11, 16, 20–1, 25, 34–5
critical irony 171
Cruikshank, J. 109
Cushman, F. A. 186
custom 14n6, 26, 35, 54, 58, 62, 77, 86, 105, 112, 176, 186

Dalton, L. 71, 80, 122, 129
Damasio, A. 18, 23, 24, 25, 26, 27, 33, 34
Davidoff, P. 126, 129
Davoudi, S. 45, 47
deliberation community 87; democratic 4, 72, 77, 96, 105–6n1, 148–52, 178,

181, 186; emotions and 25, 32, 110; institutional design 58, 60, 62; persuasion 13–4, 14n2, 126–8; plans and 51, 53–4, 90, 92, 103, 117, 122–3, 146; public 159–174, 178
democracy 81, 112, 129, 149, 160, 171, 174, 180, 182, 186–7
design 32–33n6, 67, 86, 122; institutional 2, 49–51, 58–64, 181; planning and 44–6, 57, 71, 74, 85, 88, 92, 97, 118, 124, 133, 147, 150, 160, 162, 165, 167; urban 39, 68, 119, 137, 170
detachment 4, 17, 24, 70, 77, 123, 171–4, 184
developers 56, 60, 62, 128, 133–5, 137–9, 144, 151–4
developmental naturalism 177
Dewey, J. 12, 80, 113, 128, 187
Deyle, R. 182, 187
dispute 9, 25, 47, 61–2, 96, 109, 126, 129
district 48, 117, 133, 135–8, 152, 169, 173
Ditto, P. H. 187
diversity 9, 42, 45, 47, 75, 124, 127, 145–6, 151–2, 178–9, 186
doctrine 44–5, 65–7, 70, 73–4, 134–5, 150, 153, 163, 176
Donaghy, K. 48–50, 55–6, 63–4, 86, 88–92, 105, 107
Dorner, D. 121, 126–7, 129
Duineveld, M. 73, 79
duty 178, 184
dwellings 22, 133–5, 139, 152, 168

Eaton, R. 66, 68, 80
Ecological 14n5, 51–2, 125, 146–7, 182
Education 43–4, 46n1, 47, 55, 64, 79–81, 89, 107–9, 129–31, 155, 166, 169, 187
Edwards, D. 34
efficiency diversity 127
elected officials 15n12, 60, 136, 138, 148, 152, 186
Ellis, C. 155
Elster, J. 18, 34
emotions and planning vii, 3, 9–11, 14–5n, 17–35, 70–6, 80, 91–3, 97, 105–10, 114, 121, 166, 177, 181, 187;
Engagement 100, 120, 127, 174, 187
Engel, A. K. 11, 15
environment viii, 2, 17, 23, 41, 46, 50, 52–5, 57, 67, 72, 77, 80, 92, 103–6n, 108, 113, 116, 125–6, 129–30, 137, 147– 8, 150, 154, 160, 168, 175, 179, 187
epistemic 63, 71, 75, 89, 97, 100
equilibrium 49, 51, 56, 78, 174n

equity 71, 118, 130, 145–146, 151
ethical journey 176; judgment 176–177, 183; principles 176
exclusion 146, 163
experiment 1, 4, 17–22, 35–6, 62, 79, 91, 120, 126–7, 153, 176, 187
expertise I, 19, 29, 53, 106n, 110, 115, 121–3, 126–8, 137, 152, 160, 166, 171–2, 180,
exploitation 2, 67, 175, 179, 181–2
externality 58, 103, 116, 162, 182

Fainstein, S. 41, 47, 74, 75, 80
Faludi, A. 19, 34, 42, 47, 96, 107, 127
Fazio, R. H. 22, 34
Fesmire, S. 177, 187
Fischer, F. 96, 107
flood plain 88, 178
flourishing 26, 76, 79, 178
Flyvbjerg, B. 177, 187
Forecast 16, 35, 39, 71–2, 76, 81, 108, 113, 125, 176
Forester, J. vii, 13, 15, 25, 27, 33–4, 44, 47, 54, 58, 64, 74, 80, 89, 96, 105, 107, 112, 122, 129, 130, 166, 173–4n
Forgas, J.P. 17, 18, 20, 22, 34
Foucault, M. 73, 80, 119, 129
foundation 1, 3, 4, 9, 13, 40, 45–7, 73–4, 79, 86, 112–3, 176, 187
Fox, C. J. 126, 129
framing 3, 19, 24, 32, 54, 60, 76, 94, 102, 107–8, 144–5
Frankfort Planning Department 140, 154
Frankfort, Illinois vi, 132, 135, 139–144, 151–154
freedom 57, 74, 108, 119, 162, 166, 172, 178, 187
Friedmann, J. vii, 42, 47, 63n, 64, 65, 66, 68, 75, 79, 80
Frijda, H. H. 34
Fung, A. 181, 187

Gabbe, C. J. 80
Galanter, E. 19, 35
Gallagher, S. 11, 15
Gardner, R. 56, 64
Garrison, J. 74, 80
Gavanski, I. 35
Gleicher, F. 20, 34
God 26, 67, 72, 168
Goetz, E. G. 78, 80
Goldie, P. 17, 34
Goldstein, B. E. 186–7
Graham, J. 179, 186–7

Grant, J. 122, 129
Greenleigh, N. 134, 154
Gronow, A. J. 91, 107
Gross, M. A. 31, 35
growth vii, 4, 42, 93, 99, 119, 133–5, 139–42, 147, 151, 154–5
Gunder, M. 74–5, 79–80
Gunderson, L. H. 122, 129
Guttman, A. 186–7

Haack, S. 13, 15
habit 10, 14n6, 20, 52–4, 63n, 69–78, 90, 93, 97, 105–7, 110–11, 125, 128, 128n2, 145, 147–8, 160, 162, 176, 179–81
Haidt, J. 179, 181, 187
Hall, P. 35, 41, 47, 117, 129, 127, 187
Harmon, M. M. 128–129
Harper, T. L. 64, 74, 78, 80, 112, 129–30, 174n
Hayes–Roth, B. 19, 34
Hayes–Roth, F. 19, 34
Healey, P. 40, 42, 44, 47, 49, 54, 64, 65, 71, 74, 78, 80, 81, 112, 122, 126, 129
Heath, J. 174n, 174
Hebbert, F. 80
Hendler, S. 130, 177, 187
Hendricks–Jensen, H. 13, 16
Heuristics 19, 56–7,
Hillier, J. 35, 40, 42, 47, 74, 80–1
Holden, M. 179, 182, 185, 187
Holway, J. 71, 80
Homeless 10, 79, 110, 161
HOPEVI 168
Hopkins, Lew 31, 34, 48–52, 55–8, 60, 63–4, 69–72, 80–1, 85–92, 99, 103, 107–8, 145, 149–50, 152–4, 181, 187
housing 12, 15n10, 39, 55, 58–62, 68, 70–1, 75, 78, 80–1, 89, 99, 119, 127, 134–5, 154, 166, 168–73
Houston, D. A. 22, 34

imagination v, viii, 25, 33n3, 34, 54, 63, 65, 67, 69, 71, 73, 75, 77–9, 81, 177, 187
inclusion 10, 13, 96, 159, 185
incremental 66, 73, 74, 94, 114, 128, 146, 185, 186
indivisibility 49, 51, 58, 85, 87–8, 145, 150, 181
inequality 62, 68, 146–9, 160, 163–4, 169–70
inertia 69, 148
inference 11, 90, 109, 111

infill development 134, 137
infrastructure 4, 15n13, 59, 61, 76, 78, 106n8, 135–9, 141, 151, 160, 165, 176, 182
Innes, J. 54, 57, 58, 61, 64, 74, 78, 80, 89, 96, 105, 108, 126, 130, 173, 182, 187
Innovation 2, 43, 46, 48, 50–1, 53, 57, 86, 102, 175
Instrumental 9, 13, 31, 51, 58, 66, 86, 88, 116, 124, 160, 178–82
integrate 3–4, 23, 27, 39, 42–7, 49, 61–2, 65, 72, 75–6, 85, 89, 94, 132, 137–9, 146, 151–2, 169, 171, 175, 177, 185
intelligence v, viii, 14, 17, 22–3, 31–2, 33, 35, 122, 128, 165, 172, 177
interaction effects 52, 55, 62, 68, 70, 72, 75–6, 103, 145, 152, 177, 182
interdependence 4, 5, 49–51, 57–8, 60–1, 85, 87–8, 107, 110, 145–6, 148, 150, 160, 162, 178, 181
interpretation 10, 25, 41, 66–7, 75–7, 86–7, 95–7, 100–3, 124, 128n2, 146–7, 150–1, 163, 165, 169, 180
irreversibility 49, 51, 85, 87, 145, 150, 181
Iyer, R. 187
Izard, C. E. 23, 34

Jacobs, A. 122, 130
James, William 113, 127
Johnson, J. 178, 187
Johnson, M. 94, 108
Jones, Norah 183
justification 13, 15, 42, 45, 55, 63n4, 71, 89–90, 106n, 128, 132, 153, 166, 185, 187

Kahn, H. 69, 80
Kahneman, D. 11, 16, 32, 35, 75, 81
Kamm, F. M. 179, 182, 187
Kaplan, A. 116, 130
Kaufman, S. 96, 108
Kaza, N. 145, 150, 154
Kelley, E. D. 89, 108
Keltner, D. 31, 35
Kim, A. M. 73, 81
King, C. S. 126, 130
Klosterman, R. E. 39, 47
Knapp, G. 145, 149–152, 154–155
Knight, J. 178, 187
Koleva, S. 187
Krumholz, N. 122, 126, 130

Lai, L. 89, 96, 109
Lakoff, G. 94, 108

Lally, J. 80
land use vi, 24, 59, 72, 100, 128n2, 132, 137–47, 152–5
Landry, C 41, 47
landscape 23, 42, 44, 67–8, 77, 88, 118–9, 128n2, 133, 145, 155
Lanyi, C. S. 134, 154
Lauria, M. 44, 47
LeBaron, M. 33, 35
Lee, D. B. 86, 108
Lee, S. 134, 154
legitimacy 42, 51, 58, 61, 99, 124, 127, 152, 173, 185
Lekan, T. 53–54, 64
Lerner, J. S. 31, 35
liberal 66, 76, 79, 101, 106n, 149, 159–61, 166, 172, 174, 180, 185
Lichfield, N. 115–6, 130
Light, S. S. 122, 129
Lovallo, D. 11, 16, 32, 35
Luger, M. I. 118, 130

MacIntyre, A. 176, 187
Majoor, S. J. H. 122, 130
Mandelbaum, S. 33, 35, 69, 75, 81, 85–9, 106n1, 108, 129, 159–74, 180–1, 187
Manna, D. R. 31, 35
Manson, S. M. 108
Margalit, A. 182, 187
Markets 48–51, 55, 60, 89, 109, 111, 125, 154, 180
Markman, K. D. 32, 35
Marris, P. vii, 25, 27, 32, 35, 106n4, 108, 127, 130, 181, 187
Marshall, R. 44, 46
Matthews, R. 80
McClendon, B. 122, 130
McGraw, A. P. 186
McMullen, M. N. 22, 32, 35
means–ends thinking 12, 13
mediation 34, 96
Menand, L. 113, 130
Menon, K. 31, 35
Metaphor 17, 48, 94, 105–6, 108, 115, 122–25
Meyerson, M. 107–8, 117, 130
Migration vi, 71, 99, 111, 134, 141, 184
Miller, G. A. 19, 35
Miller, H. T. 126, 129
Minsky, M. 95, 106n5, 108
Mithen, S. 10, 16
models 14n8, 20–1, 33n2, 35, 48–51, 56–7, 91, 99, 102–3, 108, 115, 117, 124–5
modernism 118–119

moral; horizon 67, 176, 181, 185; sentiments 154; superiority 173
Morris, R. 19–20, 34–6
Motyl, M. 187
Mouffe, C. 75, 81
municipal plan 15n11, 27–8, 58–62, 99, 108, 132–5, 138, 142, 144, 149–53, 169

narrative 10, 18, 21, 27, 32, 67–71, 73, 76, 81, 103, 119, 121, 124–5, 140–2, 152, 167, 176
negotiation 45, 93, 96, 108–9, 126, 170
neighborhood 27–8, 56, 63, 81, 92, 99–100, 108, 126, 133–4, 137, 139, 147, 161, 180, 185
New Urbanism 41, 47, 81, 137, 146, 155
Newell, A. 19, 35
Nijkamp, P. 116, 130
normative orientation 2, 33, 71, 74–5, 132, 147, 175–6, 181
norms 2, 45, 52, 64, 66, 73–8, 86, 90, 103, 145, 148, 151, 159, 161, 163, 175–9
Nussbaum, M. 18, 23–7, 31–2, 35

Oak Park District 97 169
objectivity 4, 14, 17–8, 22, 30–1, 72, 111, 114, 126
obligation 161, 172, 177, 179
Olson, J. M. 11, 16, 20, 35
open moral communities 35, 81, 87, 108, 159, 161, 174, 187
opportunity 28, 30, 63, 78, 133, 151, 161
optimization 73, 106n6, 115, 144
Orland Park Planning Department vi, 136, 139, 142, 155
Orland Park, Illinois vi, 132, 135–9, 142, 144, 151–2, 155
Ormerod, P. 19, 35
Ostrom, E. 49–52, 56–61, 64, 11, 187
outcomes 10, 12, 20, 33, 68, 70–3, 76–9, 89–90, 103, 105, 114–8, 121, 123, 146, 170, 175, 187
Ozzawa, C. 96, 108–9

park 68, 99, 117, 135, 178, 184
participants 50, 63, 136, 164
participation 26, 29–30, 34, 57, 69, 108, 120, 169, 185
pedestrian 137, 139, 147, 161
Pendall, R. 99, 108
perfection 67, 74, 78, 132, 163, 166, 172, 176, 182
persuasion 31–2, 34
Pierce, C. 113, 124

194   Index

Pieters, R. 31, 34
Pijanowski, B. C. 155
Pinder, D. 76, 81
Pizarro, D. A. 186
Plan for City Center Philadelphia 167, 170–1
plan blueprints 1, 9.10, 45, 52, 89, 103, 124–5, 150, 153, 178; composition 3, 43, 50, 68, 72, 75, 80, 85–6, 92, 94, 96; evaluation 110–1, 114–6, 123, 129; impact 1, 3–4, 18–21, 41, 51, 73, 76, 91–3, 99, 110, 114–16, 121, 130– 4, 142, 153, 177–9, 185; intentions 1, 2, 5, 10–5, 17, 21, 24–6, 31–2, 46, 49, 53–4, 71–5, 77–8, 80, 85–97, 103– 7n11, 114, 123, 142, 145, 149–53, 166–7, 174–7; large 'P' 1, 85, 90, 92, 171; mandate 49, 58– 61, 86, 107n11, 108, 120–1; small 'p' 1, 53–4, 57, 85, 90–2, 165, 171
Planning Accreditation Board (PAB) 43
Planning Advisory Service 120
planning craft viii, 42, 47, 95, 132, 153, 173; discipline v, viii, 3, 5, 18–9, 39–49, 62–3, 69–70, 87, 111, 129, 144, 151–2, 162, 176; field viii, 3, 33, 40–9, 56, 63, 75, 94–8, 144, 151–2, 162, 166, 181; institutions 41, 42, 52; movement v, viii, 39–47, 68, 125, 131, 144, 151, 163, 180; practice v, 33, 35, 43–7, 78, 81, 107, 115, 120–2, 129– 55, 161, 176, 182, 185; practitioners I, 1, 17, 39, 42, 44–6, 63, 78–9, 114, 121, 124, 127, 132, 176–7, 182; process 13, 34, 70, 128n, 129, 145, 187; theory v, vi, viii, 9, 10, 15, 34–6, 39–47, 58, 64, 68, 71–3, 79–81, 107–8, 112, 129, 155, 187; rational 1, 15n, 19, 121, 145; scenarios 1, 52, 65, 68–73, 76, 78–9, 89, 103, 181; vision 1, 31, 45, 50–1, 65–8, 73–5, 78, 88, 128, 150–3
plausibility 21, 52, 62, 68–72, 92, 95, 103, 105, 118, 123–4, 127, 173, 177
pluralist 87, 106n1, 159–63, 180
policy 9, 12–3, 28, 31–2, 41, 59–60, 65, 71, 79–80, 85–6, 97, 102–3, 107–8, 116–7, 121, 129–30, 133, 137, 138–41, 148–52, 165, 167, 169–70, 174, 179, 187–88
Pollock, J. 21, 33, 35
post structural planning theory 15n13, 73
postmodernism 9, 74, 112, 118, 120, 129
Potter, J. 34
practical art 32–3, 78, 120; judgment 1–5, 9–10, 13, 23, 27, 31, 43–9, 53, 62–5, 74–5, 78–9, 85–6, 89–90, 91–5,

105–6n12, 125, 149, 161, 173, 177, 179, 181; reasoning 11, 13, 53, 90–1
pragmatic planning 9, 126, 128; orientation 3, 12, 52, 58, 163
pragmatist approach 2–4, 11, 33, 45–6, 73–4, 77, 110, 144, 174–5
precedent vi, 42, 44, 69, 86, 97, 99–102, 105, 147, 162, 177
predict 2, 10, 12–3, 31, 45, 48–9, 51–2, 56–7, 64, 70, 89, 90, 92, 95, 97, 99, 113, 125, 160, 165–6, 177
prejudice 128, 173178, 185
Pribram, K. H. 19, 35
principles 1, 44, 50, 52, 71, 86, 91, 98, 100, 107n12, 115, 120, 123, 137, 139, 145–8, 151–2, 154, 159, 165, 176–7
prison planning 29, 30
private good 52, 176, 181
problem setting 97
problem solving 14n, 19, 35–6, 52, 66, 97, 129
professional planner 1, 4, 9, 17, 31–2, 39–40, 45, 49–50, 60–1, 87, 95, 97, 114, 122, 132, 144–6, 147, 148–9, 154, 159–60, 174, 184
professional planning 1, 41, 88, 112, 115, 148; best practice I, 1, 2, 53, 105
progress i, vii, 4, 26, 42, 47, 118, 148, 167, 178, 186–7
protocol 9, 42, 86, 97, 98–9, 110, 144, 149, 153
prudent 43, 127, 162, 172, 177, 185
psychology 16, 18–20, 33–6, 54, 73, 106n3, 187–8
public good 3, 5, 114–5, 118, 126, 148, 178
public housing 80–1, 168–73
public interest 48, 120, 130, 175, 178–9, 182
publicity 33n5, 145, 160, 164–5, 170, 172–3
Pueblo, Colorado 117
Pullman, Illinois 183–5
Pullman, M. E. 31, 35

Quay, R. 80, 130

rational planning (see planning, rational)
rationality 1–4, 9, 11, 13, 15n11, 42, 45, 54–7, 71, 78–9, 88, 92–3, 110–5, 119–27, 132, 145, 160, 172
reciprocity 52, 57, 61, 161, 165, 175, 185
reconcile 2, 65–6, 75, 93, 102, 161, 164, 175–7

recreation 133, 135
redevelopment 25, 102, 108, 134, 137, 146, 154, 168, 183–7
regional development 48, 142
Regional Transit Authority (RTA) 136
regulation 27, 46, 57, 59–62, 98–9, 114, 119–20, 133–4, 146, 151, 154–5
representation viii, 19, 26, 32, 55, 57, 80, 86–9, 92, 95–7, 103–5, 107, 128n2, 137, 147, 149
repression 75, 160
residential development 99, 103, 133, 142,
respect vii, 9–10, 13, 49, 62, 87–9, 97, 106n1, 111, 113, 132, 150–1, 159–62, 164–5, 168, 172–173, 180–1
responsibility 42–3, 59, 61, 69, 121, 123, 127, 129, 147, 149, 167, 170, 177–9
rhetoric 18, 35, 42, 45, 63n1, 80, 85–6, 113, 119, 130, 161, 163, 167, 169
risk 1, 6, 17, 29, 32, 35, 53, 62, 105, 127–8, 161–2, 185
Rittel, H. 106n6, 108
Robinson, K. D. 134, 155
Roese, N. J. 11, 16, 20, 35
Rogoff, B. 75, 81
Rolls, E.T. 18, 35
Rosenblum, N. 159, 174
Rousenau, H. 81
Royal Town Planning Institute (RTPI) 40
Rules 13–4n6, 43–4, 49–58, 61–4, 76–7, 86, 90, 96, 103, 144–147, 150, 155, 161, 175–81
Ryan, B. 78, 81

Saeger, T. 49, 64, 89, 96, 105, 108
Salet, W. 49, 52, 56, 64
San Francisco Planning Department 100, 108
San Francisco vi, 35, 99–101, 108
San Jose vi, 102, 108
San Jose Redevelopment Department 102, 108
Sandercock, L. 26, 35, 75, 81, 120, 130
scale 1, 14n6, 36, 42, 49–52, 54–7, 62–3, 68, 90–3, 99, 108, 119, 125–6, 128n2, 130, 133, 142, 145, 151–53, 162, 180
Scerri, A. 179, 182, 185, 187
Schon, D. 44, 47, 94, 106n9, 108, 121–2, 130
school 39, 42–4, 47, 135, 169–70, 173
Schwartz, B. 177, 181, 187
Schwartz, S. H. 179, 187
Schwarz, N. 20, 32, 35
Scott, J. C. 118–20, 130
Seabright, P. 54, 64

Index   195

Segregation 24, 60, 134, 145, 152, 169
Sen, A. 179, 187
Sennett, R. 105, 108
sensitivity 12, 17, 18, 22, 31, 49, 71, 74, 99, 122, 147, 149, 177
settlement 1, 5, 39–40, 44, 52, 66, 75, 87, 92, 95, 119, 128, 135, 145–6, 160, 170, 181, 186
Shafir, E. 22, 35
shared fate 164
Sharpe, K. 177, 181, 187
Sheppard, J. W. 176, 179, 187
Sherman, S. J. 35
Shunneli, D. F. 106, 108
Simon, H. 19, 21, 33, 34, 35, 106, 108
Simons, J. 34
simulate 19, 20, 21, 31, 71, 76, 102,
simulation 35, 69, 71, 103, 105, 121, 127
site 28–9, 59, 125, 133, 138–9, 145–8, 168, 183–5
Slotterback, C. S. 182, 187
Smith A. 179, 188
Smith A. D. 35
Smith, A. 178–9, 188
Smith, A. M. 80
Smith, C.A. 18, 20, 22, 31, 34
social complexity 106n1, 160–166, 171–172, 179–180
social learning 4, 5, 14n4, 106n4, 179
social psychology 16, 18, 34, 35, 54, 187
stakeholders 2, 31–2, 45, 50, 61–2, 65, 68–78, 95–6, 102–3, 123, 138, 175–7, 182,
State of California 98, 109
Stegman, M. 118, 130
Stein, S. M. 74, 78, 80, 112, 129
Stiftel, B. 35, 45, 47
Stivers, C. 126, 130
storytelling 35–6, 69, 76, 81, 124, 130, 135,
strategies 1, 4, 19, 41, 47, 50–1, 55, 60–1, 64, 67, 69–71, 76–8, 96, 103, 108, 130, 144, 154, 169–70
Strathman, A. J. 34
students I, 43, 66, 74, 96, 153, 169
subdivision 28, 88, 133–142, 145–8, 151, 154
subjection 119, 160, 175
suburb 4, 27, 61, 132–5, 142, 144–5, 149, 151, 154, 161, 169
Sunstein, C. 10, 14n5, 16
Susskind, L. 96, 109
synoptic rational planning 19

Talen, E. 41, 47, 68, 81, 117, 130, 144–6, 151, 155

territory 33, 88, 161
testimony I, 1, 27, 30, 126, 185
Thagard, P. 90–2, 109
Thomas, H. 177, 188
Thompson, D. 186–7
Throgmorton, J. 27, 33, 35–6, 69, 81, 122–3, 130
Tomasello, M. 95, 109
Torrens, P. M. 48, 64
Toulmin, S. 113, 130
town 22, 28, 40–1, 67, 77, 80, 108, 116, 118–9, 130, 135–6, 140–2, 171, 183–4
tradition 18, 41–2, 44, 66, 68, 73, 76, 80, 93, 125, 146, 148, 178–9
transcendent 86, 159, 174n3, 177–8
transect 146–7
transportation 2, 20, 55, 61, 89, 99, 103, 127, 142

Ullman–Margalit, E. 11, 16
uncertainty 4, 10–1, 35, 49, 51–2, 58, 60, 67, 76, 85, 87–8, 103, 108, 121, 125, 128, 130, 145, 150, 160, 164–6, 170, 181, 187
unconscious 75, 110, 129
Underwood, J. 44, 47
Unger, R. M. 176, 178, 179, 181, 188
Upton, R. 44, 47
urban development 34, 49–51, 60, 63–4, 80, 85, 87, 89, 94, 99, 102, 105, 107, 132–3, 144, 146, 148, 154, 167

Urbana, Illinois 153
utilitarian 66, 177178, 186n1
utopia v, viii, 4, 12, 48, 65, 68, 70–8

Vale, L. J. 78, 81
van Dijk, T. 72, 81
Van Hulst, M. 76, 78, 81
Verma, N. 14n, 16, 56, 64, 89, 106, 109, 127, 131, 186, 188
virtue 2, 15n, 66, 77, 79, 106n, 154, 159–61, 165, 171, 175–7
voting 111, 126

Wachs, M. 175, 177, 188
Wagner, J. A. 44, 47
Walker, J. 56, 64
Walzer, M. 159, 164, 174, 180, 188
Ward, G. 19, 20, 34–6
Watson, V. 35, 44, 47, 122, 131
web of plans 50, 85
Weber, M. 106n, 108
Webster, C. J. 54, 64, 89, 96, 109
Weiner, A. 69, 80
Wojcik, S. 187
Wright, R. 179, 188

Zapata, M. A. 69–70, 80–1, 103
zoning 27, 39, 60, 102, 107n, 114, 121, 133, 138, 145–6, 151